ABRAHAM LINCOLN

WORD FOR WORD

MAUREEN HARRISON
STEVE GILBERT
EDITORS

EXCELLENT BOOKS
SAN DIEGO, CALIFORNIA

EXCELLENT BOOKS
Post Office Box 927105
San Diego, CA 92192-7105

Publisher's Cataloging in Publication Data

Abraham Lincoln: Word for Word/
 Maureen Harrison, Steve Gilbert, editors.
 p. cm. - (Word for Word Series)
Bibliography:p.
Includes Index.
1. Abraham Lincoln, 1809-1865. 2. United States - Presidents.
I. Title. II. Harrison, Maureen. III. Gilbert, Steve.
IV. Series: Word for Word.
E457.92 1994   LC 93-72421
353.031-dc20
ISBN 1-880780-06-2

INTRODUCTION

"A house divided against itself cannot stand." I believe this government cannot endure, permanently half slave and half free. **The "House Divided" Speech**

Fourscore and seven years ago our fathers brought forth on the continent a new nation, conceived in liberty and dedicated to the proposition that all men are created equal. **The Gettysburg Address**

With malice toward none; with charity for all; with firmness in the right, as God gives us to see the right, let us strive on to finish the work we are in.
The Second Inaugural

The words of Abraham Lincoln are alive. His inate, and unshakable, beliefs in freedom, liberty, and equality reach out across the years to inspire people throughout the world.

Abraham Lincoln: Word For Word is designed to easily acquaint readers, young and old alike, with the best speeches and writings of Lincoln. We have carefully selected from a lifetime of Abraham Lincoln's diverse public speeches and private writings those documents which we think will give the reader real insight into the essential Lincoln. Some - *A House Divided Against Itself, The Gettysburg Address, The Second Inaugural* - are famous; others - *The War With Mexico, The Temperance and Intemperance Address* - are obscure. We believe that all the selected speeches and writings contained in this book are revealing of the man and his times. We hope that you find them interesting, thought-provoking, entertaining, and informative.

Abraham Lincoln: Word For Word traces the writings of Lincoln from an excerpt from his first public speech in 1832 to his last public address in Washington in 1865.

The editors offer their heartfelt thanks to the reference librarians of the Chicago Historical Society, the Illinois State Historical Society, the University of Illinois at Champaign-Urbana, the New York Public Library, Columbia University in New York City, and especially of the Library of Congress in Washington, DC.

The life, death, and continuing legacy of Abraham Lincoln have been extensively chronicled in books of varying quality and accuracy throughout the years. We have included in our bibliography what we consider to be the best of the Lincoln biographies and histories. Among our favorite biographies are Carl Sandburg's *Abraham Lincoln: The Prairie Years* and *Abraham Lincoln: The War Years*, William Herndon's *Life of Lincoln*, and Nicolay and Hay's *Abraham Lincoln: A History*. The best complete collections of Lincoln's writings are Roy Basler's *The Collected Works of Abraham Lincoln* and David Mearns' *The Lincoln Papers*. The standard (but aging) bibliography is still James Monaghan's *Lincoln Bibliography, 1839-1939*.

On November 19, 1863 President of the United States Abraham Lincoln spoke at the dedication ceremony of the Gettysburg National Cemetery. In part of that brief, brilliant, speech Lincoln said: *The world will little note, nor long remember, what we say here.* In this Abraham Lincoln was much mistaken - his words and thoughts live on.

M.H. & S.G.

TABLE OF CONTENTS

If I could save the Union without freeing any slave, I would do it; and if I could save it by freeing all the slaves, I would do it; and if I could save it by freeing some and leaving others alone, I would also do that.

If destruction be our lot we must ourselves be its author and finisher. As a nation of freemen we must live through all time, or die by suicide.

Any people anywhere, being inclined and having the power, have the right to rise up and shake off their existing government, and form a new one that suits them better. This is a most valuable, a most sacred right - a right which we hope and believe is to liberate the world.

Whether or not the world would be vastly benefitted by a total and final banishment from it of all intoxicating drinks seems to me now to be an open question. Three-fourths of mankind confess the affirmative with their tongues, and, I believe, all the rest acknowledge it in their hearts.

A HOUSE DIVIDED AGAINST ITSELF
187

*"A house divided against itself cannot stand." I believe
this government cannot endure, permanently half slave
and half free. I do not expect the Union to be dissolved -
I do not expect the house to fall - but I do expect it will
cease to be divided.*

THE SECOND
LINCOLN-DOUGLAS DEBATE
199

*It is most extraordinary that he should so far forget all
the suggestions of justice to an adversary, or of prudence
to himself, as to venture upon the assertion of that which
the slightest investigation would have shown him to be totally false.*

KEEPING THE FAITH
215

*All you have to do is keep the faith, to remain steadfast to
the right, to stand by your banner. Nothing should lead
you to leave your guns. Stand together, ready, with match
in hand. Allow nothing to turn you to the right or to the
left. . . . Victory, complete and permanent, is sure at the
last.*

SLAVERY IS WRONG
219

*I say that there is room enough for us all to be free, and
that it not only does not wrong the white man that the negro should be free, but it positively wrongs the mass of
the white men that the negro should be enslaved.*

ADDRESS AT COOPER INSTITUTE
251

Let us have faith that Right makes Might, and in that faith, let us, to the end, dare to do our duty as we understand it.

THE QUESTION OF SLAVERY
275

The question of slavery is the question, the all-absorbing topic of the day. It is true that all of us - and by that I mean not the Republican Party alone, but the whole American people here and elsewhere - all of us wish this question settled; wish it out of the way.

FAREWELL ADDRESS
289

I now leave, not knowing when or whether ever I may return, with a task before me greater than that which rested upon Washington.

ADDRESS AT INDEPENDENCE HALL
291

Can this country be saved? ... If it can, I will consider myself one of the happiest men in the world if I can help to save it. If it cannot be saved upon that principle, it will be truly awful. But if this country cannot be saved without giving up that principle ... I would rather be assassinated on the spot than surrender it.

FIRST INAUGURAL ADDRESS
293

We are not enemies, but friends. We must not be enemies. Though passion may have strained, it must not break our bonds of affection. The mystic chords of memory, stretching from every battlefield, and patriot grave, to every living heart and hearthstone, all over this broad land, will yet swell the chorus of the Union, when again touched, as surely they will be, by the better angels of our nature.

CONFEDERATE SECESSION
307

With rebellion thus sugar-coated they have been drugging the public mind of their section for more than thirty years, until at length they have brought many good men to a willingness to take up arms against the government the day after some assemblage of men have enacted the farcical pretense of taking their State out of the Union.

FIRST ANNUAL MESSAGE ON
THE STATE OF THE UNION
329

A disloyal portion of the American people have, during the whole year, been engaged in an attempt to divide and destroy the Union.

SECOND ANNUAL MESSAGE ON
THE STATE OF THE UNION
337

In giving freedom to the slave, we assure freedom to the free - honorable alike in what we give and what we preserve. We shall nobly save or meanly lose the last, best hope of earth.

A DAY OF THANKSGIVING
365

He has been pleased to animate and inspire our minds and hearts with fortitude, courage, and resolution sufficent for the great trial of civil war.

THE RE-ELECTION SPEECH
367

We cannot have free government without elections; and if the Rebellion could force us to forego or postpone a national election, it might fairly claim to have already conquered and ruined us.

FOURTH ANNUAL MESSAGE ON THE STATE OF THE UNION
369

[Jefferson Davis] would accept nothing short of severance of the Union - precisely what we will not and cannot give. His declarations to this effect are explicit and oft repeated. He does not atttempt to deceive us. He affords us no excuse to deceive ourselves. He cannot voluntary reaccept the union; we cannot voluntarily yield it.

SECOND INAUGURAL ADDRESS
375

With malice toward none; with charity for all; with firmness in the right, as God gives us to see the right, let us strive on to finish the work we are in; to bind up the nation's wounds; to care for him who shall have borne the battle, and for his widow, and his orphan - to do all which may achieve and cherish a just and lasting peace, among ourselves, and with all nations.

RECONSTRUCTION OF THE UNION
THE LAST PUBLIC SPEECH
379

We all agree that the seceded States, so called, are out of their proper practical relation with the Union; and that the sole object of the govenment, civil and military, in regard to those States is to again get them into that proper practical relation. I believe it is not only possible, but in fact, easier to do this, without deciding, or even considering, whether these States have ever been out of the Union.

LINCOLNIANA

BETTER TO BE RIGHT

It is better only sometimes to be right than at all times to be wrong.

Address to the People of Sangamon County
March 9, 1832

CAPITALISTS

These capitalists generally act harmoniously and in concert, to fleece the people, and now, that they have got into a quarrel with themselves, we are called upon to appropriate the people's money to settle the quarrel.

Speech to the Illinois Legislature
January 1837

FINDING HEAD NOR TAIL

In one faculty, at least, there can be no dispute of the gentleman's superiority over me, and most other men; and that is, the faculty of entangling a subject, so that neither himself, nor any other man can find head or tail to it.

Speech to the Illinois Legislature
January 1837

POLITICIANS

This work is exclusively the work of politicians; a set of men who have interests aside from the interests of the people, and who, to say the most of them, are, taken as a mass, at least one long step removed from honest men. I say this with the greater freedom because, being a politician myself, none can regard it as personal.

Bank Speech
January 1837

DESERTING AMERICA

Many free countries have lost their liberty, and ours may lose hers; but if she shall, be it my proudest plume, not that I was the last to desert, but that I never deserted her.

Treasury Speech
December 20, 1839

THE LAMB AND THE WIND

How true it is that "God tempers the wind to the shorn lamb," or in other words, that He renders the worst of human conditions tolerable, while He permits the best to be nothing better than tolerable.

Letter to Mary Speed
September 27, 1841

POSTERITY

Few can be induced to labor exclusively for posterity; and none will do it enthusiastically.

Temperance Address
February 22, 1842

THE NATURE OF MAN

It is not much in the nature of man to be driven to anything; still less to be driven about that which is exclusively his own business; and least of all where such driving is to be submitted to at the expense of pecuniary interest or burning appetite.

Temperance Address
February 22, 1842

HOW TO MAKE FRIENDS

"A drop of honey catches more flies than a gallon of gall."
So with men. If you would win a man to your cause, first
convince him that you are his sincere friend. Therein is a
drop of honey which catches his heart, which, say what he
will, is the great highroad to his reason.

Temperance Address
February 22, 1842

TRUTH

I never encourage deceit, and falsehood, especially if you
have got a bad memory, is the *worst* enemy a fellow can
have. The fact is, truth is your truest friend, no matter
what the circumstances are.

Letter to George Pickett
February 22, 1842

BEST OF A BAD BARGAIN

If you make a bad bargain, hug it all the tighter.

Letter to Joshua Speed
February 25, 1842

CONFIDENCE

I must gain my confidence in my own ability to keep my
resolves when they are made. In that ability you know I
once prided myself. . . . I have not yet regained it; and
until I do, I cannot trust myself in any matter of much
importance.

Letter to Joshua Speed
July 4, 1842

HOW TO GET THINGS DONE

Determine that the thing can and shall de done, and then we shall find the way.... How to do something and still not do too much is the desideratum.

Speech on Internal Improvements
June 20, 1848

SUSPICION AND JEALOUSY

The way for a young man to rise is to improve himself every way he can, never suspecting that anybody wishes to hinder him. Allow me to assure you that suspicion and jealousy never did help any man in any situation. There may sometimes be ungenerous attempts to keep a young man down; and they will succeed, too, if he allows his mind to be diverted from its true channel to brood over the attempted injury.

Letter to William Herndon
July 10, 1848

A LITTLE YELLOW DOG

A fellow once advertised that he had made a discovery by which he could make a new man out of an old one, and have enough of the stuff left to make a little yellow dog.

Speech in Congress
July 27, 1848

PRINCIPLES

I suppose I cannot reasonably hope to convince you that we have any principles. The most I can expect is to assure you that we think we have, and are quite contented with them.

Speech in Congress
July 27, 1848

FRIENDSHIP

The better part of one's life consists of his friendships.

Letter to Joseph Gillespie
July 13, 1849

TRUST THE PEOPLE

We see it, and to us it appears like principle, and the best sort of principle at that - the principle of allowing the people to do as they please with their own business.

Speech in Congress
July 27, 1848

EXTEMPORANEOUS SPEAKING

Extemporaneous speaking should be practised and cultivated. It is the lawyer's avenue to the public.

Notes for a Law Lecture
July 1, 1850

THE GOOD LAWYER

Discourage litigation. Persuade your neighbor to compromise whenever you can. . . . As a peace-maker the lawyer has a superior opportunity of being a good man. There will still be business enough.

Notes for a Law Lecture
July 1, 1850

THE HONEST LAWYER

Resolve to be honest at all events; and if in your own judgment you cannot be an honest lawyer, resolve to be honest without being a lawyer.

Notes for a Law Lecture
July 1, 1850

EQUALITY

Equality in society alike beats inequality, whether the latter be of the British aristocratic sort or of the domestic slavery sort.

On Slavery
July 1, 1854

THE OBJECT OF GOVERNMENT

The legitimate object of government is to do for a community of people whatever they need to have done, but cannot do at all, or cannot so well do, for themselves, in their separate and individual capacities. In all that the people can individually do as well for themselves, government ought not to interfere.

On Government
July 1, 1854

PUBLIC OPINION

A universal feeling, whether well or ill-founded, cannot be safely disregarded.

Speech at Peoria, Illinois
October 16, 1854

TERRITORIES OF THE MOON

Now this provision . . . had no more direct reference to Nebraska than it had to the territories of the moon.

Speech at Peoria, Illinois
October 16, 1854

RIGHT AND WRONG

Stand with anybody that stands right. Stand with him while he is right, and part with him when he goes wrong.

Speech at Peoria, Illinois
October 16, 1854

DESPOTISM

When the white man governs himself, that is self-government; but when he governs himself and also governs another man, that is more than self-government - that is despotism.

Speech at Peoria, Illinois
October 16, 1854

PRESERVATION OF LIBERTY

If there is anything which it is the duty of the whole people to never intrust to any hands but their own, that thing is the preservation and perpetuity of their own liberties and institutions.

Speech at Peoria, Illinois
October 16, 1854

SLAVERY

No man is good enough to govern another man without that other's consent.

Speech at Peoria, Illinois
October 16, 1854

LET BYGONES BE BYGONES

Let bygones be bygones; let past differences as nothing be; and with steady eye on the real issue, let us reinaugurate the good old "central ideas" of the republic. The human heart is with us. God is with us.

Speech at Chicago , Illinois
December 10, 1856

DRAGGING CHESTNUTS FROM THE FIRE

By much dragging of chestnuts from the fire for others to eat, his claws are burnt off to the gristle, and he is thrown aside as unfit for further use.

Speech at Chicago, Illinois
December 10, 1856

ORIGIN OF THE WILL

Will springs from the two elements of moral sense and self-interest.

Speech at Springfield, Illinois
June 26, 1857

NEITHER SLAVE NOR WIFE

I protest against the counterfeit logic which concludes that, because I do not want a black woman for a slave, I must necessarily want her for a wife. I need not have her for either. I can just leave her alone.

Speech at Springfield, Illinois
June 27, 1857

A HOUSE DIVIDED AGAINST ITSELF

"A house divided against itself cannot stand." I believe this government cannot endure permanently half slave and half free. I do not expect the Union to be dissolved -

I do not expect the house to fall - but I do expect it will cease to be divided.

Speech at Springfield, Illinois
June 16, 1858

INDIVIDUAL RIGHTS

I believe each individual is naturally entitled to do as he pleases with himself and the fruit of his labor, so far as it in no wise interferes with any other man's rights.

Speech at Chicago, Illinois
July 10, 1858

FREEDOM TO EVERY CREATURE

If we cannot give freedom to every creature, let us do nothing that will impose slavery upon any other creature.

Speech at Chicago, Illinois
July 10, 1858

THE NEGRO

All I ask for the negro is that if you do not like him, let him alone. If God gave him but little, that little let him enjoy.

Speech at Springfield, Illinois
July 17, 1858

MISREPRESENTATIONS

When a man hears himself somewhat misrepresented, it provokes him - at least, I find it so with myself; but when misrepresentation becomes very gross and palpable, it is more apt to amuse him.

The Lincoln-Douglas Debate, Ottawa, Illinois
August 21, 1858

POWER OF PUBLIC OPINION

In this age, and in this country, public sentiment is everything. With it, nothing can fail; against it, nothing can succeed.

Notes for Speeches
October 1, 1858

BALLOTS, NOT BULLETS

To give the victory to the right, not bloody bullets, but peaceful ballots only are necessary. Thanks to our good old Constitution, and organization under it, these alone are necessary. It only needs that every right thinking man shall go to the polls, and without fear or prejudice vote as he thinks.

Notes for Speeches
October 1, 1858

LIBERTY

I am for the people of the whole nation doing just as they please in all matters which concern the whole nation; for those of each part doing just as they choose in all matters which concern no other part; and for each individual doing just as he chooses in all matters which concern nobody else.

Notes for Speeches
October 1, 1858

DIFFERENCE IN CONSCIENCES

Consciences differ in different individuals.

Notes for Speeches
October 1, 1858

HOMEOPATHIC SOUP

Has it not got down as thin as the homeopathic soup that was made by boiling the shadow of a pigeon that had starved to death?

Lincoln-Douglas Debate, Quincy, Illinois
October 13, 1858

THE TYRANNICAL PRINCIPLE

The same spirit says, "You toil and work and earn bread, and I'll eat it." No matter in what shape it comes, whether from the mouth of a king who seeks to bestride the people of his own nation and live by the fruit of their labor, or from one race of men as an apology for enslaving another race, it is the same tyrannical principle.

Lincoln-Douglas Debate, Alton, Illinois
October 15, 1858

THE SERPENT'S TAIL

The last tip of the last joint of the old serpent's tail was just drawing out of view.

Lincoln-Douglas Debate, Alton, Illinois
October 15, 1858

LONG AFTER I AM GONE

The race gave me a hearing on the great and durable question of the age, which I could have had in no other way; and though I now sink out of view, and shall be forgotten, I believe I have made some marks which will tell for the cause of civil liberty long after I am gone.

Letter to A.G. Henry
November 19, 1858

ALL SLAVE OR ALL FREE

I think we have fairly entered upon a durable struggle as to whether this nation is to ultimately become all slave or all free, and though I fall early in the contest, it is nothing if I shall have contributed, in the least degree, to the final restful result.

Letter to H.D. Sharpe
December 18, 1858

ADAM AND EVE

The very first invention was a joint operation, Eve having shared with Adam the getting up of the apron.   And, indeed, judging from the fact that sewing has come down to our times as "woman's work" it is very probable she took the leading part - he, perhaps, doing no more than to stand by and thread the needle.

Lecture on Discoveries, Inventions and Improvements
February 22, 1859

THE GREAT COAT FIGHT

I remember being once much amused at seeing two particularly intoxicated men engaged in a fight with their great coats on, which fight, after a long and rather harmless contest, ended in each having fought himself out of his own coat and into that of the other.

Letter to H.L. Pierce
April 6, 1859

POPULAR SOVEREIGNTY

I think a definition of "popular sovereignty" in the abstract, would be about this: That each man shall do precisely as he pleases with himself, and with all those things that exclusively concern him . . . that a general government shall do all those things which pertain to it, and all the local governments shall do precisely as they please in respect to those matters which exclusively concern them.

Speech at Columbus, Ohio
September 16, 1859

SILENCE IS NOT ALWAYS SAFE

It is not entirely safe, when one is misrepresented under his very nose, to allow the misrepresentation to go uncorrected.

Speech at Columbus, Ohio
September 16, 1859

REASON AND AUTHORITY

There are two ways of establishing a proposition. One is by trying to demonstrate it upon reason, and the other is to show that great men in former times have thought so and so, and thus to pass it by the weight of pure authority.

Speech at Columbus, Ohio
September 16, 1859

EMBARRASSMENT

When one is embarrassed, usually the shortest way to get through with it is to quit talking or thinking about it, and go at something else.

Speech at Cincinnati, Ohio
September 17, 1859

THE ANCIENT APHORISM

It is said an Eastern monarch once charged his wise men to invent him an aphorism to be ever in view, and which should be true and appropriate in all times and situations.

They presented him the words, "And this, too, shall pass away."

Agricultural Address
September 30, 1859

POVERTY

If any continue through life in the condition of the hired laborer, it is not the fault of the system, but because of either a dependent nature which prefers it, or improvidence, folly, or singular misfortune.

Agricultural Address
September 30, 1859

BLADES OF GRASS

Every blade of grass is a study; and to produce two where there was but one is both a profit and a pleasure.

Agricultural Address
September 30, 1859

SELF-PORTRAIT

I am, in height, six feet four inches, nearly; lean in flesh, weighing on average one hundred and eighty pounds; dark complexion, with coarse black hair and grey eyes. No other marks or brands recollected.

Letter to J.W. Fell
December 20, 1859

EDUCATION

No qualification was ever required of a teacher beyond "readin', writin', and cipherin'" to the rule of three. If a

straggler supposed to understand Latin happened to
sojourn in the neighborhood, he was looked upon as a
wizard.

Letter to J. W. Fell
December 20, 1859

FAITH THAT RIGHT MAKES MIGHT

Let us have faith that right makes might, and in that faith
let us to the end dare to do our duty as we understand it.

Address at Cooper Institute
February 27, 1860

POOR MAN'S SON

I am not ashamed to confess that twenty-five years ago I
was a hired laborer, mauling rails, at work on a flatboat -
just what might happen to any poor man's son. I want
every man to have a chance.

Speech at New Haven, Connecticut
March 6, 1860

LARGE ENOUGH FOR ALL

If it was like two wrecked seamen on a narrow plank;
where each must push the other off or drown himself, I
would push the negro off - or the white man either; but it
is not: the plank is large enough for both.

Speech at New Haven, Connecticut
March 6, 1860

THE SLAVERY QUESTION

Our best and greatest men have greatly underestimated
the size of this question. They have constantly brought

LAWS AND FRIENDS

Can aliens make treaties easier than friends can make laws? Can treaties be more faithfully enforced between aliens than laws can among friends?

First Inaugural Address
March 4, 1861

DEEDS, NOT WORDS, WANTED

Tell him, when he starts, to put it through - not to be writing or telegraphing back here, but put it through.

Letter to Secretary Cameron
June 20, 1861

THE SUGAR COATED REBELLION

With rebellion thus sugar coated, they have been drugging the public mind of their section for more than thirty years.

Message to Congress
July 4, 1861

POLITICAL SOVEREIGNTY

What is "sovereignty" in the political sense of the term? Would it be far wrong to define it a "political community without a poltical superior?"

Message to Congress
July 4, 1861

MEN WORTHY OF TRUST

No men living are more worthy to be trusted than those who toil up from poverty - none less inclined to take or touch aught which they have not honestly earned.

State of the Union Address
December 3, 1861

LEADERSHIP

He who does *something* at the head of one regiment, will eclipse him who does *nothing* at the head of a hundred.

Letter to General Hunter
December 31, 1861

THE UNION ARMY

It is called the Army of the Potomac, but it is only McClellan's bodyguard. . . . If McClellan is not using the Army I should like to borrow it for awhile.

Letter to General McClellan
April 9, 1862

LOSS OF FRIENDS

The loss of enemies does not compensate for the loss of friends.

Telegram to Secretary Seward
June 30, 1862

HOLD YOUR POSITION

If you can hold your present position, we shall hive the enemy yet.

Telegram to General McClellan
July 5, 1862

CUTTING EACH OTHER'S THROATS

How much better . . . than to sink both the things to be sold and the price of it in cutting one another's throats?
Appeal in Favor of Compensated Emancipation
July 12, 1862

SEVERE JUSTICE

The severest justice may not always be the best policy.
Message to Congress
July 17, 1862

MALICE

I shall do nothing in malice. What I deal with is too vast for malicious dealing.
Letter to Cuthbert Bullitt
July 28, 1862

SELF-INTEREST

Unless among those deficient of intellect, everybody you trade with makes something.
Address on Negro Colonization
August 14, 1862

A MAN'S WORTH

It is difficult to make a man miserable while he feels he is worthy of himself and claims kindred to the great God who made him.
Address on Negro Colonization
August 14, 1862

SAVING THE UNION

If I could save the Union without freeing any slave, I would do it; and if I could save it by freeing all the slaves, I would do it; and if I could save it by freeing some and leaving others alone, I would also do that.

Letter to Horace Greeley
August 22, 1862

REVELATIONS

If it is probable that God would reveal His will to others on a point so connected with my duty, it might be supposed He would reveal it directly to me.

To The Religious Denominations of Chicago
September 13, 1862

REBEL PRAYERS

The rebel soldiers are praying with a great deal more earnestness, I fear, than our own troops, and expecting God to favor their side; for one of our soldiers . . . said that he met with nothing so discouraging as the evident sincerity of those he was among in their prayers.

To The Religious Denominations of Chicago
September 13, 1862

MORE THAN BREATH WANTED

The North responds to the proclamation sufficiently in breath; but breath alone kills no rebels.

Letter to Hannibal Hamlin
September 28, 1862

NONSENSE HURTS NO ONE

In my present position it is hardly proper for me to make speeches. Every word is so closely noted that it will not do to make foolish ones, and I cannot be expected to be prepared to make sensible ones. If I were as I have been for most of my life, I might, perhaps, talk nonsense to you for half an hour, and it wouldn't hurt anybody.

Remarks at Frederick, Maryland
October 4, 1862

TRY

I say "try"; if we never try, we shall never succeed.

Letter to General McClellan
October 13, 1862

WORKING TOGETHER

We can succeed only by concert. It is not "Can any of us imagine better?" but, "Can we all do better?"

State of the Union Address
December 1, 1862

PRACTICE AND THEORY

Practice proves more than theory, in any case.

State of the Union Address
December 1, 1862

QUIET PAST AND STORMY PRESENT

The dogmas of the quiet past are inadequate to the stormy present.

State of the Union Address
December 1, 1862

THE SPIRIT OF THE CONSTITUTION

It is said the devil takes care of his own. Much more should a good spirit - the spirit of the Constitution and the Union - take care of its own. I think it cannot do less and live.

Opinion on Admission of West Virginia
December 31, 1862

THE VOTERS

It is not the qualified voters, but the qualified voters who choose to vote, that constitute the political power of the State.

Opinion on Admission of West Virginia
December 31, 1862

MILITARY SUCCESS

Only those generals who gain successes can set up dictators. What I now ask of you is military success, and I will risk the dictatorship.

Letter to General Hooker
January 26, 1863

SAVE THE GOVERNMENT

Let the friends of the government first save the government and then administer it to their own liking.

Letter to Henry Davis
March 18, 1863

COWARDS

If the Lord gives a man a pair of cowardly legs, how can he help their running away with him?

Telegram to General Meade
September 11, 1863

THE SHORT AND FEEBLE REBELLION

This rebellion can eke out a short and feeble existence, as an animal sometimes may with a thorn in its vitals.

Letter to General Halleck
September 21, 1863

THE MISSISSIPPI

The Father of Waters again goes unvexed to the sea.

Letter to James Conkling
August 26, 1863

A NEW NATION CONCEIVED IN LIBERTY

Fourscore and seven years ago our fathers brought forth on this continent a new nation, conceived in liberty, and dedicated to the proposition that all men are created equal.

Gettysburg Address
November 19, 1863

GOVERNMENT OF THE PEOPLE

We here highly resolve that these dead shall not have died in vain; that this nation, Under God, shall have a new birth of freedom; and that government of the people, by the people, for the people, shall not perish from the earth.

Gettysburg Address
November 19, 1863

STANDING FIRM

I am very glad the elections this autumn have gone favorably, and that I have not, by native depravity or under evil influences, done anything bad enough to prevent the good result. I hope to "stand firm" enough to not go backward, and yet not go forward enough to wreck the country's cause.

Letter to Zachariah Chandler
November 20, 1863

FORGIVENESS

On principle I dislike an oath which requires a man to swear he has not done wrong. It rejects the Christian principle of forgiveness on terms of repentance. I think it is enough if the man does no wrong hereafter.

Indorsement
February 5, 1864

THE LAST SHRIEK OF RETREAT

His idea was that it would be considered our last shriek on the retreat.

Account of the Emancipation Proclamation
February 6, 1864

THE JEWEL OF LIBERTY

[The negroes in Louisiana] would probably help, in some trying time to come, to keep the jewel of liberty within the family of freedom.

Letter to Governor Hahn
March 13, 1864

GOD BLESS THE WOMEN OF AMERICA

I am not accustomed to the use of language of eulogy; I have never studied the art of playing compliments to women; but I must say, that if all that has been said by orators and poets since the creation of the world in praise of women were applied to the women of America, it would not do them justice for their conduct during this war. I close by saying, God bless the women of America.

Remarks at the Sanitary Fair in Washington, D.C.
March 18, 1864

SAFETY FROM VIOLENCE

Let not him who is houseless pull down the house of another, but let him work diligently and build one for himself, thus by example assuring that his own shall be safe from violence when built.

Reply to New York Working-Men
March 21, 1864

SOLIDARITY OF LABOR

The strongest bond of human sympathy, outside of the family relation, should be one uniting all working people, of all nations, and tongues, and kindreds.

Reply to New York Working-Men
March 21, 1864

CONTROLLED BY EVENTS

I claim not to have controlled events, but confess plainly that events have controlled me.

Letter to A.G. Hodges
April 4, 1864

LIFE AND LIMB

By general law, life and limb must be protected, yet often a limb must be amputated to save a life; but a life is never wisely given to save a limb.

Letter to A.G. Hodges
April 4, 1864

THE SHEEP AND THE WOLF

The shepherd drives the wolf from the sheep's throat, for which the sheep thanks the shepherd as his liberator, while the wolf denounces him for the same act, as the destroyer of liberty, especially if the sheep was a black one. Plainly, the sheep and the wolf are not agreed upon a definition of the word liberty; and precisely the same difference prevails today among us human creatures, even in the North, and all professing to love liberty.

Address at the Sanitary Fair, Baltimore, Maryland
April 18, 1864

IF GOD IS WITH US

If we do right God will be with us, and if God is with us we cannot fail.

Proclamation for Day of Prayer
July 7, 1864

THE CABINET

I propose continuing to be myself the judge as to when a member of the Cabinet shall be dismissed.

Letter to Secretary Stanton
July 14, 1864

VIGILANCE

It will neither be done nor attempted, unless you watch it every day and hour, and force it.

Telegram to General Grant
August 3, 1864

DEVOTION TO THE UNION

I cannot fly from my thoughts - my solicitude for this great country follows me wherever I go. I do not think it is personal vanity or ambition, though I am not free from these infirmities, but I cannot but feel that the weal or woe of this great nation will be decided in November.

Interview with John Mills
August 15, 1864

HOLD ON TO THE ENEMY

Hold on with a bull-dog grip, and chew and choke as much as possible.

Telegram to General Grant
August 17, 1864

IN HIS OWN GOOD TIME

I shall do more whenever I shall believe doing more will help the cause.

Letter to Charles D. Robinson
August 17, 1864

TAXES

If we should wait before collecting a tax, to adjust the taxes upon each man in exact proportion with every other man, we should never collect any tax at all.

Address to the 164th Ohio Regiment
August 18, 1864

A CLEAR CONSCIENCE

At least I should have done my duty, and have stood clear before my own conscience.

Memorandum
August 23, 1864

SMOKY LOCALITIES

Experience has already taught us in this war that holding these smoky localities responsible for the conflagrations within them has a very salutary effect.

Letter to J.R. Underwood
October 26, 1864

WHERE THERE'S SMOKE

We better know there is fire whence we see much smoke rising than we could know it by one or two witnesses swearing to it. The witnesses may commit perjury, but the smoke cannot.

Letter to J.R. Underwood
October 26, 1864

PATRIOTIC MEN

Gold is good in its place, but living, brave, patriotic men are better than gold.

Reconstruction of the Union
November 10, 1864

ALL MEN SHOULD BE FREE

I have always thought that all men should be free; but if any should be slaves, it should first those who desire it for themselves, and secondly, those who desire it for others.

Address to an Indiana Regiment
March 17, 1865

TRYING SLAVERY

When I hear anyone arguing for slavery, I feel a strong impulse to see it tried on him personally.

Address to an Indiana Regiment
March 17, 1865

LET THE THING BE PRESSED

General Sheridan says "If the thing be pressed I think that Lee will surrender." Let the *thing* be pressed.

Telegram to General Grant
April 7, 1865

SMASHED EGGS

Concede that the new government of Louisiana is only what it should be, as the egg to the fowl, we shall sooner have the fowl by hatching the egg than by smashing it.

Last Public Address
April 11, 1865

INFLEXIBILITY OF PRINCIPLES

Important principles may and must be inflexible.

Last Public Address
April 11, 1865

THE PERPETUATION OF OUR
POLITICAL INSTITUTIONS
SPRINGFIELD, ILLINOIS
January 27, 1837

In the great journal of things happening under the sun, we, the American people, find our account running under date of the nineteenth century of the Christian era. We find ourselves in the peaceful possession of the fairest portion of the earth as regards extent of territory, fertility of soil, and salubrity of climate. We find ourselves under the government of a system of political institutions conducing more essentially to the ends of civil and religious liberty than any of which the history of former times tells us. We, when mounting the stage of existence, found ourselves the legal inheritors of these fundamental blessings. We toiled not in the acquirement or establishment of them; they are a legacy bequeathed us by a once hardy, brave, and patriotic, but now lamented and departed, race of ancestors. Theirs was the task (and nobly they performed it) to possess themselves, and through themselves us, of this goodly land, and to uprear upon its hills and its valleys a political edifice of liberty and equal rights; 'tis ours only to transmit these - the former unprofaned by the foot of an invader, the latter undecayed by the lapse of time and untorn by usurpation - to the latest generation that fate shall permit the world to know. This task: gratitude to our fathers, justice to ourselves, duty to posterity, and love for our species in general, all imperatively require us faithfully to perform.

How then shall we perform it? At what point shall we expect the approach of danger? By what means shall we fortify against it? Shall we expect some transatlantic military giant to step the ocean and crush us at a blow? Never! All the armies of Europe, Asia, and Africa combined, with all the treasure of the earth (our own excepted) in their military chest, with a Bonaparte for a commander, could not by force take a drink from the Ohio or make a track on the Blue Ridge in a trial of a thousand years.

At what point then is the approach of danger to be expected? I answer, if it ever reach us it must spring up amongst us; it cannot come from abroad. If destruction be our lot we must ourselves be its author and finisher. As a nation of freemen we must live through all time, or die by suicide.

I hope I am over wary; but if I am not, there is even now something of ill omen amongst us. I mean the increasing disregard for law which pervades the country - the growing disposition to substitute the wild and furious passions in lieu of the sober judgment of courts, and the worse than savage mobs for the executive ministers of justice. This disposition is awfully fearful in any community; and that it now exists in ours, though grating to our feelings to admit, it would be a violation of truth and an insult to our intelligence to deny. Accounts of outrages committed by mobs form the every-day news of the times. They have pervaded the country from New England to Louisiana; they are neither peculiar to the eternal snows of the former nor the burning suns of the latter; they are not the creature of climate, neither are they confined to the slaveholding or the non-slaveholding States. Alike they spring up among the pleasure-hunting masters of Southern slaves, and the order-loving citizens of the land of steady habits. Whatever then their cause may be, it is common to the whole country.

It would be tedious as well as useless to recount the horrors of all of them. Those happening in the State of Mississippi and at St. Louis are perhaps the most dangerous in example and revolting to humanity. In the Mississippi case they first commenced by hanging the regular gamblers - a set of men certainly not following for a livelihood a very useful or very honest occupation, but one which, so far from being forbidden by the laws, was actually licensed by an act of the legislature passed but a single year before. Next, negroes suspected of conspiring to raise an insurrection were caught up and hanged in all parts of the State; then, white men supposed to be leagued with the negroes; and finally, strangers from neighboring States, going thither on business, were in many instances subjected to the same fate. Thus went on this process of hanging, from gamblers to negroes, from negroes to white citizens, and from these to strangers, till dead men were seen literally dangling from the boughs of trees upon every roadside, and in numbers almost sufficient to rival the native Spanish moss of the country as a drapery of the forest.

Turn then to that horror-striking scene at St. Louis. A single victim only was sacrificed there. This story is very short, and is perhaps the most highly tragic of anything of its length that has ever been witnessed in real life. A mulatto man by the name of McIntosh was seized in the street, dragged to the suburbs of the city, chained to a tree, and actually burned to death; and all within a single hour from the time he had been a freeman attending to his own business and at peace with the world.

Such are the effects of mob law, and such are the scenes becoming more and more frequent in this land so lately famed for love of law and order, and the stories of which have even now grown too familiar to attract anything more than an idle remark.

But you are perhaps ready to ask, "What has this to do with the perpetuation of our political institutions?" I answer, "It has much to do with it." Its direct consequences are, comparatively speaking, but a small evil, and much of its danger consists in the proneness of our minds to regard its direct as its only consequences. Abstractly considered, the hanging of the gamblers at Vicksburg was of but little consequence. They constitute a portion of population that is worse than useless in any community; and their death, if no pernicious example be set by it, is never matter of reasonable regret with any one. If they were annually swept from the stage of existence by the plague or smallpox, honest men would perhaps be much profited by the operation. Similar too is the correct reasoning in regard to the burning of the negro at St. Louis. He had forfeited his life by the perpetration of an outrageous murder upon one of the most worthy and respectable citizens of the city, and had he not died as he did, he must have died by the sentence of the law in a very short time afterward. As to him alone, it was as well the way it was as it could otherwise have been. But the example in either case was fearful. When men take it in their heads to-day to hang gamblers or burn murderers, they should recollect that in the confusion usually attending such transactions they will be as likely to hang or burn some one who is neither a gambler nor a murderer as one who is, and that, acting upon the example they set, the mob of to-morrow may, and probably will, hang or burn some of them by the very same mistake. And not only so; the innocent, those who have ever set their faces against violations of law in every shape, alike with the guilty fall victims to the ravages of mob law; and thus it goes on, step by step, till all the walls erected for the defense of the persons and property of individuals are trodden down and disregarded. But all this, even, is not the full extent of the evil. By such examples, by instances of the perpetrators of such acts going unpunished, the lawless in spirit are encouraged to become lawless in practice; and having been used to no restraint but dread of punishment, they thus become absolutely unrestrained. Having ever regarded government as their deadliest bane, they make a jubilee of the suspension of its operations, and pray for nothing so much as its total annihilation. While, on the other hand, good men, men who love tranquillity, who desire to abide by the laws and enjoy their benefits, who would gladly spill their blood in the defense of their country, seeing their property destroyed, their families insulted, and their lives endangered, their persons injured, and seeing nothing in prospect that forebodes a change for the better, become tired of and disgusted with a government that offers them no protection, and are not much averse to a change in which they imagine they have nothing to lose. Thus, then, by the operation of this mobocratic spirit which all must admit is now abroad in the land, the strongest bulwark of any government, and particularly of those constituted like ours, may effectually be broken down and destroyed - I mean the attachment of the people. Whenever this effect shall be produced among us; whenever the vicious portion of population shall be permitted to gather in bands of hundreds and thousands, and burn churches, ravage and rob provision-stores, throw printing-presses into rivers, shoot editors, and hang and burn obnoxious persons at pleasure and with impunity, depend on it, this government cannot last. By such things the feelings of the best citizens will become more or less alienated from it, and thus it will be left without friends, or with too few, and those few too weak to make their friendship effectual. At such a time, and under such circumstances, men of sufficient talent and ambition will not be wanting to seize the opportunity, strike the blow, and overturn that fair fabric which for the last half century has been the fondest hope of the lovers of freedom throughout the world.

I know the American people are much attached to their government; I know they would suffer much for its sake; I know they would endure evils long and patiently before they would ever think of exchanging it for another - yet, notwithstanding all this, if the laws be continually despised and disregarded, if their rights to be secure in their persons and property are held by no better tenure than the caprice of a mob, the alienation of their affections from the government is the natural consequence; and to that, sooner or later, it must come.

Here then is one point at which danger may be expected.

The question recurs, "How shall we fortify against it?" The answer is simple. Let every American, every lover of liberty, every well-wisher to his posterity swear by the blood of the Revolution never to violate in the least particular the laws of the country, and never to tolerate their violation by others. As the patriots of seventy-six did to the support of the Declaration of Independence, so to the support of the Constitution and laws let every American pledge his life, his property, and his sacred honor - let every man remember that to violate the law is to trample on the blood of his father, and to tear the charter of his own and his children's liberty. Let reverence for the laws be breathed by every American mother to the lisping babe that prattles on her lap; let it be taught in schools, in seminaries, and in colleges; let it be written in primers, spelling-books, and in almanacs; let it be preached from the pulpit, proclaimed in legislative halls, and enforced in courts of justice. And, in short, let it become the political religion of the nation; and let the old and the young, the rich and the poor, the grave and the gay of all sexes and tongues and colors and conditions, sacrifice unceasingly upon its altars.

While ever a state of feeling such as this shall universally or even very generally prevail throughout the nation, vain will be every effort, and fruitless every attempt, to subvert our national freedom.

When I so pressingly urge a strict observance of all the laws, let me not be understood as saying there are no bad laws, or that grievances may not arise for the redress of which no legal provisions have been made. I mean to say no such thing. But I do mean to say that although bad laws, if they exist, should be repealed as soon as possible, still, while they continue in force, for the sake of example they should be religiously observed. So also in unprovided cases. If such arise, let proper legal provisions be made for them with the least possible delay, but till then let them, if not too intolerable, be borne with.

There is no grievance that is a fit object of redress by mob law. In any case that may arise, as, for instance, the promulgation of abolitionism, one of two positions is necessarily true - that is, the thing is right within itself, and therefore deserves the protection of all law and all good citizens, or it is wrong, and therefore proper to be prohibited by legal enactments; and in neither case is the interposition of mob law either necessary, justifiable, or excusable.

But it may be asked, "Why suppose danger to our political institutions? Have we not preserved them for more than fifty years? And why may we not for fifty times as long?"

We hope there is no sufficient reason. We hope all danger may be overcome; but to conclude that no danger may ever arise would itself be extremely dangerous. There are now, and will hereafter be, many causes, dangerous in their tendency, which have not existed heretofore, and which are not too insignificant to merit attention. That our government should have been maintained in its original form, from its establishment until now, is not much to be wondered at. It had many props to support it through that period, which now are decayed and crumbled away. Through that period it was felt by all to be an undecided experiment; now it is understood to be a successful one. Then, all that sought celebrity and fame and distinction expected to find them in the success of that experiment. There all was staked upon it; their destiny was inseparably linked with it. Their ambition aspired to display before an admiring world a practical demonstration of the truth of a proposition which had hitherto been considered at best no better than problematical - namely, the capability of a people to govern themselves. If they succeeded they were to be immortalized; their names were to be transferred to counties, and cities, and rivers, and mountains; and to be revered and sung, toasted through all time. If they failed, they were to be called knaves, and fools, and fanatics for a fleeting hour; then to sink and be forgotten. They succeeded. The experiment is successful, and thousands have won their deathless names in making it so. But the game is caught; and I believe it is true that with the catching end the pleasures of the chase. This field of glory is harvested, and the crop is already appropriated. But new reapers will arise, and they too will seek a field. It is to deny what the history of the world tells us is true, to suppose that men of ambition and talents will not continue to spring up amongst us. And when they do, they will as naturally seek the gratification of their ruling passion as others have done before them. The question then is, Can that gratification be found in supporting and maintaining an edifice that has been erected by others? Most certainly it cannot. Many great and good men, sufficiently qualified for any task they should undertake, may ever be found whose ambition would aspire to nothing beyond a seat in Congress, a gubernatorial or a presidential chair; but such belong not to the family of the lion, or the tribe of the eagle. What! think you these places would satisfy an Alexander, a Caesar, or a Napoleon? Never! Towering genius disdains a beaten path. It seeks regions hitherto unexplored. It sees no distinction in adding story to story upon the monuments of fame erected to the memory of others. It denies that it is glory enough to serve under any chief. It scorns to tread in the footsteps of any predecessor, however illustrious. It thirsts and burns for distinction; and if possible, it will have it, whether at the expense of emancipating slaves or enslaving freemen. Is it unreasonable, then, to expect that some man possessed of the loftiest genius, coupled with ambition sufficient to push it to its utmost stretch, will at some time spring up among us? And when such a one does, it will require the people to be united with each other, attached to the government and laws, and generally intelligent, to successfully frustrate his designs.

Distinction will be his paramount object, and although he would as willingly, perhaps more so, acquire it by doing good as harm, yet, that opportunity being past, and nothing left to be done in the way of building up, he would set boldly to the task of pulling down.

Here then is a probable case, highly dangerous, and such a one as could not have well existed heretofore.

Another reason which once was, but which, to the same extent, is now no more, has done much in maintaining our institutions thus far.   I mean the powerful influence which the interesting scenes of the Revolution had upon the passions of the people as distinguished from their judgment. By this influence, the jealousy, envy, and avarice incident to our nature, and so common to a state of peace, prosperity, and conscious strength, were for the time in a great measure smothered and rendered inactive, while the deep-rooted principles of hate, and the powerful motive of revenge, instead of being turned against each other, were directed exclusively against the British nation. And thus, from the force of circumstances, the basest principles of our nature were either made to lie dormant, or to become the active agents in the advancement of the noblest of causes - that of establishing and maintaining civil and religious liberty.

But this state of feeling must fade, is fading, has faded, with the circumstances that produced it.

I do not mean to say that the scenes of the Revolution are now or ever will be entirely forgotten, but that, like everything else, they must fade upon the memory of the world, and grow more and more dim by the lapse of time. In history, we hope, they will be read of, and recounted, so long as the Bible shall be read; but even granting that they will, their influence cannot be what it heretofore has been. Even then they cannot be so universally known nor so vividly felt as they were by the generation just gone to rest. At the close of that struggle, nearly every adult male had been a participator in some of its scenes. The consequence was that of those scenes, in the form of a husband, a father, a son, or a brother, a living history was to be found in every family - a history bearing the indubitable testimonies of its own authenticity, in the limbs mangled, in the scars of wounds received, in the midst of the very scenes related - a history, too, that could be read and understood alike by all, the wise and the ignorant, the learned and the unlearned. But those histories are gone. They can be read no more forever. They were a fortress of strength; but what invading foeman could never do, the silent artillery of time has done - the leveling of its walls. They are gone. They were a forest of giant oaks; but the all-restless hurricane has swept over them, and left only here and there a lonely trunk, despoiled of its verdure, shorn of its foliage, unshading and unshaded, to murmur in a few more gentle breezes, and to combat with its mutilated limbs more ruder storms, then to sink and be no more.

They were pillars of the temple of liberty; and now that they have crumbled away that temple must fall unless we, their descendants, supply their places with other pillars, hewn from the solid quarry of sober reason. Passion has helped us, but can do so no more. It will in future be our enemy. Reason - cold, calculating, unimpassioned reason - must furnish all the materials for our future support and defense. Let those materials be molded into general intelligence, sound morality, and, in particular, a reverence for the Constitution and laws; and that we improved to the last, that we remained free to the last, that we revered his name to the last, that during his long sleep we permitted no hostile foot to pass over or desecrate his resting-place, shall be that which to learn the last trump shall awaken our Washington.

Upon these let the proud fabric of freedom rest, as the rock of its basis, and, as truly as has been said of the only greater institution, "the gates of hell shall not prevail against it."

THE WAR WITH MEXICO
THE HOUSE OF REPRESENTATIVES
WASHINGTON, DC
January 12, 1848

Some if not all the gentlemen on the other side of the House who have addressed the committee within the last two days have spoken rather complainingly, if I have rightly understood them, of the vote given a week or ten days ago declaring that the war with Mexico was unnecessarily and unconstitutionally commenced by the President. I admit that such a vote should not be given in mere party wantonness, and that the one given is justly censurable, if it have no other or better foundation. I am one of those who joined in that vote; and I did so under my best impression of the truth of the case. How I got this impression, and how it may possibly be remedied, I will now try to show. When the war began, it was my opinion that all those who because of knowing too little, or because of knowing too much, could not conscientiously oppose the conduct of the President in the beginning of it should nevertheless, as good citizens and patriots, remain silent on that point, at least till the war should be ended. Some leading Democrats, including ex-President Van Buren, have taken this same view, as I understand them; and I adhered to it and acted upon it, until since I took my seat here; and I think I should still adhere to it were it not that the President and his friends will not allow it to be so. Besides the continual effort of the President to argue every silent vote given for supplies into an indorsement of the justice and wisdom of his conduct; besides that singularly candid paragraph in his late message in which he tells us that Congress with great unanimity had declared that "by the act of the Republic of Mexico, a state of war exists between that Government and the United States," when the same journals that informed him of this also informed him that when that declaration stood disconnected from the question of supplies sixty-seven in the House, and not fourteen merely, voted against it; besides this open attempt to prove by telling the truth what he could not prove by telling the whole truth - demanding of all who will not submit to be misrepresented, in justice to themselves, to speak out - besides all this, one of my colleagues [Mr. Richardson] at a very early day in the session brought in a set of resolutions expressly indorsing the original justice of the war on the part of the President. Upon these resolutions when they shall be put on their passage I shall be compelled to vote; so that I cannot be silent if I would. Seeing this, I went about preparing myself to give the vote understandingly when it should come. I carefully examined the President's message, to ascertain what he himself had said and proved upon the point. The result of this examination was to make the impression that, taking for true all the President states as facts, he falls far short of proving his justification; and that the President would have gone farther with his proof if it had not been for the small matter that the truth would not permit him. Under the impression thus made I gave the vote before mentioned. I propose now to give concisely the process of the examination I made, and how I reached the conclusion I did. The President, in his first war message of May, 1846, declares that the soil was ours on which hostilities were commenced by Mexico, and he repeats that declaration almost in the same language in each successive annual message, thus showing that he deems that point a highly essential one. In the importance of that point I entirely agree with the President. To my judgment it is the very point upon which he should be justified, or condemned. In his message of December,

1846, it seems to have occurred to him, as is certainly true, that title - ownership - to soil or anything else is not a simple fact, but is a conclusion following on one or more simple facts; and that it was incumbent upon him to present the facts from which he concluded the soil was ours on which the first blood of the war was shed.

Accordingly, a little below the middle of page twelve in the message last referred to he enters upon that task; forming an issue and introducing testimony, extending the whole to a little below the middle of page fourteen. Now, I propose to try to show that the whole of this - issue and evidence - is from beginning to end the sheerest deception. The issue, as he presents it, is in these words: "But there are those who, conceding all this to be true, assume the ground that the true western boundary of Texas is the Nueces, instead of the Rio Grande; and that, therefore, in marching our army to the east bank of the latter river, we passed the Texas line and invaded the territory of Mexico." Now this issue is made up of two affirmatives and no negative. The main deception of it is that is assumes as true that one river or the other is necessarily the boundary; and cheats the superficial thinker entirely out of the idea that possibly the boundary is somewhere between the two, and not actually at either. A further deception is that it will let in evidence which a true issue would exclude. A true issue made by the President would be about as follows: "I say the soil was ours, on which the first blood was shed; there are those who say it was not."

I now proceed to examine the President's evidence as applicable to such an issue. When that evidence is analyzed, it is all included in the following propositions:

(1) That the Rio Grande was the western boundary of Louisiana as we purchased it of France in 1803.

(2) That the Republic of Texas always claimed the Rio Grande as her western boundary.

(3) That by various acts she had claimed it on paper.

(4) That Santa Anna in his treaty with Texas recognized the Rio Grande as her boundary.

(5) That Texas before, and the United States after, annexation had exercised jurisdiction beyond the Nueces - between the two rivers.

(6) That our Congress understood the boundary of Texas to extend beyond the Nueces.

Now for each of these in its turn. His first item is that the Rio Grande was the western boundary of Louisiana, as we purchased it of France in 1803; and seeming to expect this to be disputed, he argues over the amount of nearly a page to prove it true; at the end of which he lets us know that by the treaty of 1819 we sold to Spain the whole country from the Rio Grande eastward to the Sabine. Now, admitting for the present that the Rio Grande was the boundary of Louisiana, what, under heaven, had that to do with the present boundary between us and Mexico? How, Mr. Chairman, the line that once divided your land from mine can still be the boundary between us after I have sold my land to you is to me beyond all comprehension. And how any man, with an honest purpose only of proving the truth, could ever have thought of introducing such a fact to prove such an issue is equally incomprehensible. His next piece of evidence is that "the Republic of Texas always claimed this river (Rio Grande) as her western boundary." That is not true, in fact. Texas has claimed it, but she has not always claimed it. There is at least one distinguished exception. Her State constitution - the republic's most solemn and well-considered act; that which may, without impropriety, be called her last will and testament, revoking all others - makes no such claim. But suppose she had always claimed it. Has not Mexico always claimed the contrary? So that there is but claim against claim, leaving nothing proved until we get back of the claims and find which has the better foundation. Though not in the order in which the President presents his evidence, I now consider that class of his statements which are in substance nothing more than that Texas has, by various acts of her Convention and Congress, claimed the Rio Grande as her boundary, on paper. I mean here what he says about the fixing of the Rio Grande as her boundary in her old constitution (not her State constitution), about forming congressional districts, counties, etc. Now all of this is but naked claim; and what I have already said about claims is strictly applicable to this. If I should claim your land by word of mouth, that certainly would not make it mine; and if I were to claim it by a deed which I had made myself, and with which you had had nothing to do, the claim would be quite the same in substance - or rather, in utter nothingness. I next consider the President's statement that Santa Anna in his treaty with Texas recognized the Rio Grande as the western boundary of Texas. Besides the position so often taken, that Santa Anna while a prisoner of war, a captive, could not bind Mexico by a treaty, which I deem conclusive - besides this, I wish to say something in relation to this treaty, so called by the President, with Santa Anna. If any

clear to the Rio Grande is quite certain, by the fact of their joint resolutions for admission expressly leaving all questions of boundary to future adjustment. And it may be added that Texas herself is proved to have had the same understanding of it that our Congress had, by the fact of the exact conformity of her new constitution to those resolutions.

I am now through the whole of the President's evidence; and it is a singular fact that if any one should declare the President sent the army into the midst of a settlement of Mexican people who had never submitted, by consent or by force, to the authority of Texas or of the United States, and that there and thereby the first blood of the war was shed, there is not one word in all the President has said which would either admit or deny the declaration. This strange omission it does seem to me could not have occurred but by design. My way of living leads me to be about the courts of justice; and there I have sometimes seen a good lawyer, struggling for his client's neck in a desperate case, employing every artifice to work round, befog, and cover up with many words some point arising in the case which he dared not admit and yet could not deny. Party bias may help to make it appear so, but with all the allowance I can make for such bias, it still does appear to me that just such, and from just such necessity, is the President's struggle in this case.

Some time after my colleague [Mr. Richardson] introduced the resolutions I have mentioned, I introduced a preamble, resolution, and interrogations, intended to draw the President out, if possible, on this hitherto untrodden ground. To show their relevancy, I propose to state my understanding of the true rule for ascertaining the boundary between Texas and Mexico. It is that wherever Texas was exercising jurisdiction was hers; and wherever Mexico was exercising jurisdiction was hers; and that whatever separated the actual exercise of jurisdiction of the one from that of the other was the true boundary between them. If, as is probably true, Texas was exercising jurisdiction along the western bank of the Nueces, and Mexico was exercising it along the eastern bank of the Rio Grande, then neither river was the boundary; but the uninhabited country between the two was. The extent of our territory in that region depended not on any treaty-fixed boundary (for no treaty had attempted it), but on revolution. Any people anywhere being inclined and having the power have the right to rise up and shake off the existing government, and form a new one that suits them better. This is a most valuable, a most sacred right - a right which we hope and believe is to liberate the world. Nor is this right confined to cases in which the whole people of an existing government may choose to exercise it. Any portion of such people that can may revolutionize and make their own of so much of the territory as they inhabit. More than this, a majority of any portion of such people may revolutionize, putting down a minority, intermingled with or near about them, who may oppose this movement. Such minority was precisely the case of the Tories of our own revolution. It is a quality of revolutions not to go by old lines or old laws; but to break up both, and make new ones.

As to the country now in question, we bought it of France in 1803, and sold it to Spain in 1819, according to the President's statements. After this, all Mexico, including Texas, revolutionized against Spain; and still later Texas revolutionized against Mexico. In my view, just so far as she carried her resolution by obtaining the actual, willing or unwilling, submission of the people, so far the country was hers, and no farther. Now, sir, for the purpose of obtaining the very best evidence as to whether Texas had actually carried her revolution to the place where the hostilities of the present war commenced, let the President answer the interrogatories I proposed, as before mentioned, or some other similar ones. Let him answer fully, fairly, and candidly. Let him answer with facts and not with arguments. Let him remember he sits where Washington sat, and so remembering, let him answer as Washington would answer. As a nation should not, and the Almighty will not, be evaded, so let him attempt no evasion - no equivocation. And if, so answering, he can show that the soil was ours where the first blood of the war was shed - that it was not within an inhabited country, or, if within such, that the inhabitants had submitted themselves to the civil authority of Texas or of the United States, and that the same is true of the site of Fort Brown - then I am with him for his justification. In that case I shall be most happy to reverse the vote I gave the other day. I have a selfish motive for desiring that the President may do this - I expect to gain some votes, in connection with the war, which, without his so doing, will be of doubtful propriety in my own judgment, but which will be free from the doubt if he does so. But if he can not or will not do this - if on any pretense or no pretense he shall refuse or omit it - then I shall be fully convinced of what I more than suspect already - that he is deeply conscious of being in the wrong; that he feels the blood of this war, like the blood of Abel, is crying to Heaven against him; that originally having some strong motive - what, I will not stop now to give my opinion concerning - to involve the two countries in a war, and trusting to escape scrutiny by fixing the public gaze upon the exceeding brightness of military glory - that attractive rainbow that rises in showers of blood - that serpent's eye that charms to destroy - he plunged into it, and has swept on and on till, disappointed in his calculation of the ease with which Mexico might be subdued, he now finds himself he knows not where. How like the half-insane mumbling of a fever dream is the whole war part of his late message! At one time telling us that Mexico has nothing whatever that we can get but territory; at another showing us how we can support the war by levying contributions on Mexico. At one time urging the national honor, the security of the future, the prevention of foreign interference, and even the good of Mexico herself as among the objects of the war; at another telling us that "to reject indemnity, by refusing to accept a cession of territory, would be to abandon all our just demands, and to wage the war bearing all its expenses, without a purpose or definite object." So then this national honor, security of the future, and everything but territorial indemnity may be considered the no-purposes and indefinite objects of the war! But, having it now settled that territorial indemnity is the only object, we are urged to seize, by legislation here, all that he was content to take a few months ago, and the whole province of Lower California to boot, and to still carry on the war - to take all we are fighting for, and still fight on. Again, the President is resolved under all circumstances to have full territorial indemnity for the expenses of the war; but he forgets to tell us how we are to get the excess after those expenses shall have surpassed the value of the whole of the Mexican territory. So again, he insists that the separate national existence of Mexico shall be maintained; but he does not tell us how this can be done, after we shall have taken all her territory. Lest the questions I have suggested be considered speculative merely, let me be indulged a moment in trying to show they are not. The war has gone on some twenty months; for the expenses of which, together with an inconsiderable old score, the President now claims about one half of the Mexican territory, and that by far the better half, so far as concerns our ability to make anything out of it. It is comparatively uninhabited; so that we could establish land offices in it, and raise some money in that way. But the other half is already inhabited, as I understand it, tolerably densely for the nature of the country, and all its lands, or all that are valuable, already appropriated as private property. How then are we to make anything out of these lands with this encumbrance on them? or how remove the encumbrance? I suppose no one would say we should kill the people, or drive them out, or make slaves of them; or confiscate their property. How, then, can we make much out of this part of the territory? If the prosecution of the war has in expenses already equaled the better half of the country, how long its future prosecution will be in equaling the less valuable half is not a speculative, but a practical, question, pressing closely upon us. And yet it is a question which the President seems never to have thought of. As to the mode of terminating the war and securing peace, the President is equally wandering and indefinite. First, it is to be done by a more vigorous prosecution of the war in the vital parts of the enemy's country; and after apparently talking himself tired on this point, the President drops down into a half-despairing tone, and tells us that "with a people distracted and divided by contending actions, and a government subject to constant changes by successive revolutions, the continued success of our arms may fail to secure a satisfactory peace." Then he suggests the propriety of wheedling the Mexican people to desert the counsels of their own leaders, and, trusting in our protestations, to set up a government from which we can secure a satisfactory peace; telling us that "this may become the only mode of obtaining such a peace." But soon he falls into doubt of this too; and then drops back onto the already half-abandoned ground of "more vigorous prosecution." All this shows that the President is in nowise satisfied with his own positions. First he takes up one, and in attempting to argue us into it he argues himself out of it, then seizes another and goes through the same process, and then, confused at being able to think of nothing new, he snatches up the old one again, which he has some time before cast off. His mind, taxed beyond its power, is running hither and thither, like some tortured creature on a burning surface, finding no position on which it can settle down and be at ease.

Again, it is a singular omission in this message that it nowhere intimates when the President expects the war to terminate. At its beginning, General Scott was by this same President driven into disfavor, if not disgrace, for intimating that peace could not be conquered in less than three or four months. But now, at the end of about twenty months, during which time our arms have given us the most splendid successes, every department and every part, land and water, officers and privates, regulars and volunteers, doing all that men could do, and hundreds of things which it had ever before been thought men could not do - after all this, this same President gives a long message, without showing us that as to the end he himself has even an imaginary conception. As I have before said, he knows not where he is. He is a bewildered, confounded, and miserably perplexed man. God grant he may be able to show there is not something about his conscience more painful than all his mental perplexity.

TEMPERANCE AND INTEMPERANCE
SPRINGIELD TEMPERANCE SOCIETY
FEBRUARY 22, 1842

Although the Temperance cause has been in progress for near twenty years, it is apparent to all, that it is, *just now*, being crowned with a degree of success, hitherto unparalleled.

The list of its friends is daily swelled by the additions of fifties, of hundreds, and of thousands. The cause itself seems suddenly transformed from a cold abstract theory, to a living, breathing, active, and powerful chieftain, going forth "conquering and to conquer." The citadels of his great adversary are daily being stormed and dismantled; his temples and his altars, where the rites of his idolatrous worship have long been performed, and where human sacrifices have long been wont to be made, are daily desecrated and deserted. The trump of the conqueror's fame is sounding from hill to hill, from sea to sea, and from land to land, and calling millions to his standard at a blast.

For this new and splendid success, we heartily rejoice. That that success is so much greater *now* than *heretofore*, is doubtless owing to rational causes; and if we would have it to continue, we shall do well to enquire what those causes are. The warfare heretofore waged against the demon of Intemperance, has, some how or other, been erroneous. Either the champions engaged, or the tactics they adopted, have not been the most proper. These champions for the most part, have been Preachers, Lawyers, and hired agents. Between these and the mass of mankind, there is a want of *approachability*, if the term be admissible, partially at least, fatal to their success. They are sup-

posed to have no sympathy of feeling or interest, with
those very persons whom it is their object to convince and
persuade.

And again, it is so easy and so common to ascribe motives
to men of these classes, other than those they profess to
act upon. The *preacher*, it is said, advocates temperance
because he is a fanatic, and desires a union of the Church
and State; the *lawyer*, from his pride and vanity of hearing himself speak; and the *hired agent*, for his salary. But
when one, who has long been known as a victim of intemperance, bursts the fetters that have bound him, and appears before his neighbors "clothed, and in his right
mind," a redeemed specimen of long lost humanity, and
stands up with tears of joy trembling in eyes, to tell of the
miseries *once* endured, *now* to be endured no more forever; of his once naked and starving children, now clad and
fed comfortably; of a wife, long weighed down with woe,
weeping, and a broken heart, now restored to health, happiness and renewed affection; and how easily it all is
done, once it is resolved to be done; however simple his
language, there is a logic, and an eloquence in it, that few,
with human feelings, can resist. They cannot say that *he*
desires a union of church and state, for he is not a church
member; they can not say *he* is vain of hearing himself
speak, for his whole demeanor shows, he would gladly
avoid speaking at all; they cannot say *he* speaks for pay
for he receives none, and asks for none. Nor can his sincerity in any way be doubted; or his sympathy for those
he would persuade to imitate his example, be denied.

In my judgment, it is to the battles of this new class of
champions that our late success is greatly, perhaps chiefly,
owing. But, had the old school champions themselves,
been of the most wise selecting, was their *system* of tac-

tics, the most judicious? It seems to me, it was not. Too much denunciation against dram sellers and dram drinkers was indulged in. This I think, was both impolitic and unjust. It was *impolitic*, because, it is not much in the nature of man to be driven to any thing; still less to be driven about that which is exclusively his own business; and least of all, where such driving is to be submitted to, at the expense of pecuniary interest, or burning appetite. When the dram-seller, and drinker, were incessantly told, not in the accents of entreaty and persuasion, diffidently addressed by erring man to an erring brother, but in the thundering tones of anathema and denunciation, with which the lordly Judge often groups together all the crimes of the felon's life, and thrusts them in his face just ere he passes sentence of death upon him, that *they* were the authors of all the vice and misery and crime in the land; that *they* were the manufacturers and material of all the thieves and robbers and murderers that infested the earth; that *their* houses were the workshops of the devil; and that *their persons* should be shunned by all the good and virtuous, as moral pestilences - I say, when they were told all this, and in this way, it is not wonderful that they were slow, *very slow*, to acknowledge the truth of such denunciations, and to join the ranks of their denouncers, in a hue and cry against themselves.

To have expected them to do otherwise than as they did - to have expected them not to meet denunciation with denunciation, crimination with crimination, and anathema with anathema, was to expect a reversal of human nature, which is God's decree, and never can be reversed. When the conduct of men is designed to be influenced, *persuasion*, kind, unassuming persuasion, should ever be adopted. It is an old and a true maxim "that a drop of honey catches more flies than a gallon of gall." So with men. If you

ing and buying of flour, beef, bacon, or any other of the real necessaries of life. Universal public opinion not only tolerated, but recognized and adopted its use.

It is true, that even *then*, it was known and acknowledged, that many were greatly injured by it; but none seemed to think the injury arose the the *use* of a *bad thing*, but from the *abuse* of a *very good thing*. The victims to it were pitied, and compassionated, just as now are, the heirs of consumptions, and other hereditary diseases. Their failing was treated as a *misfortune*, and not as a *crime*, or even as a *disgrace*.

If, then, what I have been saying be true, is it wonderful that *some* should think and act *now*, as *all* thought and acted *twenty years ago*? And is it *just* to assail, contemn, or despise them, for doing so? The universal *sense* of mankind, on any subject, is an argument, or at least an *influence*, not easily overcome. The success of the argument in favor of the existence of an overruling Providence, mainly depends upon that sense; and men ought not, in justice, to be denounced for yielding to it in any case, or for giving it up slowly, *especially*, where they are backed by interest, fixed habits, or burning appetites.

Another error, as it seems to me, into which the old reformers fell, was, the position that all habitual drunkards were utterly incorrigible, and therefore, must be turned adrift, and damned without remedy, in order that the grace of temperance might abound to the temperate *then*, and to all mankind some hundred years *thereafter*. There is in this something so repugnant to humanity, so uncharitable, so cold-blooded and feelingless, that it never did, nor ever can enlist the enthusiasm of a popular cause. We could not love the man who taught it - we could not hear him with patience. The heart could not throw open its portals to it. The generous man could not adopt it. It could not mix with his blood. It looked so fiendishly self-ish, so like throwing fathers and brothers overboard, to lighten the boat for our security - that the noble minded shrank from the manifest meanness of the thing.

And besides this, the benefits of a reformation to be ef-fected by such a system, were too remote in point of time, to warmly engage many in its behalf. Few can be induced to labor exclusively for posterity; and none will do it en-thusiastically. Posterity has done nothing for us; and the-orise on it as we may, practically we shall do very little for it, unless we are made to think, we are, at the same time, doing something for ourselves. What an ignorance of human nature does it exhibit, to ask or expect a whole community to rise up and labor for the *temporal* happi-ness of *others*, after *themselves* shall be consigned to the dust, a majority of which community take no pains what-ever to secure their own eternal welfare, at no greater dis-tant day? Great distance, in either time or space, has won-derful power to lull and render quiescent the human mind. Pleasures to be enjoyed, or pains to be endured, *af-ter* we shall be dead and gone, are but little regarded, even in our *own* cases, and much less in the cases of others.

Still, in addition to this, there is something so ludicrous in *promises* of good, or *threats* of evil, a great way off, as to render the whole subject with which they are connected, easily turned into ridicule. "Better lay down that spade you're stealing, Paddy - if you don't you'll pay for it at the day of judgment." "By the powers, if ye'll credit me so long, I'll take another, jist."

By the Washingtonians, this system of consigning the habitual drunkard to hopeless ruin, is repudiated. *They* adopt a more enlarged philanthropy. *They* go for present as well as future good. *They* labor for all *now* living, as well as all *hereafter* to live. *They* teach *hope* to all - *despair* to none. As applying to *their* cause, *they* deny the doctrine of unpardonable sin. As in Christianity it is taught, so in this *they* teach, that

> "While the lamp holds out to burn,
> The vilest sinner may return."

And, what is a matter of the most profound gratulation, they, by experiment upon experiment, and example upon example, prove the maxim to be no less true in the one case than in the other. On every hand we behold those, who but yesterday, were the chief of sinners, now the chief apostles of the cause. Drunken devils are cast out by ones, by sevens, and by legions; and their unfortunate victims, like the poor possessed, who was redeemed from his long and lonely wanderings in the tombs, are publishing to the ends of the earth how great things have been done for them.

To these *new champions*, and this *new* system of tactics, our late success is mainly owing; and to *them* we must chiefly look for the final consummation. The ball is now rolling gloriously on, and none are so able as *they* to increase its speed and its bulk - to add to its momentum, and its magnitude. Even though unlearned in letters, for this task, none others are so well educated. To fit them for this work, they have been taught in the true school. *They* have been in *that* gulf, from which they would teach others the means of escape. *They* have passed that prison wall, which others have long declared impassable; and who that has not, shall dare to weigh opinions with *them*, as to the mode of passing?

But it it be true, as I have insisted, that those who have suffered by intemperance *personally*, and have reformed, are the most powerful and efficient instruments to push the reformation to ultimate success, it does not follow, that those who have not suffered, have no part left them to perform. Whether or not the world would be vastly benefitted by a total and final banishment from it of all intoxicating drinks, seems to me not *now* to be an open question. Three-fourths of mankind confess the affirmative with their *tongues*, and, I believe, all the rest acknowledge it in their *hearts*.

Ought *any*, then, to refuse their aid in doing what the good of the *whole* demands? Shall he, who cannot do *much*, be for that reason, excused if he do *nothing*? "But," says one, "what good can I do by signing the pledge? I never drink even without signing." This question has already been asked and answered more than millions of times. Let it be answered once more. For the man to suddenly, or in any other way, to break off from the use of drams, who has indulged in them for a long course of years, and until his appetite for them has become ten or a hundred fold stronger, and more craving, than any natural appetite can be, requires a most powerful moral effort. In such an undertaking, he needs every moral support and influence, that can possibly be brought to his aid, and thrown around him. And not only so; but every moral prop, should be taken *from* whatever argument might rise in his mind to lure him to his backsliding. When he casts his eyes around him, he should be able to see, all that he respects, all that he admires, and all that he loves, kindly and anxiously pointing him onward; and none beckoning him back, to his former miserable "wallowing in the mire."

But it is said by some, that men will *think* and *act* for themselves; that none will disuse spirits or anything else, merely because his neighbors do; and that *moral influence* is not that powerful engine contended for. Let us examine this. Let me ask the man who would maintain this position most stiffly, what compensation he will accept to go to church some Sunday and sit during the sermon with his wife's bonnet upon his head? Not a trifle, I'll venture. And why not? There would be nothing irreligious in it: nothing immoral, nothing uncomfortable. Then why not? Is it not because there would be something egregiously unfashionable in it? Then it is the influence of *fashion*, and what is the influence of fashion, but the influence that *other* people's actions have on our actions, the strong inclination each of us feels to do as we see all our neighbors do? Nor is the influence of fashion confined to any particular thing or class of things. It is just as strong on one subject as another. Let us make it as unfashionable to withhold our names from the temperance pledge as for husbands to wear their wives' bonnets to church, and instances will be just as rare in the one case as the other.

"But," say some, "we are no drunkards; and we shall not acknowledge ourselves such by joining a reformed drunkards' society, whatever our influence might be." Surely no Christian will adhere to this objection. If they believe, as they profess, that Omnipotence condescended to take on himself the form of sinful man, and as such, to die an ignominious death for their sakes, surely they will not refuse submission to the infinitely lesser condescension, for the temporal, and perhaps eternal salvation, of a large, erring, and unfortunate class of their own fellow creatures. Nor is the condescension very great.

In my judgment, such of us as have never fallen victims, have been spared more from the absence of appetite, than from any mental or moral superiority over those who have. Indeed, I believe, if we take habitual drunkards as a class, their heads and their hearts will bear an advantageous comparison with those of any other class. There seems ever to have been a proneness in the brilliant, and the warm-blooded, to fall into this vice - the demon of intemperance ever seems to have delighted in sucking the blood of genius and of generosity. What one of us but can call to mind some dear relative, more promising in youth than all his fellows, who has fallen a sacrifice to his rapacity? He ever seems to have gone forth, like the Egyptian angel of death, commissioned to slay if not the first, the fairest born of every family. Shall he now be arrested in his desolating career? In that arrest, all can give aid that will; and who shall be excused that *can* and will not? Far around as human breath has ever blown, he keeps our fathers, our brothers, our sons, and our friends prostrate in the chains of moral death. To all the living every where, we cry, "come sound the moral resurrection trump, that these may rise and stand up, an exceeding great army" - "Come from the four winds, O breath! and breathe upon these slain, that they may live."

If the relative grandeur of revolutions shall be estimated by the great amount of human misery they alleviate, and the small amount they inflict, then indeed, will this be the grandest the world shall ever have seen. Of our political revolution of '76 we all are justly proud. It has given us a degree of political freedom, far exceeding that of any other of the nations of the earth. In it the world has found a

solution of the long mooted problem, as to the capability
of man to govern himself. In it was the germ which has
vegetated, and still is to grow and expand into the universal liberty of mankind.

But with all these glorious results, past, present, and to
come, it had its evils too. It breathed forth famine, swam
in blood and rode on fire; and long, long after, the orphan's cry, and the widow's wail, continued to break the
sad silence that ensued. These were the price, the inevitable price, paid for the blessings it bought.

Turn now, to the temperance revolution. In *it* we shall
find a stronger bondage broken; a viler slavery manumit-
ted; a greater tyrant deposed. In *it*, more of want supplied, more disease healed, more sorrow assuaged. By *it*
no orphans starving, no widows weeping. By *it*, none
wounded in feeling, none injured in interest. Even the
dram maker and dram seller, will have glided into other
occupations *so* gradually, as never to have felt the shock
of change; and will stand ready to join all others in the
universal song of gladness.

And what a noble ally this, to the cause of political freedom. With such an aid, its march cannot fail to be on and
on, till every son of earth shall drink in rich fruition, the
sorrow quenching draughts of perfect liberty. Happy day,
when, all appetites controlled, all passions subdued, all
matters subjected, *mind*, all conquering *mind*, shall live
and move the monarch of the world. Glorious consummation? Hail, fall of Fury! Reign of Reason, all hail!

And when the victory shall be complete - when there shall
be neither a slave nor a drunkard on the earth - how
proud the title of that *Land*, which may truly claim to be

the birthplace and the cradle of both those revolutions, that shall have ended in that victory. How nobly distinguished that People, who shall have planted, and nurtured to maturity, both the political and moral freedom of their species.

This is the one hundred and tenth anniversary of the birthday of Washington. We are met to celebrate this day. Washington is the mightiest name of earth - *long since* mightiest in the cause of civil liberty; *still* mightiest in moral reformation. On that name an eulogy is expected. It cannot be. To add brightness to the sun, or glory to the name of Washington, is alike impossible. Let none attempt it. In solemn awe pronounce the name, and in its naked deathless splendor, leave it shining on.

THE PRESIDENTIAL CANDIDATES
HOUSE OF REPRESENTATIVES
July 27, 1848

Mr. Speaker: Our Democratic friends seem to be in great
distress because they think our candidate for the Presidency don't suit *us.* Most of them cannot find out that General Taylor has any principles at all; some, however, have
discovered that he has *one,* but that that one is entirely
wrong. This one principle is his position on the veto power. The gentleman from Tennessee who has just taken his
seat, indeed, has said there is very little if any difference
on this question between General Taylor and all the Presidents; and he seems to think it sufficient detraction from
General Taylor's position on it, that it has nothing new in
it. But all others, whom I have heard speak, assail it furiously. A new member from Kentucky, of very considerable ability, was in particular concern about it. He thought
it altogether novel and unprecedented for a President, or a
Presidential candidate, to think of approving bills whose
constitutionality may not be entirely clear to his own
mind. He thinks the ark of our safety is gone, unless
Presidents shall always veto such bills as, in their judgment, may be of *doubtful* constitutionality. However
clear Congress may be of their authority to pass any particular act, the gentleman from Kentucky thinks the President must veto it if *he* has *doubts* about it. Now I have
neither time nor inclination to argue with the gentleman
on the veto power as an original question; but I wish to
show that General Taylor, and not he, agrees with the earlier statesmen on this question. When the bill chartering
the first Bank of the United States passed Congress, its
constitutionality was questioned; Mr. Madison, then in the
House of Representatives, as well as others, had opposed it

on that ground. General Washington, as President, was called on to approve or reject it. He sought and obtained, on the constitutional question, the separate written opinion of Jefferson, Hamilton, and Edmund Randolph, they then being respectively Secretary of State, Secretary of the Treasury, and Attorney-General. Hamilton's opinion was for the power; while Randolph's and Jefferson's were both against it. Mr. Jefferson, after giving his opinion decidedly against the constitutionality of that bill, closes his letter with the paragraph which I now read: "It must be admitted, however, that unless the President's mind, on a view of everything which is urged for and against this bill, is tolerably clear that it is unauthorized by the Constitution; if the pro and the con hang so even as to balance his judgment, a just respect for the wisdom of the legislature would naturally decide the balance in favor of their opinion; it is chiefly for cases where they are clearly misled by error, ambition, or interest, that the Constitution has placed a check in the negative of the President."

General Taylor's opinion, as expressed in his Allison letter, is as I now read: "The power given by the veto is a high conservative power; but, in my opinion, should never be exercised, except in cases of clear violation of the Constitution, or manifest haste and want of consideration by Congress."

It is here seen that, in Mr. Jefferson's opinion, if, on the constitutionality of any given bill, the President *doubts,* he is not to veto it, as the gentleman from Kentucky would have him do, but is to defer to Congress and approve it. And if we compare the opinions of Jefferson and Taylor, as expressed in these paragraphs, we shall find them more exactly alike than we can often find any two expressions having any literal difference. None but interested fault-finders, I think, can discover any substantial variation.

But gentlemen on the other side are unanimously agreed that General Taylor has no other principles. They are in utter darkness as to his opinions on any of the questions of policy which occupy the public attention. But is there any doubt as to what he will *do* on the prominent questions, if elected? Not the least. It is not possible to know what he will or would do in every imaginable case; because many questions have passed away, and others doubtless will arise which none of us have yet thought of; but on the prominent questions of currency, tariff, internal improvements, and Wilmot Proviso, General Taylor's course is at least as well defined as is General Cass's. Why, in their eagerness to get at General Taylor, several Democratic members here have desired to know whether, in case of his election, a bankrupt law is to be established. Can they tell us General Cass's opinion on this question? [Some member answered, "He is against it."] Aye, how do you know he is? There is nothing about it in the platform, nor elsewhere, that I have seen. If the gentleman knows anything which I do not, he can show it. But to return: General Taylor, in his Allison letter, says: "Upon the subject of the tariff, the currency, the improvement of our great highways, rivers, lakes, and harbors, the will of the people, as expressed through their Representatives in Congress, ought to be respected and carried out by the Executive."

Now, this is the whole matter - in substance, it is this: The people say to General Taylor, "If you are elected, shall we have a national bank?" He answers, "*Your* will, gentlemen, not *mine.*" "What about the tariff?" "Say yourselves." "Shall our rivers and harbors be improved?"

"Just as you please. If you desire a bank, an alteration of
the tariff, internal improvements, any or all, I will not
hinder you; if you do not desire them, I will not attempt
to force them on you. Send up your members of Congress
from the various districts, with opinions according to your
own, and if they are for these measures, or any of them, I
shall have nothing to oppose; if they are not for them, I
shall not, by any appliances whatever, attempt to dragoon
them into their adoption." Now, can there be any difficulty in understanding this? To you, Democrats, it may not
seem like principle; but surely you cannot fail to perceive
the position plainly enough. The distinction between it
and the position of your candidate is broad and obvious,
and I admit you have a clear right to show it is wrong, if
you can; but you have no right to pretend you cannot see
it at all. We see it, and to us it appears like principle, and
the best sort of principle at that - the principle of allowing the people to do as they please with their own business. My friend from Indiana has aptly asked, "Are you
willing to trust the people?" Some of you answered, substantially, "We are willing to trust the people; but the
President is as much the representative of the people as
Congress." In a certain sense, and to a certain extent, he is
the representative of the people. He is elected by them, as
well as Congress is.

But can he, in the nature of things, know the wants of the
people as well as three hundred other men coming from
all the various localities of the nation? If so, where is the
propriety of having a Congress? That the Constitution
gives the President a negative on legislation, all know; but
that this negative should be so combined with platforms
and other appliances as to enable him, and, in fact, almost
compel him, to take the whole of legislation into his own
hands, is what we object to - is what General Taylor ob-

jects to - and is what constitutes the broad distinction between you and us. To thus transfer legislation is clearly to take it from those who understand with minuteness the interest of the people, and give it to one who does not and cannot so well understand it. I understand your idea, that if a Presidential candidate avow his opinion upon a given question, or rather upon all questions, and the people, with full knowledge of this, elect him, they thereby distinctly approve all those opinions. This, though plausible, is a most pernicious deception. By means of it measures are adopted or rejected, contrary to the wishes of the whole of one party, and often nearly half of the other. The process is this: Three, four, or half a dozen questions are prominent at a given time; the party selects its candidate, and he takes his position on each of these questions. On all but one his positions have already been endorsed at former elections, and his party fully committed to them; but that one is new, and a large portion of them are against it. But what are they to do? The whole are strung together, and they must take all or reject all. They cannot take what they like and leave the rest. What they are already committed to, being the majority, they shut their eyes and gulp the whole. Next election, still another is introduced in the same way. If we run our eyes along the line of the past, we shall see that almost, if not quite, all the articles of the present Democratic creed have been at first forced upon the party in this very way. And just now, and just so, opposition to internal improvements is to be established if General Cass shall be elected. Almost half the Democrats here are for improvements, but they will vote for Cass, and if he succeeds, their votes will have aided in closing the doors against improvements. Now, this is a process which we think is wrong. We prefer a candidate who, like General Taylor, will allow the people to have their own way regardless of his private opinion;

and I should think the internal-improvement Democrats at least, ought to prefer such a candidate. He would force nothing on them which they don't want, and he would allow them to have improvements, which their own candidate, if elected, will not.

Mr. Speaker, I have said General Taylor's position is as well defined as is that of General Cass. In saying this, I admit I do not certainly know what he would do on the Wilmot Proviso. I am a northern man, or rather, a western free State man, with a constituency I believe to be, and with personal feelings I know to be, against the extension of slavery. As such, and with what information I have, I hope, and *believe*, General Taylor, if elected, would not veto the proviso; but I do not *know* it. Yet, if I knew he would, I still would vote for him. I should do so, because, in my judgment, his election alone can defeat General Cass; and because, *should* slavery thereby go into the territory we now have, just so much will certainly happen by the election of Cass; and, in addition, a course of policy leading to new wars, new acquisitions of territory, and still further extensions of slavery. One of the two is to be President: which is preferable?

But there is as much doubt of Cass on improvements as there is of Taylor on the proviso. I have no doubt myself of General Cass on this question, but I know the Democrats differ among themselves as to his position. My internal-improvement colleague stated on this floor the other day, that he was satisfied Cass was for improvements, because he had voted all the bills that he (Mr. W.) had. So far so good. But Mr. Polk vetoed some of these very bills; the Baltimore Convention passed a set of resolutions, among other things, approving these vetoes, and Cass declares, in his letter accepting the nomination, that he has carefully read these resolutions, and that he adheres to them as firmly as he approves them cordially. In other words, General Cass voted for the bills, and thinks the President did right to veto them; and his friends here are amiable enough to consider him as being on one side or the other, just as one or the other may correspond with their own respective inclinations. My colleague admits that the platform declares against the constitutionality of a general system of improvements, and that General Cass endorses the platform; but he still thinks General Cass is in favor of some sort of improvements. Well, what are they? As he is against *general* objects, those he is *for*, must be *particular* and *local.* Now, this is taking the subject precisely by the wrong end. *Particularity* - expending the money of the *whole* people for an object which will benefit only a *portion* of them, is the greatest real objection to improvements, and has been so held by General Jackson, Mr. Polk, and all others, I believe, till now. But now, behold, the objects most general, nearest free from this objection, are to be rejected, while those most liable to it are to be embraced. To return: I cannot help believing that General Cass, when he wrote his letter of acceptance, well understood he was to be claimed by the advocates of both sides of this question, and that he then closed the door against all further expressions of opinion, purposely to retain the benefits of that double position. His subsequent equivocation at Cleveland, to my mind, proves such to have been the case.

One word more, and I shall have done with this branch of the subject. You Democrats, and your candidate, in the main, are in favor of laying down, in advance, a platform - a set of party positions, as a unit; and then of enforcing the people, by every sort of appliance, to ratify them, however unpalatable some of them may be. We, and our candidate, are in favor of making Presidential elections and the legislation of the country distinct matters; so that the people can elect whom they please, and afterwards, legislate just *as* they please, without any hindrance, save only so much as may guard against infractions of the Constitution, undue haste, and want of consideration. The difference between us is clear as noon-day. That we are right we cannot doubt. We hold the true Republican position. In leaving the people's business in their hands, we cannot be wrong. We are willing, and even anxious, to go to the people on this issue.

But I suppose I cannot reasonably hope to convince you that we have any principles. The most I can expect is, to assure you that we think we have, and are quite contented with them. The other day, one of the gentlemen from Georgia [Mr. Iverson], an eloquent man, and a man of learning, so far as I can judge, not being learned myself, came down upon us astonishingly. He spoke in what the *Baltimore American* calls the "scathing and withering style." At the end of his second severe flash I was struck blind, and found myself feeling with my fingers for an assurance of my continued physical existence. A little of the bone was left, and I gradually revived. He eulogized Mr. Clay in high and beautiful terms, and then declared that we had deserted all our principles, and had turned Henry Clay out, like an old horse, to root. This is terribly severe. It cannot be answered by argument; at least, I cannot so answer it. I merely wish to ask the gentleman if the Whigs are the only party he can think of, who sometimes turn old horses out to root. Is not a certain Martin Van Buren an old horse, which your own party have turned out to root? and is he not rooting a little to your discomfort about now? But in not nominating Mr. Clay, we deserted our principles, you say. Ah! in what? Tell us, ye men of principles, what principle we violated? We say you did violate principle in discarding Van Buren, and we can tell you how. You violated the primary, the cardinal, the one great living principle of all Democratic representative government - the principle that the representative is bound to carry out the known will of his constituents. A large majority of the Baltimore Convention of 1844 were, by their constituents, instructed to procure Van Buren's nomination if they could. In violation, in utter, glaring contempt of this, you rejected him - rejected him, as the gentleman from New York, the other day expressly admitted, for *availability* - that same "General Availability" which you charge upon us, and daily chew over here, as something exceedingly odious and unprincipled. But the gentleman from Georgia gave us a second speech yesterday, all well considered and put down in writing, in which Van Buren was scathed and withered a "few" for his present position and movements. I cannot remember the gentleman's precise language, but I do remember he put Van Buren down, down, till he got him where he was finally to "stink" and "rot."

Mr. Speaker, it is no business or inclination of mine to defend Martin Van Buren. In the war of extermination now waging between him and his old admirers, I say, devil take the hindmost - and the foremost. But there is no mistaking the origin of the breach; and if the curse of "stinking" and "rotting" is to fall on the first and greatest violators of principle in the matter, I disinterestedly suggest, that the gentleman from Georgia and his present co-workers are bound to take it upon themselves.

But the gentleman from Georgia further says, we have deserted all our principles, and taken shelter under General Taylor's military coat tail; and he seems to think this is exceedingly degrading. Well, as his faith is, so be it unto him. But can he remember no other military coat tail under which a certain other party have been sheltering for near a quarter of a century? Has he no acquaintance with the ample military coat tail of General Jackson? Does he not know that his own party have run the last five Presidential races under that coat tail, and that they are now running the sixth under that same cover? Yes, sir, that coat tail was used, not only for General Jackson himself, but has been clung to with the grip of death by every Democratic candidate since. You have never ventured, and dare not now venture, from under it. Your campaign papers have constantly been "Old Hickories," with rude likenesses of the old General upon them; hickory poles and hickory brooms your never-ending emblems; Mr. Polk, himself, was "Young Hickory," "Little Hickory," or something so; and even now your campaign paper here is proclaiming that Cass and Butler are of the true "Hickory stripe."

No, sir; you dare not give it up. Like a horde of hungry ticks, you have stuck to the tail of the Hermitage lion to the end of his life, and you are still sticking to it, and drawing a loathsome sustenance from it after he is dead. A fellow once advertised that he had made a discovery, by which he could make a new man out of an old one, and have enough of the stuff left to make a little yellow dog. Just such a discovery has General Jackson's popularity been to you. You not only twice made President of him out of it, but you have had enough of the stuff left to make Presidents of several comparatively small men since; and it is your chief reliance now to make still another.

Mr. Speaker, old horses and military coat tails, or tails of any sort, are not figures of speech such as I would be the

first to introduce into discussions here; but as the gentleman from Georgia has thought fit to introduce them, he
and you are welcome to all you have made, or can make,
by them. If you have any more old horses, trot them out;
any more tails, just cock them, and come at us.

I repeat, I would not introduce this mode of discussion
here; but I wish gentlemen on the other side to understand, that the use of degrading figures is a game at which
they may not find themselves able to take all the win-
nings. [We give it up.] Aye, you give it up, and well you
may, but from a very different reason from that which
you would have us understand. The point - the power to
hurt - of all figures, consists in the *truthfulness* of their
application; and understanding this, you may well give it
up. They are weapons which hit you, but miss us.

But, in my hurry, I was very near closing on the subject of
military tails, before I was done with it. There is one entire article of the sort I have not discussed yet; I mean the
military tail you Democrats are now engaged in dovetail-
ing on to the great Michigander. Yes, sir, all his biographers (and they are legion) have him in hand, tying him
to a military tail, like so many mischievous boys tying a
dog to a bladder of beans. True, the material they have is
very limited; but they drive at it, might and main. He *in*-
vaded Canada without resistance, and he *out*vaded it without pursuit. As he did both under orders, I suppose there
was, to him, neither credit nor discredit in them; but they
are made to constitute a large part of the tail. He was not
at Hull's surrender, but he was close by. He was volunteer
aid to General Harrison on the day of the battle of the
Thames; and, as you said in 1840, Harrison was picking
whortleberries two miles off, while the battle was fought,
I suppose it is a just conclusion, with you, to say Cass was

aiding Harrison to pick whortleberries. This is about all, except the mooted question of the broken sword. Some authors say he broke it; some say he threw it away; and some others, who ought to know, say nothing about it. Perhaps it would be a fair historical compromise to say, if he did not break it, he did not do anything else with it.

By the way, Mr. Speaker, did you know I am a military hero? Yes, sir, in the days of the Black Hawk war, I fought, bled, and came away. Speaking of General Cass's career, reminds me of my own. I was not at Stillman's defeat, but I was about as near it as Cass was to Hull's surrender; and, like him, I saw the place very soon afterwards. It is quite certain I did not break my sword, for I had none to break; but I bent a musket pretty badly on one occasion. If Cass broke his sword, the idea is, he broke it in desperation; I bent the musket by accident. If General Cass went in advance of me in picking whortleberries, I guess I surpassed him in charges upon the wild onions. If he saw any live fighting Indians, it was more than I did, but I had a good many bloody struggles with the mosquitoes; and although I never fainted from loss of blood, I can truly say I was often very hungry.

Mr. Speaker, if I should ever conclude to doff whatever our Democratic friends may suppose there is of black-cockade Federalism about me, and, thereupon, they shall take me up as their candidate for the Presidency, I protest they shall not make fun of me, as they have of General Cass, by attempting to write me into a military hero.

While I have General Cass in hand, I wish to say a word about his political principles. As a specimen, I take the record of his progress on the Wilmot Proviso. In the *Washington Union*, of March 2, 1847, there is a report of a speech of General Cass, made the day before in the Senate, on the Wilmot Proviso, during the delivery of which Mr. Miller, of New Jersey, is reported to have interrupted him as follows, to wit:

> "Mr. Miller expressed his great surprise at the change in the sentiments of the Senator from Michigan, who had been regarded as the great champion of freedom in the northwest, of which he was a distinguished ornament. Last year the Senator from Michigan was understood to be decidedly in favor of the Wilmot proviso; and, as no reason had been stated for the change, he (Mr. M.) could not refrain from the expression of his extreme surprise."

To this General Cass is reported to have replied as follows, to wit:

> "Mr. Cass said, that the course of the Senator from New Jersey was most extraordinary. Last year he (Mr. C.) should have voted for the proposition had it come up. But circumstances had altogether changed. The honorable Senator then read several passages from the remarks as given above, which he had committed to writing, in order to refute such a charge as that of the Senator from New Jersey."

In the "remarks above committed to writing," is one numbered 4, as follows, to wit:

> "4th. Legislation would now be wholly inoperative, because no territory hereafter to be acquired can be governed without an act of Congress pro-

viding for its government. And such an act, on its passage, would open the whole subject, and leave the Congress, called on to pass it, free to exercise its own discretion, entirely uncontrolled by any declaration found in the statute book."

In Niles's Register, vol. 73, page 293, there is a letter of General Cass to A.O.P. Nicholson, of Nashville, Tennessee, dated December 24, 1847, from which the following are correct extracts:

"The Wilmot Proviso has been before the country some time. It has been repeatedly discussed in Congress, and by the public press. I am strongly impressed with the opinion that a great change has been going on in the public mind upon this subject - in my own as well as others; and that doubts are resolving themselves into convictions, that the principle it involves should be kept out of the National Legislature, and left to the people of the Confederacy in their respective local Governments. . . .

"Briefly, then, I am opposed to the exercise of any jurisdiction by Congress over this matter; and I am in favor of leaving the people of any territory which may be hereafter acquired the right to regulate it themselves, under the general principles of the Constitution. Because,

"1. I do not see in the Constitution any grant of the requisite power to Congress; and I am not disposed to extend a doubtful precedent beyond its necessity - the establishment of territorial governments when needed - leaving to the inhabitants all the rights compatible with the relations they bear to the Confederation."

These extracts show that, in 1846, General Cass was for the Proviso *at once,* that in March, 1847, he was still for it, *but not just then,* and that, in December, 1847, he was *against* it altogether. This is a true index to the whole man. When the question was raised in 1846, he was in a blustering hurry to take ground for it. He sought to be in advance, and to avoid the uninteresting position of a mere follower; but soon he began to see glimpses of the great Democratic ox-gad waving in his face, and to hear, indistinctly, a voice saying, "Back," "back, sir," "back a little." He shakes his head; and bats his eyes, and blunders back to his position of March 1847; but still the gad waves, and the voice grows more distinct, and sharper still - "Back, sir!" "Back, I say!" "Further back!" and back he goes to the position of December, 1847; at which the gad is still, and the voice soothingly says - "So!" "Stand at that."

Have no fears, gentlemen, of your candidate; he exactly suits you, and we congratulate you upon it. However much you may be distressed about *our* candidate, you have all cause to be contented and happy with your own. If elected, he may not maintain all, or even any, of his positions previously taken; but he will be sure to do whatever the party exigency, for the time being, may require; and that is precisely what you want. He and Van Buren are the same "manner of men"; and, like Van Buren, he will never desert *you* till you first desert *him.*

Mr. Speaker, I adopt the suggestion of a friend, that General Cass is a general of splendidly successful *charges* - charges, to be sure, not upon the public enemy, but upon the public treasury.

He was Governor of Michigan Territory, and, *ex-officio*, superintendent of Indian affairs, from the 9th of October, 1813, till the 31st of July, 1831 - a period of seventeen years, nine months, and twenty-two days. During this period, he received from the United States treasury, for personal services and personal expenses, the aggregate sum of $96,028 - being an average sum of $14.79 per day for every day of the time. This large sum was reached by assuming that he was doing service and incurring expenses at several different *places*, and in several different *capacities* in the *same* place, all at the same *time*. By a correct analysis of his accounts during that period, the following propositions may be deduced:

First. He was paid in *three* different capacities during the *whole* of the time - that is to say:

1. As Governor's salary, at the rate, per year, of $2,000.

2. As estimated for office rent, clerk hire, fuel, etc., in superintendence of Indian affairs *in* Michigan, at the rate, per year of $1,500.

3. As compensation and expenses, for various miscellaneous items of Indian service *out* of Michigan, an average, per year, of $625.

Second. During *part* of the time, that is, from the 9th of October, 1813, to the 29th of May, 1822, he was paid in *four* different capacities - that is to say:

The three as above, and in addition thereto the commutation of ten rations per day, amounting per year, to $730.

Third. During *another* part of the time, that is, from the beginning of 1822 to the 31st of July, 1831, he was also paid in *four* different capacities - that is to say:

The *first* three, as above, (the rations being dropped after the 29th of May, 1822,) and, in addition thereto, for superintending Indian agencies at Piqua, Ohio, Fort Wayne, Indiana, and Chicago, Illinois, at the rate, per year, of $1,500. It should be observed here, that the last item, commencing at the beginning of 1822, and the item of rations, ending on the 29th of May 1822, lap on each other during so much of the time as lies between those two dates.

Fourth. Still another part of the time, that is, from the 31st of October, 1821, to the 29th of May, 1822, he was paid in *six* different capacities - that is to say:

The three first, as above; the item of rations, as above; and, in addition thereto, another item of ten rations per day while at Washington, settling his accounts; being at the rate, per year, of $730.

And, also, an allowance for expenses travelling to and from Washington, and while there, of $1,022; being at the rate, per year, of $1,793.

Fifth. And yet, during the little portion of time
which lies between the 1st of January, 1822, and
the 29th of May, 1822, he was paid in *seven* different capacities; that is to say:

The six last mentioned, and also at the rate of
$1,500 per year for the Piqua, Fort Wayne, and
Chicago service, as mentioned above.

These accounts have already been discussed some here;
but when we are amongst them, as when we are in the
Patent Office, we must peep about a good while before we
can see all the curiosities. I shall not be tedious with
them. As to the large item of $1,500 per year, amounting
in the aggregate to $26,715, for office rent, clerk hire,
fuel, etc., I barely wish to remark that, so far as I can discover in the public documents, there is no evidence, by
word or inference, either from any disinterested witness,
or of General Cass himself, that he ever rented or kept a
separate office, ever hired or kept a clerk, or ever used
any extra amount of fuel, etc., in consequence of his Indian services. Indeed, General Cass's entire silence in regard
to these items in his two long letters, urging his claims
upon the Government, is, to my mind, almost conclusive
that no such items had any real existence.

But I have introduced General Cass's accounts here, chiefly to show the wonderful physical capacities of the man.
They show that he not only did the labor of several men
at the same *time,* but that he often did it at several *places*
many hundred miles apart, *at the same time.* And at eating, too, his capacities are shown to be quite as wonderful.
From October, 1821, to May, 1822, he ate ten rations a
day in Michigan, ten rations a day here in Washington,
and near five dollars' worth a day besides, partly on the

road between the two places. And then there is an important discovery in his example - the art of being paid for what one eats, instead of having to pay for it. Hereafter, if any nice young man shall owe a bill which he cannot pay in any other way, he can just board it out. Mr. Speaker, we have all heard of the animal standing in doubt between two stacks of hay, and starving to death; the like of that would never happen to General Cass. Place the stacks a thousand miles apart, he would stand stock-still midway between them, and eat them both at once; and the green grass along the line would be apt to suffer some too, at the same time. By all means, make him President, gentlemen. He will feed you bounteously - if - if there is any left after he shall have helped himself!

SLAVERY AND THE REPEAL OF
THE MISSOURI COMPROMISE
PEORIA, ILLINOIS
October 16, 1854

Fellow-citizens: The repeal of the Missouri Compromise, and the propriety of its restoration, constitute the subject of what I am about to say.

As I desire to present my own connected view of this subject, my remarks will not be, specifically, an answer to Judge Douglas; yet, as I proceed, the main points he has presented will arise, and will receive such respectful attention as I may be able to give them.

I wish further to say, that I do not propose to question the patriotism, or to assail the motives of any man, or class of men; but rather to strictly confine myself to the naked merits of the question.

I also wish to be no less than National in all the positions I may take; and whenever I take ground which others have thought, or may think, narrow, sectional, and dangerous to the Union, I hope to give a reason, which will appear sufficient, at least to some, why I think differently.

And, as this subject is no other, than part and parcel of the larger general question of domestic slavery, I wish to MAKE and to KEEP the distinction between the *existing* institution, and the EXTENSION of it, so broad, and so clear, that no honest man can misunderstand me, and no dishonest one, successfully misrepresent me.

In order to get a clear understanding of what the Missouri Compromise is, a short history of the preceding kindred subjects will perhaps be proper. When we established our independence, we did not own, or claim, the country to which this compromise applies. Indeed, strictly speaking, the confederacy then owned no country at all; the States respectively owned the country within their limits; and some of them owned territory beyond their strict State limits. Virginia thus owned the North-Western territory - the country out of which the principal part of Ohio, all Indiana, all Illinois, all Michigan and all Wisconsin, have since been formed. She also owned (perhaps within her then limits) what has since been formed into the State of Kentucky. North Carolina thus owned what is now the State of Tennessee; and South Carolina and Georgia, in separate parts, owned what are now Mississippi and Alabama. Connecticut, I think, owned the little remaining part of Ohio - being the same where they now send Giddings to Congress, and beat all creation at making cheese. These territories, together with the States themselves, constituted all the country over which the confederacy then claimed any sort of jurisdiction. We were then living under the Articles of Confederation, which were superseded by the Constitution several years afterwards. The question of ceding these territories to the general government was set on foot. Mr. Jefferson, the author of the Declaration of Independence, and otherwise a chief actor in the Revolution; then a delegate in Congress; afterwards twice President; who was, is, and perhaps will continue to be, the most distinguished politician of our history; a Virginian by birth and continued residence, and withal, a slaveholder; conceived the idea of taking that occasion, to prevent slavery ever going into the northwestern territory. He prevailed on the Virginia legislature to adopt his views, and to cede the territory, making the prohibition of slavery therein, a condition of the deed. Congress accepted the cession, with the condition; and in the first Ordinance (which the acts of Congress were then called) for the government of the territory, provided that slavery should never be permitted therein. This is the famed ordinance of '87 so often spoken of. Thenceforward, for sixty-one years, and until in 1848, the last scrap of this territory came into the Union as the State of Wisconsin, all parties acted in quiet obedience to this ordinance. It is now what Jefferson foresaw and intended - the happy home of teeming millions of free, white, prosperous people, and no slave amongst them.

Thus, with the author of the Declaration of Independence, the policy of prohibiting slavery in new territory originated. Thus, away back of the Constitution, in the pure, fresh, free breath of the Revolution, the State of Virginia, and the National Congress put that policy in practice. Thus, through sixty odd of the best years of the republic did that policy steadily work to its great and beneficent end. And thus, in those five states, and five millions of free, enterprising people, we have before us the rich fruits of this policy. But *now* new light breaks upon us. Now Congress declares this ought never to have been; and the like of it, must never be again. The sacred right of self-government is grossly violated by it! We even find some men, who drew their first breath, and every other breath of their lives, under this very restriction, now live in dread of absolute suffocation, if they should be restricted in the "sacred right" of taking slaves to Nebraska. That *perfect* liberty they sigh for - the liberty of making slaves of other people - Jefferson never thought of; their own father never thought of, they never thought of themselves, a year ago. How fortunate for them, they did not sooner become sensible of their great misery! Oh, how

difficult it is to treat with respect such assaults upon all
we have ever really held sacred!

But to return to history. In 1803 we purchased what was
then called Louisiana, of France. It included the now
States of Louisiana, Arkansas, Missouri, and Iowa; also the
territory of Minnesota, and the present bone of contention, Kansas and Nebraska. Slavery already existed among
the French at New Orleans; and to some extent at St.
Louis. In 1812 Louisiana came into the Union as a slave
state, without controversy. In 1818 or '19, Missouri
showed signs of a wish to come in with slavery. This was
resisted by Northern members of Congress; and thus began the first great slavery agitation in the nation. This
controversy lasted several months, and became very angry
and exciting; the House of Representatives voting steadily
for the prohibition of slavery in Missouri, and the Senate
voting as steadily against it. Threats of breaking up the
Union were freely made; and the ablest public men of the
day became seriously alarmed. At length a compromise
was made, in which, like all compromises, both sides yielded something. It was a law passed on the 6th day of
March, 1820, providing that Missouri might come into the
Union *with* slavery, but that in all the remaining part of
the territory purchased of France, which lies north of 36
degrees and 30 minutes north latitude, slavery should never be permitted. This provision of law, *is the Missouri
Compromise.* In excluding slavery north of the line, the
same language is employed as in the ordinance of '87. It
directly applied to Iowa, Minnesota, and to the present
bone of contention, Kansas and Nebraska. Whether there
should or should not, be slavery south of that line, nothing
was said in the law; but Arkansas constituted the principal
remaining part, south of the line; and it has since been admitted as a slave state, without serious controversy. More

recently, Iowa, north of the line, came in as a free state without controversy. Still later, Minnesota, north of the line, had a territorial organization without controversy. Texas principally south of the line, and west of Arkansas; though originally within the purchase from France, had, in 1819, been traded off to Spain, in our treaty for the acquisition of Florida. It had thus become a part of Mexico. Mexico revolutionized and became independent of Spain. American citizens began settling rapidly, with their slaves, in the southern part of Texas. Soon they revolutionized against Mexico, and established an independent government of their own, adopting a constitution, with slavery, strongly resembling the constitutions of our slave states. By still another rapid move, Texas, claiming a boundary much further West, than when we parted with her in 1819, was brought back to the United States, and admitted into the Union as a slave state. There then was little or no settlement in the northern part of Texas, a considerable portion of which lay north of the Missouri line; and in the resolutions admitting her into the Union, the Missouri restriction was expressly extended westward across her territory. This was in 1845, only nine years ago.

Thus originated the Missouri Compromise; and thus has it been respected down to 1845. And even four years later, in 1849, our distinguished Senator, in a public address, held the following language in relation to it:

> "The Missouri Compromise had been in practical operation for about a quarter of a century, and had received the sanction and approbation of men of all parties in every section of the Union. It had allayed all sectional jealousies and irritations growing out of this vexed question, and harmonized and tranquillized the whole country. It has

given to Henry Clay, as its prominent champion, the proud sobriquet of the "*Great Pacificator*," and by that title and for that service, his political friends had repeatedly appealed to the people to rally under his standard, as a presidential candidate, as the man who had exhibited the patriotism and the power to suppress, an unholy and treasonable agitation, and preserve the Union. He was not aware that any man or any party from any section of the Union, had ever urged as an objection to Mr. Clay, that he was the great champion of the Missouri Compromise. On the contrary, the effort was made by the opponents of Mr. Clay, to prove that he was not entitled to the exclusive merit of that great patriotic measure, and that the honor was equally due to others as well as to him, for securing its adoption - that it had its origin in the hearts of all patriotic men, who desired to preserve and perpetuate the blessings of our glorious Union - an origin akin that of the Constitution of the United States, conceived in the same spirit of fraternal affection, and calculated to remove forever, the only danger, which seemed to threaten, at some distant day, to sever the social bond of union. All the evidences of public opinion at that day, seemed to indicate that this Compromise had been canonized in the hearts of the American people, as a sacred thing which no ruthless hand would ever be reckless enough to disturb."

I do not read this extract to involve Judge Douglas in an inconsistency - if he afterwards thought he had been wrong, it was right for him to change - I bring this forward merely to show the high estimate placed on the Missouri Compromise by all parties up to so late as the year 1849.

But, going back a little, in point of time, our war with Mexico broke out in 1846. When Congress was about adjourning that session, President Polk asked them to place two millions of dollars under his control, to be used by him in the recess, if found practicable and expedient, in negotiating a treaty of peace with Mexico, and acquiring some part of her territory. A bill was duly got up, for the purpose, and was progressing swimmingly, in the House of Representatives, when a member by the name of David Wilmot, a democrat from Pennsylvania, moved as an amendment "Provided that in any territory thus acquired, there shall never be slavery."

This is the origin of the far-famed "Wilmot Proviso." It created a great flutter; but it stuck like wax, was voted into the bill, and the bill passed with it through the House. The Senate, however, adjourned without final action on it and so both appropriation and proviso were lost, for the time. The war continued, and at the next session, the President renewed his request for the appropriation, enlarging the amount, I think, to three million. Again came the Proviso; and defeated the measure. Congress adjourned again, and the war went on. In December 1847, the new congress assembled. I was in the lower House that term. The "Wilmot Proviso" or the principle of it, was constantly coming up in some shape or other, and I think I may venture to say I voted for it at least forty times during the short term I was there. The Senate, however, held it in check, and it never became a law. In the spring of 1848 a treaty of peace was made with Mexico by which we obtained that portion of her country which now constitutes the territories of New Mexico and Utah, and the now state of California. By this treaty the Wilmot Proviso was defeated, as so far as it was intended to be a condition of the acquisition of territory. Its friends, however, were still determined to find some way to restrain slavery from getting into the new country. This new acquisition lay directly west of our old purchase from France, and extended west to the Pacific Ocean - and was so situated that if the Missouri line should be extended straight west, the new country would be divided by such extended line, leaving some north and some south of it. On Judge Douglas' motion a bill, or provision of a bill, passed the Senate to so extend the Missouri line. The Proviso men in the House, including myself, voted it down, because by implication, it gave up the southern part to slavery, while we were bent on having it *all* free.

In the fall of 1848 the gold mines were discovered in California. This attracted people to it with unprecedented rapidity, so that on, or soon after, the meeting of the new congress in December, 1849, she already had a population of nearly a hundred thousand, had called a convention, formed a state constitution, excluding slavery, and was knocking for admission into the Union. The Proviso men, of course, were for letting her in, but the Senate, always true to the other side, would not consent to her admission. And there California stood, kept *out* of the Union, because she would not let slavery *into* her borders. Under all the circumstances perhaps this was not wrong. There were other points of dispute, connected with the general question of slavery, which equally needed adjustment. The South clamored for a more efficient fugitive slave law. The North clamored for the abolition of a peculiar species of slave trade in the District of Columbia, in connection with which, in view from the windows of the capitol, a sort of negro-livery stable, where droves of negroes were collected, temporarily kept, and finally taken to Southern markets, precisely like droves of horses, had been openly maintained for fifty years. Utah and New Mexico needed territorial governments; and whether slavery should or should not be prohibited within them, was another question. The indefinite western boundary of Texas was to be settled. She was received a slave state; and consequently the farther west the slavery men could push her boundary, the more slave country they secured. And the farther east the slavery opponents could thrust the boundary back, the less slave ground was secured. Thus this was just as clearly a slavery question as any of the others.

These points all needed adjustment; and they were held up, perhaps wisely, to make them help to adjust one another. The Union, now, as in 1820, was thought to be in danger; and devotion to the Union rightfully inclined men to yield somewhat, in points where nothing else could have so inclined them. A compromise was finally effected. The South got their new fugitive-slave law; and the North got California, (the far best part of our acquisition from Mexico,) as a free State. The South got a provision that New Mexico and Utah, *when admitted as States,* may come in *with* or *without* slavery as they may then choose; and the North got the slave-trade abolished in the District of Columbia. The North got the western boundary of Texas, thence further back eastward than the South desired; but, in turn, they gave Texas ten millions of dollars, with which to pay her old debts. This is the Compromise of 1850.

Preceding the presidential election of 1852, each of the great political parties, democrats and whigs, met in convention and adopted resolutions endorsing the Compromise of '50, as a "finality," a final settlement, so far as these parties could make it so, of all slavery agitation. Previous to this, in 1851, the Illinois Legislature had indorsed it.

During this long period of time Nebraska had remained substantially an uninhabited country, but now emigration to, and settlement within it began to take place. It is about one third as large as the present United States, and its importance, so long overlooked, begins to come into view. The restriction of slavery by the Missouri Compromise directly applies to it; in fact, was first made, and has since been maintained, expressly for it. In 1853, a bill to give it a territorial government passed the House of Representatives, and, in the hands of Judge Douglas, failed of passing the Senate only for want of time. This bill contained no repeal of the Missouri Compromise. Indeed, when it was assailed because it did not contain such repeal, Judge Douglas defended it in its existing form.

On January, 4th, 1854, Judge Douglas introduces a new bill to give Nebraska territorial government. He accompanies this bill with a report, in which last, he expressly recommends that the Missouri Compromise shall neither be affirmed nor repealed. Before long the bill is so modified as to make two territories instead of one; calling the southern one Kansas.

Also, about a month after the introduction of the bill, on the Judge's own motion, it is so amended as to declare the Missouri Compromise inoperative and void; and, substantially, that the people who go and settle there may establish slavery, or exclude it, as they may see fit. In this shape the bill passed both branches of congress, and became a law.

This is the *repeal* of the Missouri Compromise. The foregoing history may not be precisely accurate in every particular; but I am sure it is sufficiently so, for all the uses I shall attempt to make of it, and in it, we have before us, the chief material enabling us to correctly judge whether the repeal of the Missouri Compromise is right or wrong.

I think, and shall try to show, that it is wrong; wrong in its direct effect, letting slavery into Kansas and Nebraska - and wrong in its prospective principle, allowing it to spread to every other part of the wide world, where men can be found inclined to take it.

This *declared* indifference, but, as I must think, covert *real zeal* for the spread of slavery, I can not but hate. I hate it because of the monstrous injustice of slavery itself. I hate it because it deprives our republican example of its just influence in the world - enables the enemies of free institutions, with plausibility, to taunt us as hypocrites - causes the real friends of freedom to doubt our sincerity, and especially because it forces so many really good men amongst ourselves into an open war with the very fundamental principles of civil liberty - criticizing the Declaration of Independence, and insisting that there is no right principle of action but *self-interest.*

Before proceeding, let me say that I think I have no prejudice against the Southern people. They are just what we would be in their situation. If slavery did not now exist amongst them, they would not introduce it. If it did now exist amongst us, we should not instantly give it up. This I believe of the masses north and south. Doubtless there are individuals on both sides, who would not hold slaves under any circumstances; and others who would gladly introduce slavery anew, if it were out of existence. We know that some southern men do free their slaves, go north, and become tip-top abolitionists; while some northern ones go south, and become most cruel slave-masters.

When southern people tell us they are no more responsible for the origin of slavery, that we; I acknowledge the fact. When it is said that the institution exists, and that it is very difficult to get rid of it, in any satisfactory way, I can understand and appreciate the saying. I surely will not blame them for not doing what I should not know how to do myself. If all earthly power were given me, I should not know what to do, as to the existing institution. My first impulse would be to free all the slaves, and send them to Liberia, - to their own native land. But a moment's reflection would convince me, that whatever of high hope, (as I think there is) there may be in this, in the long run, its sudden execution is impossible. If they were all landed there in a day, they would all perish in the next ten days; and there are not surplus shipping and surplus money enough in the world to carry them there in many times ten days. What then? Free them all, and keep them among us as underlings? Is it quite certain that this betters their condition? I think I would not hold one in slavery, at any rate; yet the point is not clear enough to me to denounce people upon. What next? Free them, and make them, politically and socially, our equals? My own feelings will not admit of this; and if mine would, we well know that those of the great mass of white people will not. Whether this feeling accords with justice and sound judgment, is not the sole question, if indeed, it is any part of it. A universal feeling, whether well or ill-founded, can not be safely disregarded. We can not, then, make them equals. It does seem to me that systems of gradual emancipation might be adopted; but for their tardiness in this, I will not undertake to judge our brethren of the south.

When they remind us of their constitutional rights, I acknowledge them, not grudgingly, but fully, and fairly; and I would give them any legislation for the reclaiming of their fugitives, which should not, in its stringency, be more likely to carry a free man into slavery, than our ordinary criminal laws are to hang an innocent one.

But all this, to my judgment, furnishes no more excuse for permitting slavery to go into our own free territory, than it would for reviving the African slave trade by law. The law which forbids the bringing of slaves *from* Africa; and that which has so long forbid the taking them *to* Nebraska, can hardly be distinguished on any moral principle; and the repeal of the former could find quite as plausible excuses as that of the latter.

The arguments by which the repeal of the Missouri Compromise is sought to be justified, are these:

First, that the Nebraska country needed a territorial government.

Second, that in various ways, the public had repudiated it, and demanded the repeal; and therefore should not now complain of it.

And lastly, that the repeal establishes a principle, which is intrinsically right.

I will attempt an answer to each of them in its turn.

First, then, if that country was in need of a territorial organization, could it not have had it as well without as with
the repeal? Iowa and Minnesota, to both of which the
Missouri restriction applied, had, without its repeal, each
in succession, territorial organizations. And even, the year
before, a bill for Nebraska itself, was within an ace of
passing, without the repealing clause; and this in the
hands of the same men who are now the champions of repeal. Why no necessity then for the repeal? But still later, when this very bill was first brought in, it contained no
repeal. But, say they, because the public had demanded,
or rather commanded the repeal, the repeal was to accom-
pany the organization, whenever that should occur.

Now, I deny that the public ever demanded any such thing
- ever repudiated the Missouri Compromise - ever commanded its repeal. I deny it, and call for the proof. It is
not contended, I believe, that any such command has ever
been given in express terms. It is only said that it was
done in *principle.* The support of the Wilmot Proviso, is
the first fact mentioned, to prove that the Missouri restriction was repudiated in *principle,* and the second is,
the refusal to extend the Missouri line over the country
acquired from Mexico. These are near enough alike to be
treated together. The one was to exclude the chances of
slavery from the *whole* new acquisition by the lump; and
the other was to reject a division of it, by which one *half*
was to be given up to those chances. Now whether this
was a repudiation of the Missouri line, in *principle,* depends upon whether the Missouri law contained any *principle* requiring the line to be extended over the country
acquired from Mexico. I contend it did not. I insist that it
contained no general principle, but that it was, in every
sense, specific. That its terms limit it to the country purchased from France, is undenied and undeniable. It could

have no principle beyond the intention of those who made it. They did not intend to extend the line to country which they did not own. If they intended to extend it, in the event of acquiring additional territory, why did they not say so? It was just as easy to say, that "in all the country west of the Mississippi, which we now own, or *may hereafter acquire* there shall never be slavery," as to say what they did say; and they would have said it if they had meant it. An intention to extend the law is not only not mentioned in the law, but is not mentioned in any contemporaneous history. Both the law itself, and the history of the times are a blank a to any *principle* of extension; and by neither the known rules of construing statutes and contracts, nor by common sense, can any such *principle* be inferred.

Another fact showing the *specific* character of the Missouri law - showing that it intended no more than it expressed - showing that the line was not intended as a universal dividing line between free and slave territory, present and prospective - north of which slavery could never go - is the fact that by that very law, Missouri came in as a slave State, *north* of the line. If that law contained any prospective *principle*, the whole law must be looked to in order to ascertain what the *principle* was. And by this rule, the South could fairly contend that inasmuch as they got one slave state north of the line at the inception of the law, they have the right to have another given them *north* of it occasionally - now and then in the indefinite westward extension of the line. This demonstrates the absurdity of attempting to deduce a prospective *principle* from the Missouri Compromise line.

When we voted for the Wilmot Proviso, we were voting to keep slavery *out* of the whole Mexican acquisition; and little did we think we were thereby voting, to let it *into* Nebraska, laying several hundred miles distant. When we voted against extending the Missouri line, little did we think we were voting to destroy the old line, then of near thirty years' standing. To argue that we thus repudiated the Missouri Compromise is no less absurd than it would be to argue that because we have, so far, forborne to acquire Cuba, we have thereby, *in principle*, repudiated our former acquisitions, and determined to throw them out of the Union! No less absurd than it would be to say that because I may have refused to build an addition to my house, I thereby have decided to destroy the existing house! And if I catch you setting fire to my house, you will turn upon me and say I INSTRUCTED you to do it! The most conclusive argument, however, that, while voting for the Wilmot Proviso, and while voting against the EXTENSION of the Missouri line, we never thought of disturbing the original Missouri Compromise, is found in the fact that there was then, and still is, an unorganized tract of fine country, nearly as large as the State of Missouri, lying immediately west of Arkansas, and south of the Missouri Compromise line; and that we never attempted to prohibit slavery as to it. I wish particular attention to this. It adjoins the original Missouri Compromise line, by its northern boundary; and consequently is part of the country, into which, by implication, slavery was permitted to go, by that compromise. There it has lain open ever since, and there it still lies. And yet no effort has been made at any time to wrest it from the South. In all our struggles to prohibit slavery within our Mexican acquisitions, we never so much as lifted a finger to prohibit it, as to this tract. Is not this entirely conclusive that at all times, we have held the Missouri Compromise as a sacred thing; even when against ourselves, as well as when for us?

Senator Douglas sometimes says the Missouri line itself
was, *in principle*, only an extension of the line of the ordinance of '87 - that is to say, an extension of the Ohio River. I think this is weak enough on its face. I will remark,
however, that, as a glance at the map will show, the Missouri line is a long way farther south than the Ohio; and
that if our Senator, in proposing his extension, had stuck
to the *principle* of jogging southward, perhaps it might
not have been voted down so readily.

But next it is said that the Compromises of '50 and the
ratification of them by both political parties, in '52, established a *new principle*, which required the repeal of the
Missouri Compromise. This again I deny. I deny it, and
demand the proof. I have already stated fully what the
Compromises of '50 are. The particular part of those
measures, for which the virtual repeal of the Missouri
Compromise is sought to be inferred (for it is admitted
they contain nothing about it, in express terms) is the provision in the Utah and New Mexico laws, which permits
them then they seek admission into the Union as States, to
come in with or without slavery as they shall then see fit.
Now I insist this provision was made for Utah and New
Mexico, and for no other place whatever. It had no more
direct reference to Nebraska then it had to the territories
of the moon. But, say they, it had reference to Nebraska,
in principle. Let us see. The North consented to this provision, not because they considered it right in itself; but
because they were compensated - paid for it. They, at the
same time, got California into the Union as a free State.
This was far the best part of all they had struggled for by
the Wilmot Proviso. They also got the area of slavery
somewhat narrowed in the settlement of the boundary of
Texas. Also, they got the slave trade abolished in the District of Columbia. For all these desirable objects the

North could afford to yield something; and they did yield to the South the Utah and New Mexico provision. I do not mean that the whole North, or even a majority, yielded, when the law passed; but enough yielded, when added to the vote of the South, to carry the measure. Now can it be pretended that the *principle* of this arrangement requires us to permit the same provision to be applied to Nebraska, *without any equivalent at all?* Give us another free State; press the boundary of Texas still further back; give us another step toward the destruction of slavery in the District, and you present us a similar case. But ask us not to repeat, for nothing, what you paid for in the first instance. If you wish the thing again, pay again. That is the *principle* of the Compromises of '50, if indeed they had any principles beyond their specific terms - it was the system of equivalents.

Again, if Congress, at that time, intended that all future territories should, when admitted as States, come in with or without slavery, at their own option, why did it not say so? With such an universal provision, all know the bills could not have passed. Did they, then - could they - establish a *principle* contrary to their own intention? Still further, if they intended to establish the principle that wherever Congress had control, it should be left to the people to do as they thought fit with slavery, why did they not authorize the people of the District of Columbia at their adoption to abolish slavery within these limits? I personally know that this has not been left undone, because it was unthought of. It was frequently spoken of by members of Congress and by citizens of Washington six years ago; and I heard no one express a doubt that a system of gradual emancipation, with compensation to owners, would meet the approbation of a large majority of the white people of the District. But without the action of Congress they could say nothing; and Congress said "no." In the measures of 1850, Congress had the subject of slavery in the District expressly on hand. If they were then establishing the *principle* of allowing the people to do as they please with slavery, why did they not apply the *principle* to that people?

Again, it is claimed that by the Resolutions of the Illinois Legislature, passed in 1851, the repeal of the Missouri Compromise was demanded. This I deny also. Whatever may be worked out by a criticism of the language of those resolutions, the people have never understood them as being any more than an endorsement of the Compromises of 1850, and a release of our Senators from voting for the Wilmot Proviso. The whole people are living witnesses, that this only, was their view. Finally, it is asked "if we did not mean to apply the Utah and New Mexico provision, to all future territories, what did we mean, when we, in 1852, endorsed the Compromise of '50?"

For myself, I can answer this question most easily. I meant not to ask a repeal, or modification of the fugitive slave law. I meant not to ask for the abolition of slavery in the District of Columbia. I meant not to resist the admission of Utah and New Mexico, even should they ask to come in as slave States. I meant nothing about additional territories, because, as I understood, we then had no territory whose character as to slavery was not already settled. As to Nebraska, I regarded its character as being fixed, by the Missouri Compromise, for thirty years - as unalterably fixed as that of my own home in Illinois. As to new acquisitions I said "sufficient unto the day is the evil thereof." When we make new acquisitions, we will, as heretofore, try to manage them somehow. That is my answer. That is what I meant and said; and I appeal to the people to say, each for himself, whether that was not also the universal meaning of the free States.

And now, in turn, let me ask a few questions. If by any, or all these matters, the repeal of the Missouri Compromise was commanded, why was not the command sooner obeyed? Why was the repeal omitted in the Nebraska bill of 1853? Why was it omitted in the original bill of 1854? Why, in the accompanying report, was such a repeal characterized as a *departure* from the course pursued in 1850? and its continued omission recommended?

I am aware Judge Douglas now argues that the subsequent express repeal is no substantial alteration of the bill. This argument seems wonderful to me. It is as if one should argue that white and black are not different. He admits, however, that there is a literal change in the bill; and that he made the change in deference to other Senators, who would not support the bill without. This proves that those other Senators thought the change a substantial one; and that the Judge thought their opinions worth deferring to. His own opinions, therefore, seem not to rest on a very firm basis even in his own mind - and I suppose the world believes, and will continue to believe, that precisely on the substance of that change this whole agitation has arisen.

I conclude then, that the public never demanded the repeal of the Missouri Compromise.

I now come to consider whether the repeal, with its avowed principle, is intrinsically right. I insist that it is not. Take the particular case. A controversy had arisen between the advocates and opponents of slavery, in relation to its establishment within the country we had purchased of France. The southern, and then best part of the purchase, was already in as a slave State. The controversy was settled by also letting Missouri in as a slave State; but with the agreement that within all the remaining part of the purchase, north of a certain line, there should never be slavery. As to what was to be done with the remaining part south of the line, nothing was said; but perhaps the fair implication was, that it should come in with slavery if it should so choose. The southern part, except a portion heretofore mentioned, afterwards did come in with slavery, as the State of Arkansas. All these many years since 1820, the Northern part had remained a wilderness. At length settlements began in it also. In due course Iowa came in as a free State, and Minnesota was given a territorial government, without removing the slavery restriction. Finally the sole remaining part, north of the line, Kansas and Nebraska, was to be organized; and it is proposed, and carried, to blot out the old dividing line of thirty-four years' standing, and to open the whole of that country to the introduction of slavery. Now, this, to my mind, is manifestly unjust. After an angry and dangerous controversy, the parties made friends by dividing the bone of contention. The one party first appropriates her own share, beyond all power to be disturbed in the possession of it; and then seizes the share of the other party. It is as if two starving men had divided their only loaf; the one had hastily swallowed his half, and then grabbed the other half just as he was putting it to his mouth.

Equal justice to the South, it is said, requires us to consent to the extending of slavery to new countries. That is to say, inasmuch as you do not object to my taking my hog to Nebraska, therefore I must not object to you taking your slave. Now, I admit this is perfectly logical, if there is no difference between hogs and negroes. But while you thus require me to deny the humanity of the negro, I wish to ask whether you of the south yourselves, have ever been willing to do as much? It is kindly provided that of all those who come into the world, only a small percentage are natural tyrants. That percentage is no larger in the slave States than in the free. The great majority, south as well as north, have human sympathies, of which they can no more divest themselves than they can of their sensibility to physical pain. These sympathies in the bosoms of the southern people, manifest in many ways their sense of the wrong of slavery, and their consciousness that, after all, there is humanity in the negro. If they deny this, let me address them a few plain questions. In 1820 you joined the north, almost unanimously, in declaring the African slave trade piracy, and in annexing to it the punishment of death. Why did you do this? If you did not feel that it was wrong, why did you join in providing that men should be hung for it? The practice was no more than bringing wild negroes from Africa, to sell to such as would buy them. But you never thought of hanging men for catching and selling wild horses, wild buffaloes or wild bears.

Again, you have amongst you, a sneaking individual, of the class of native tyrants, known as the "SLAVE-DEALER." He watches your necessities, and crawls up to buy your slave, at a speculating price. If you cannot help it, you sell to him; but if you can help it, you drive him from your door. You despise him utterly. You do not recognize him as a friend, or even as an honest man. Your children must not play with his; they may rollick freely with the little negroes, but not with the "slave-dealer's" children. If you are obliged to deal with him, you try to get through the job without so much as touching him. It is common with you to join hands with the men you meet; but with the slave-dealer you avoid the ceremony - instinctively shrinking from the snaky contact. If he grows rich and retires from business, you still remember him, and still keep up the ban of non-intercourse upon him and his family. Now why is this? You do not so treat the man who deals in corn, cattle or tobacco.

And yet again, there are in the United States and territories, including the District of Columbia, 433,643 free blacks. At $500 per head they are worth over two hundred millions of dollars. How comes this vast amount of property to be running about without owners? We do not see free horses or free cattle running at large. How is this? All these free blacks are the descendants of slaves, or have been slaves themselves, and they would be slaves now, but for SOMETHING which has operated on their white owners, inducing them, at vast pecuniary sacrifices, to liberate them. What is that SOMETHING? Is there any mistaking it? In all these cases it is your sense of justice, and human sympathy, continually telling you, that the poor negro has some natural right to himself - that those who deny it, and make mere merchandise of him, deserve kickings, contempt and death.

And now, why will you ask us to deny the humanity of the slave? and estimate him only as the equal of the hog? Why ask us to do what you will not do yourselves? Why ask us to do for *nothing*, what two hundred million of dollars could not induce you to do?

But one great argument in the support of the repeal of the Missouri Compromise, is still to come. That argument is "the sacred right of self government." It seems our distinguished Senator has found great difficulty in getting his antagonists, even in the Senate, to meet him fairly on this argument. Some poet has said:

"Fools rush in where angels fear to tread."

At the hazard of being thought one of the fools of this quotation, I meet that argument - I rush in, I take the bull by the horns.

I trust I understand, and truly estimate the right of self-government. My faith in the proposition that each man should do precisely as he pleases with all which is exclusively his own, lies at the foundation of the sense of justice there is in me. I extend the principles to communities of men, as well as to individuals. I so extend it, because it is politically wise, as well as naturally just; politically wise in saving us from broils about matters which do not concern us. Here or at Washington, I would not trouble myself with the oyster laws of Virginia, or the cranberry laws of Indiana.

The doctrine of self-government is right - absolutely and eternally right - but it has no just application, as here attempted. Or perhaps I should rather say that whether it has such application depends upon whether a negro is *not* or *is* a man. If he is *not* a man, why in that case, he who *is* a man may, as a matter of self-government, do just as he pleases with him. But if the negro *is* a man, is it not to that extent a total destruction of self-government, to say that he too shall not govern *himself?* When the white man governs himself that is self-government; but when he govern himself, and also governs *another* man, that is *more* than self-government - that is despotism. If the negro is a *man*, why then my ancient faith teaches me that "all men are created equal"; and that there can be no moral right in connèction with one man's making a slave of another.

Judge Douglas frequently, with bitter irony and sarcasm, paraphrases our argument by saying: "The white people of Nebraska are good enough to govern themselves, *but they are not good enough to govern a few miserable negroes!*"

Well I doubt not that the people of Nebraska are, and will continue to be as good as the average of people elsewhere. I do not say the contrary. What I do say is, that no man is good enough to govern another man, *without that other's consent.* I say this is the leading principle - the sheet anchor of American republicanism. Our Declaration of Independence says:

> "We hold these truths to be self evident: That all men are created equal; that they are endowed by their Creator with certain inalienable rights; that among these are life, liberty and the pursuit of happiness. That to secure these rights, governments are instituted among men, DERIVING THEIR JUST POWERS FROM THE CONSENT OF THE GOVERNED."

I have quoted so much at this time merely to show that according to our ancient faith, the just powers of governments are derived from the consent of the governed. Now the relation of masters and slaves is PROTANTO, a total violation of this principle. That master not only governs the slave without his consent; but he governs him by a set of rules altogether different from those which he prescribes for himself. Allow ALL the governed an equal voice in the government, and that, and that only, is self-government.

Let it not be said I am contending for the establishment of political and social equality between the whites and blacks. I have already said the contrary. I am not now combating the argument of NECESSITY, arising from the fact that the blacks are already amongst us; but I am combating what is set up as MORAL argument for allowing them to be taken where they have never yet been - arguing against the EXTENSION of a bad thing, which where it already exists we must of necessity, manage as we best can.

In support of his application of the doctrine of self-government, Senator Douglas has sought to bring to his aid the opinions and examples of our revolutionary fathers. I am glad he has done this. I love the sentiments of those old-time men; and shall be most happy to abide by their opinions. He shows us that when it was in contemplation for the colonies to break off from Great Britain, and set up a new government for themselves, several of the states instructed their delegates to go for the measure, PROVIDED EACH STATE SHOULD BE ALLOWED TO REGULATE ITS DOMESTIC CONCERNS IN ITS OWN WAY. I do not quote; but this in substance. This was right. I see nothing objectionable in it. I also think it probable that it had some reference to the existence of slavery amongst them. I will not deny that it had. But had it, in any reference, to the carrying of slavery into NEW COUNTRIES? That is the question; and we will let the fathers themselves answer it.

This same generation of men, and mostly the same individuals of the generation, who declared this principle - who declared independence - who fought the War of the Revolution through - who afterwards made the Constitution under which we still live - these same men passed the

Ordinance of '87, declaring that slavery should never go to the north-west territory. I have no doubt Judge Douglas thinks they were very inconsistent in this. It is a question of discrimination between them and him. But there is not an inch of ground left for his claiming that their opinions - their example - their authority - are on his side in this controversy.

But you say this question should be left to the people of Nebraska, because they are more particularly interested. If this be the rule, you must leave it to each individual to say for himself whether he will have slaves. What better moral right have thirty-one citizens of Nebraska to say, that the thirty-second shall not hold slaves, than the people of the thirty-one States have to say that slavery shall not go into the thirty-second State at all?

But if it is a sacred right for the people of Nebraska to take and hold slaves there, it is equally their sacred right to buy them where they can buy them cheapest; and that undoubtedly will be on the coast of Africa; provided you will consent to not hang them for going there to buy them. You must remove this restriction too, from the sacred right of self-government. I am aware you say that taking slaves from the States to Nebraska, does not make slaves of freemen; but the African slave-trader can say just as much. He does not catch free negroes and bring them here. He finds them already slaves in the hands of their black captors, and he honestly buys them at the rate of about a red cotton handkerchief a head. This is very cheap, and it is a great abridgement of the sacred right of self-government to hang men for engaging in this profitable trade!

Another important objection to this application of the right of self-government, is that it enables the first FEW, to deprive the succeeding MANY, of a free exercise of the right of self-government. The first few may get slavery IN, and the subsequent many cannot easily get it OUT. How common is the remark now in the slave States - "If we were only clear of our slaves, how much better it would be for us." They are actually deprived of the privilege of governing themselves as they would, by the action of a very few, in the beginning. The same thing was true of the whole nation at the time our Constitution was formed.

Whether slavery shall go into Nebraska, or other new territories, is not a matter of exclusive concern to the people who may go there. The whole nation is interested that the best use shall be made of these territories. We want them for the homes of free white people. This they cannot be, to any considerable extent, if slavery shall be planted within them. Slave States are places for poor white people to remove FROM; not to remove TO. New free States are the places for poor people to go to and better their condition. For this use, the nation needs these territories.

Still further; there are constitutional relations between the slave and free States, which are degrading to the latter. We are under legal obligations to catch and return their runaway slaves to them - a sort of dirty, disagreeable job which I believe, as a general rule, the slave-holders will not perform for one another. Then again, in the control of the government - the management of the partnership affairs - they have greatly the advantage of us. By the Constitution, each State has two Senators, each has a number of Representatives, in proportion to the number of its people - and each has a number of presidential elec-

tors, equal to the whole number of its Senators and Representatives together. But in ascertaining the number of the
people, for this purpose, five slaves are counted as being
equal to three whites. The slaves do not vote; they are
only counted and so used as to swell the influence of the
white people's votes. The practical effect of this is more
aptly shown by a comparison of the States of South Carolina and Maine. South Carolina has six representatives,
and so has Maine; South Carolina has eight presidential
electors, and so has Maine. This is precise equality so far;
and, of course they are equal in Senators, each having two.
Thus in the control of the government, the two States are
equals precisely. But how are they in the number of their
white people? Maine has 581,813 - while South Carolina
has 274,567. Maine has twice as many as South Carolina,
and 32,679 over. Thus each white man in South Carolina
is more than the double of any man in Maine. This is all
because South Carolina, besides her free people, has
384,984 slaves. The South Carolinian has precisely the
same advantage over the white man in every other free
State, as well as in Maine. He is more than the double of
any one of us in this crowd. The same advantage, but not
to the same extent, is held by all the citizens of the slave
States, over those of the free; and it is an absolute truth,
without an exception, that there is no voter in any slave
State, but who has more legal power in the government,
than any voter in any free State. There is no instance of
exact equality; and the disadvantage is against us the
whole chapter through. This principle, in the aggregate,
gives the slave States in the present Congress, twenty additional representatives - being seven more than the whole
majority by which they passed the Nebraska bill.

Now all this is manifestly unfair; yet I do not mention it
to complain of it, in so far as it is already settled. It is in

the Constitution; and I do not, for that cause, or any other cause, propose to destroy, or alter, or disregard the Constitution. I stand to it, fairly, fully, and firmly.

But when I am told I must leave it altogether to OTHER PEOPLE to say whether new partners are to be bred up and brought into the firm, on the same degrading terms against me, I respectfully demur. I insist, that whether I shall be a whole man, or only the half of one, in comparison with others, is a question in which I am somewhat concerned; and one which no other man can have a sacred right of deciding for me. If I am wrong in this - if it really be a sacred right of self-government, in the man who shall go to Nebraska, to decide whether he will be the EQUAL of me or the DOUBLE of me, then, after he shall have exercised that right, and thereby shall have reduced me to a still smaller fraction of a man than I already am, I should like for some gentleman, deeply skilled in the mysteries of sacred rights, to provide himself with a microscope, and peep about, and find out, if he can, what has become of *my* sacred rights! They will surely be too small for detection with the naked eye.

Finally, I insist that if there is ANYTHING which it is the duty of the WHOLE PEOPLE to never entrust to any hands but their own, that thing is the preservation and perpetuity of their own liberties and institutions. And if they shall think, as I do, that the extension of slavery endangers them, more than any, or all other causes, how recreant to themselves, if they submit the question, and with it, the fate of their country, to a mere handful of men, bent only on temporary self-interest. If this question of slavery extension were an insignificant one - one having no power to do harm - it might be shuffled aside in this way. But being, as it is, the great Behemoth of danger,

shall the strong gripe of the nation be loosened upon him
to entrust him to the hands of such feeble keepers?

I have done with this mighty argument, of self-
government. Go, sacred thing! Go in peace.

But Nebraska is urged as a great Union-saving measure.
Well, I too, go for saving the Union. Much as I hate slavery, I would consent to the extension of it rather than see
the Union dissolved, just as I would consent to any
GREAT evil, to avoid a GREATER one. But when I go to
Union saving, I must believe, at least, that the means I employ have some adaptation to the end. To my mind, Nebraska has no such adaptation.

   "It hath no relish of salvation in it."

It is an aggravation, rather, of the only one thing which
ever endangers the Union. When it came upon us, all was
peace and quiet. The nation was looking to the forming
of new bonds of Union; and a long course of peace and
prosperity seemed to lie before us. In the whole range of
possibility, there scarcely appears to me to have been any
thing, out of which the slavery agitation could have been
revived, except the very project of repealing the Missouri
Compromise. Every inch of territory we owned, already
had a definite settlement of the slavery question, and by
which all parties were pledged to abide. Indeed, there was
no uninhabited country on the continent, which we could
acquire; if we except some extreme northern regions,
which are wholly out of the question. In this state of case,
the genius of Discord himself, could scarcely have invented a way of again setting us by the ears, but by turning
back and destroying the peace measures of the past. The
councils of that genius seem to have prevailed, the Mis-

souri Compromise was repealed; and here we are, in the
midst of a new slavery agitation, such, I think, as we have
never seen before. Who is responsible for this? Is it
those who resist the measure; or those who, causelessly,
brought it forward, and pressed it through, having reason
to know, and, in fact, knowing it must and would be so resisted? It could not but be expected by its author, that it
would be looked upon as a measure for the extension of
slavery, aggravated by a gross breach of faith. Argue as
you will, and long as you will, this is the naked FRONT
and ASPECT, of the measure. And in this aspect, it could
not but produce agitation. Slavery is founded in the self-
ishness of man's nature - opposition to it, in his love of
justice. These principles are an eternal antagonism; and
when brought into collision so fiercely, as slavery extension bring them, shocks, and throes, and convulsions must
ceaselessly follow. Repeal the Missouri Compromise - repeal all compromises - repeal the Declaration of Independence - repeal all past history, you still can not repeal human nature. It still will be the abundance of man's heart,
that slavery extension is wrong; and out of the abundance
of his heart, his mouth will continue to speak.

The structure, too, of the Nebraska bill is very peculiar.
The people are to decide the question of slavery for themselves; but WHEN they are to decide, or HOW they are to
decide; or whether, when the question is once decided, it is
to remain so, or is to be subject to an indefinite succession
of new trials, the law does not say. Is it to be decided by
the first dozen settlers who arrive there? or is to await the
arrival of a hundred? Is it to be decided by a vote of the
people? or a vote of the legislature? or, indeed, by a vote
of any sort? To these questions, the law gives no answer.
There is a mystery about this; for when a member proposed to give the legislature express authority to exclude

slavery, it was hooted down by the friends of the bill.
This fact is worth remembering. Some Yankees, in the
east, are sending emigrants to Nebraska to exclude slavery
from it; and, so far as I can judge, they expect the question to be decided by voting, in some way or other. But
the Missourians are awake too. They are within a stone's
throw of the contested ground. They hold meetings, and
pass resolutions, in which not the slightest allusion to voting is made. They resolve that slavery already exists in
the territory; that more shall go there; that they, remaining in Missouri, will protect it; and that abolitionists shall
be hung, or driven away. Through all this, bowie-knives
and six-shooters are seen plainly enough; but never a
glimpse of the ballot-box. And, really, what is to be the
result of this? Each party WITHIN, having numerous and
determined backers WITHOUT, is it not probable that the
contest will come to blows, and bloodshed? Could there
be a more apt invention to bring about collision and violence, on the slavery question, than this Nebraska project
is? I do not charge, or believe, that such was intended by
Congress; but if they had literally formed a ring, and
placed champions within it to fight out the controversy,
the fight could be no more likely to come off, than it is.
And if this fight should begin, is it likely to take a very
peaceful, Union-saving turn? Will not the first drop of
blood so shed, be the real knell of the Union?

The Missouri Compromise ought to be restored. For the
sake of the Union, it ought to be restored. We ought to
elect a House of Representatives which will vote its restoration. If by any means, we omit to do this, what follows!
Slavery may or may not be established in Nebraska. But
whether it be or not, we shall have repudiated - discarded
from the councils of the Nation - the SPIRIT OF COM-
PROMISE; for who after this will ever trust in a national

compromise? The spirit of mutual concession - that spirit which first gave us the Constitution, and which has thrice saved the Union - we shall have strangled and cast from us forever. And what shall we have in lieu of it? The South flushed with triumph and tempted to excesses; the North, betrayed, as they believe, brooding on wrong and burning for revenge. One side will provoke; the other resent. The one will taunt, the other defy; one aggresses, the other retaliates. Already a few in the North, defy all constitutional restraints, resist the execution of the fugitive slave law, and even menace the institution of slavery in the states where it exists.

Already a few in the South, claim the constitutional right to take and to hold slaves in the free states - demand the revival of the slave trade: and demand a treaty with Great Britain by which fugitive slaves may be reclaimed from Canada. As yet they are but few on either side. It is a grave question for the lovers of the Union, whether the final destruction of the Missouri Compromise, and with it the spirit of all compromise, will or will not embolden and embitter each of these, and fatally increase the numbers of both.

But restore the compromise, and what then? We thereby restore the national faith, the national confidence, the national feeling of brotherhood. We thereby reinstate the spirit of concession and compromise - that spirit which has never failed us in past perils, and which may be safely trusted for all the future. The South ought to join in doing this. The peace of the nations is as dear to them as to us. In memories of the past and hopes of the future, they share as largely as we. It would be on their part a great act - great in its spirit, and great in its effect. It would be worth to the nation a hundred years' purchase of peace and prosperity. And what of sacrifice would they make? They only surrender to us, what they gave us for a consideration long, long ago; what they have not now asked for, struggled or cared for; what has been thrust upon them, not less to their own astonishment than to ours.

But it is said we cannot restore it; that though we elect every member of the lower house, the Senate is still against us. It is quite true, that of the Senators who passed the Nebraska bill, a majority of the whole Senate will retain their seats in spite of the elections of this and the next year. But if at these elections, their several constituencies shall clearly express their will against Nebraska, will these Senators disregard their will? Will they neither obey, nor make room for those who will?

But even if we fail to technically restore the compromise, it is still a great point to carry a popular vote in favor of the restoration. The moral weight of such a vote can not be estimated too highly. The authors of Nebraska are not at all satisfied with the destruction of the compromise - an endorsement of this PRINCIPLE they proclaim to be the great object. With them, Nebraska alone is a small matter - to establish a principle, for FUTURE USE, is what they particularly desire.

That future use is to be the planting of slavery wherever in the wide world, local and unorganized opposition can not prevent it. Now if you wish to give them this endorsement - if you wish to establish this principle - do so. I shall regret it; but it is your right. On the contrary if you are opposed to the principle - intend to give it no such endorsement - let no wheedling, no sophistry, divert you from throwing a direct vote against it.

Some men, mostly whigs, who condemn the repeal of the Missouri Compromise, nevertheless hesitate to go for its restoration, lest they be thrown in company with the abolitionists. Will they allow me as an old whig to tell them good humoredly, that I think this is very silly? Stand with anybody that stands RIGHT. Stand with him while he is right and PART with him when he goes wrong. Stand WITH the abolitionist in restoring the Missouri Compromise; and stand AGAINST him when he attempts the repeal of the fugitive slave law. In the latter case you stand with the southern disunionist. What of that? you are still right. In both cases you are right. In both cases you expose the dangerous extremes. In both you stand on middle ground and hold the ship level and steady. In both you are national and nothing less than national. This is the good old whig ground. To desert such ground, because of any company, is to be less than a whig - less than a man - less than an American.

I particularly object to the NEW position which the avowed principle of this Nebraska law gives to slavery in the body politic. I object to it because it assumes that there can be MORAL RIGHT in the enslaving of one man by another. I object to it as a dangerous dalliance for a few people - a sad evidence that, feeling prosperity, we forget right - that liberty, as a principle, we have ceased to revere. I object to it because the fathers of the Republic eschewed, and rejected it. The argument of "Necessity" was the only argument they ever admitted in favor of slavery; and so far, and so far only as it carried them, did they ever go. They found the institution existing among us, which they could not help; and they cast blame upon the British King for having permitted its introduction. BEFORE the Constitution, they prohibited its introduction into the northwestern Territory - the only country we

owned, then free from it. At the framing and adoption of
the Constitution, they forbore to so much as mention the
word "slave" or "slavery" in the whole instrument. In the
provision for the recovery of fugitives, the slave is spoken
of as a "PERSON HELD TO SERVICE OR LABOR." In
that prohibiting the abolition of the African slave trade
for twenty years, that trade is spoken of as "The migration or importation of such persons as any of the States
NOW EXISTING, shall think proper and admit," etc.
These are the only provisions alluding to slavery. Thus,
the thing is hid away, in the Constitution, just as an afflicted man hides away a wen or a cancer, which he dares
not cut out at once, lest he bleed to death; with the promise, nevertheless, that the cutting may begin at the end of
a given time. Less than this our fathers COULD not do;
and NOW they WOULD not do. Necessity drove them so
far, and further, they would not go. But this is not all.
The earlier Congress, under the Constitution, took the
same view of slavery. They hedged and hemmed it in to
the narrowest limits of necessity.

In 1794, they prohibited an out-going slave trade - that is,
the taking of slaves FROM the United States to sell.

In 1798, they prohibited the bringing of slaves from Africa INTO the Mississippi Territory, this territory then
comprising what are now the States of Mississippi and
Alabama. This was TEN YEARS before they had the authority to do the same thing as to the States existing at the
adoption of the Constitution.

In 1800 they prohibited AMERICAN CITIZENS from
trading in slaves between foreign countries - as, for instance, from Africa to Brazil.

Our republican robe is soiled, and trailed in the dust. Let us re-purify it. Let us turn and wash it white, in the spirit, if not the blood, of the Revolution. Let us turn slavery from its claims of "moral right" back upon its existing legal rights, and its arguments of "necessity." Let us return it to the position our fathers gave it; and there let it rest in peace. Let us re-adopt the Declaration of Independence, and with it, the practices, and policy, which harmonize with it. Let north and south - let all Americans - let all lovers of liberty everywhere - join in the great and good work. If we do this, we shall not only have saved the Union; but we shall have so saved it, as to make, and to keep it, forever worthy of the saving. We shall have so saved it, that the succeeding millions of free happy people, the world over, shall rise up, and call us blessed, to the latest generations.

"BLEEDING KANSAS"
LINCOLN'S LOST SPEECH
BLOOMINGTON, ILLINOIS
May 29, 1856

(No true draft or stenographic copy of this speech exists. In September 1896 McClure's *Magazine published this version of the "Lost Speech" based on the notes and recollections of Henry Clay Whitney, an Illinois lawyer, present that night. The Whitney Manuscript is now in the possession of the Chicago Historical Society. See Elwell Crissey's* Lincoln's Lost Speech *in the bibliography).*

Mr. Chairman and Gentlemen: I was over at [*Cries of "Platform!" "Take the platform!"*] - I say, that while I was at Danville Court, some of our friends of anti-Nebraska got together in Springfield and elected me as one delegate to represent old Sangamon with them in this convention, and I am here certainly as a sympathizer in this movement and by virtue of that meeting and selection. But we can hardly be called delegates strictly, inasmuch as, properly speaking, we represent nobody but ourselves. I think it altogether fair to say that we have no anti-Nebraska party in Sangamon, although there is a good deal of anti-Nebraska feeling there; but I say for myself, and I think I may speak also for my colleagues, that we who are here fully approve of the platform and of all that has been done [*a voice: "Yes!"*]; and even if we are not regularly delegates, it will be right for me to answer your call to speak. I suppose we truly stand for the public sentiment of Sangamon on the great question of the repeal, although we do not yet represent many numbers who have taken a distinct position on the question.

We are in a trying time - it ranges above mere party - and this movement to call a halt and turn our steps backward needs all the help and good counsels it can get; for unless popular opinion makes itself very strongly felt, and change is made in our present course, *blood will flow on account of Nebraska, and brother's hand will be raised against brother!* [*The last sentence was uttered in such an earnest, impressive, if not, indeed, tragic, manner, as to make a cold chill creep over me. Others gave a similar experience.*]

I have listened with great interest to the earnest appeal made to Illinois men by the gentleman from Lawrence [James S. Emery] who has just addressed us so eloquently and forcibly. I was deeply moved by his statement of the wrongs done to free-State men out there. I think it just to say that all true men North should sympathize with them, and ought to be willing to do any possible and needful thing to right their wrongs. But we must not promise what we ought not, lest we be called on to perform what we cannot; we must be calm and moderate, and consider the whole difficulty, and determine what is possible and just. We must not be led by excitement and passion to do that which our sober judgments would not approve in our cooler moments. We have higher aims; we will have more serious business than to dally with temporary measures.

We are here to stand firmly for a principle - to stand firmly for a right. We know that great political and moral wrongs are done, and outrages committed, and we denounce those wrongs and outrages, although we cannot, at present, do much more. But we desire to reach out beyond those personal outrages and establish a rule that will apply to all, and so prevent any future outrages.

We have seen to-day that every shade of popular opinion is represented here, with *Freedom* or rather *Free-Soil* as the basis. We have come together as in some sort representatives of popular opinion against the extension of slavery into territory now free in fact as well as by law, and the pledged word of the statesmen of the nation who are now no more. We come - we are here assembled together - to protest as well as we can against a great wrong, and to take measures, as well as we now can, to make that wrong right; to place the nation, as far as it may be possible now, as it was before the repeal of the Missouri Compromise; and the plain way to do this is to restore the Compromise and to demand and determine that *Kansas shall be free!* [*Immense applause.*] While we affirm, and reaffirm, if necessary, our devotion to the principles of the Declaration of Independence, let our practical work here be limited to the above. We know that there is not a perfect agreement of sentiment here on the public questions which might be rightfully considered in this convention, and that the indignation which we all must feel cannot be helped; but all of us must give up something for the good of the cause. There is one desire which is uppermost in the mind, one wish common to us all - to which no dissent will be made; and I counsel you earnestly to bury all resentment, to sink all personal feeling, make all things work to a common purpose in which we are united and agreed about, and which all present will agree is absolutely necessary - which *must* be done by any rightful mode if there be such: *Slavery must be kept out of Kansas!* [*Applause.*] The test - the pinch - is right there. If we lose Kansas to freedom, an example will be set which will prove fatal to freedom in the end. We, therefore, in the language of the *Bible*, must "lay the axe to the root of the tree." Temporizing will not do longer; now is the time for decision - for firm, persistent, resolute action. [*Applause.*]

The Nebraska bill, or rather Nebraska law, is not one of wholesome legislation, but was and is an act of legislative usurpation, whose result, if not indeed intention, is to make slavery national; and unless headed off is some effective way, we are in a fair way to see this land of boasted freedom converted into a land of slavery in fact. [*Sensation.*] Just open your two eyes, and see if this be not so. I need do no more than state, to command universal approval, that almost the entire North, as well as a large following in the border States, is radically opposed to the planting of slavery in free territory. Probably in a popular vote throughout the nation nine-tenths of the voters in the free States, and at least one-half in the border States, if they could express their sentiments freely, would vote NO on such an issue; and it is safe to say that two-thirds of the votes of the entire nation would be opposed to it. And yet, in spite of this overbalancing of sentiment in this free country, we are in a fair way to see Kansas present itself for admission as a slave State. Indeed, it is a felony, by the local law of Kansas, to deny that slavery exists there even now. By every principle of law, a Negro in Kansas is free; yet the *bogus* legislature makes it an infamous crime to tell him that he is free!

The party lash and the fear of ridicule will overawe justice and liberty; for it is a singular fact, but none the less a fact, and well known by the most common experience, that men will do things under the terror of the party lash that they would not on any account or for any consideration do otherwise; while men who will march up to the mouth of a loaded cannon without shrinking, will run from the terrible name of "Abolitionist," even when pronounced by a worthless creature whom they, with good reason, despise. For instance - to press this point a little - Judge Douglas introduced his anti-Nebraska bill in January; and we had an extra session of our legislature in the succeeding February, in which were seventy-five Democrats; and at a party caucus, fully attended, there were just three votes out of the whole seventy-five, for the measure. But in a few days orders came on from Washington, commanding them to approve the measure; the party lash was applied, and it was brought up again in caucus, and passed

by a large majority. The masses were against it, but party
necessity carried it; and it was passed through the lower
house of Congress against the will of the people, for the
same reason. Here is where the greatest danger lies - that,
while we profess to be a government of law and reason,
law will give way to violence on demand of this awful and
crushing power. Like the great Juggernaut - I think that
is the name - the great idol, it crushes everything that
comes in its way, and makes a - or as I read once, in a
black-letter law book, "a slave is a human being who is legally not a *person* but a *thing.*" And if the safeguards to
liberty are broken down, as is now attempted, when they
have made *things* of all the free Negroes, how long, think
you, before they will begin to make *things* of poor white
men? [*Applause.*] Be not deceived. Revolutions do not
go backward. The founder of the Democratic party declared that *all* men were created equal. His successor in
the leadership has written the word "white" before men,
making it read "all *white* men are created equal." Pray,
will or may not the Know-nothings, if they should get in
power, add the word "protestant," making it read "*all Protestant white men*"?

Meanwhile the hapless Negro is the fruitful subject of re-
prisals in other quarters. John Pettit, whom Tom Benton
paid his respects to, you will recollect, calls the immortal
Declaration "a self-evident lie"; while at the birthplace of
freedom - in the shadow of Bunker Hill and of the "cradle
of liberty," at the home of the Adamses and Warren and
Otis - Choate, from our side of the House, dares to fritter
away the birthday promise of liberty by proclaiming the
Declaration to be "a string of glittering generalities"; and
the Southern Whigs, working hand in hand with pro-
slavery Democrats, are making Choate's theories practical.
Thomas Jefferson, a slaveholder, mindful of the moral
element in slavery, solemnly declared that he "trembled
for his country when he remembered that God is just";

while Judge Douglas, with an insignificant wave of the hand, "don't care whether slavery is voted up or voted down." Now, if slavery is right, or even negative, he has a right to treat it in this trifling manner. But if it is a moral and political wrong, as all Christendom considers it to be, how can he answer to God for this attempt to spread and fortify it? [*Applause.*]

But no man, and Judge Douglas no more than any other, can maintain a negative, or merely neutral, position on this question; and, accordingly, he avows that the Union was made *by* white men and *for* white men and their descendants. As matter of fact, the first branch of the proposition is historically true; the government was made by white men, and they were and are the superior race. This I admit. But the corner-stone of the government, so to speak, was the declaration that "*all* men are created equal," and all entitled to "life, liberty, and the pursuit of happiness." [*Applause.*]

And not only so, but the framers of the Constitution were particular to keep out of that instrument the word "slave," the reason being that slavery would ultimately come to an end, and they did not wish to have any reminder that in this free country human beings were ever prostituted to slavery. [*Applause.*] Nor is it any argument that we are superior and the Negro inferior - that he has but one talent while we have ten. Let the Negroes possess the little he has in independence; if he has but one talent, he should be permitted to keep the little he has. [*Applause.*] But slavery will endure no test of reason or logic; and yet its advocates, like Douglas, use a sort of bastard logic, or noisy assumption, it might better be termed, like the above, in order to prepare the mind for the gradual, but none the less certain, encroachments of the Moloch slavery upon the fair domain of freedom. But however much you may argue upon it, or smother it in soft phrases, slavery can only be maintained by force - by violence. The repeal of the Missouri compromise was by violence. It was a violation of both law and the sacred obligations of honor, to overthrow and trample underfoot, a solemn compromise, obtained by the fearful loss to freedom of one of the fairest of our Western domains. Congress violated the will and confidence of its constituents in voting for the bill; and while public sentiment, as shown by the elections of 1854, demanded the restoration of this compromise, Congress violated its trust by refusing, simply because it had the force of numbers to hold on to it. And murderous violence is being used now, in order to force slavery on to Kansas; for it cannot be done in any other way. [*Sensation.*]

The necessary result was to establish the rule of violence - force, instead of the rule of law and reason; to perpetuate and spread slavery, and, in time, to make it general. We see it at both ends of the line. In Washington, on the very spot where the outrage was started, the fearless Sumner is beaten to insensibility, and is now slowly dying; while senators who claim to be gentlemen and Christians stood by, countenancing the act, and even applauding it afterward in their places in the Senate. Even Douglas, our man, saw it all and was within helping distance, yet let the murderous blows fall unopposed. Then, at the other end of the line, at the very time Sumner was being murdered, Lawrence was being destroyed for the crime of Freedom. It was the most prominent stronghold of liberty in Kansas, and must give way to the all-dominating power of slavery. Only two days ago, Judge Trumbull found it necessary to propose a bill in the Senate to prevent a general civil war and to restore peace in Kansas.

We live in the midst of alarms; anxiety beclouds the future; we expect some new disaster with each newspaper we read. Are we in a healthful political state? Are not the tendencies plain? Do not the signs of the times point plainly the way in which we are going? [*Sensation.*]

In the early days of the Constitution slavery was recognized, by South and North alike, as an evil, and the division of sentiment about it was not controlled by geographical lines or considerations of climate, but by moral and philanthropic views. Petitions for the abolition of slavery were presented to the very first Congress by Virginia and Massachusetts alike. To show the harmony which prevailed, I will state that a fugitive slave law as passed in 1793, with no dissenting voice in the Senate, and but seven dissenting votes in the House. It was, however, a wise law, moderate, and, under the Constitution, a just one. Twenty-five years later, a more stringent law was proposed and defeated; and thirty-five years after that, the present law, drafted by Mason of Virginia, was passed by Northern votes. I am not, just now, complaining of this law, but I am trying to show how the current sets; for the proposed law of 1817 was far less offensive than the present one. In 1774 the Continental Congress pledged itself, without a dissenting vote, to wholly discontinue the slave trade, and to neither purchase nor import any slave; and less than three months before the passage of the Declaration of Independence, the same Congress which adopted that declaration unanimously resolved "that *no slave be imported into any of the thirteen United Colonies.*" [*Great applause.*]

On the second day of July, 1776, the draft of a Declaration of Independence was reported to Congress by the committee, and in it the slave trade was characterized as "an execrable commerce," as "a piratical warfare," as the "opprobrium of infidel powers," and as "a cruel war against human nature." [*Applause.*] All agreed on this except South Carolina and Georgia, and in order to preserve harmony, and from the necessity of the case, these expressions were omitted. Indeed, abolition societies existed as far south as Virginia; and it is a well-known fact that Washington, Jefferson, Madison, Lee, Henry, Mason, and Pendleton were qualified abolitionists, and much more radical on that subject than we of the Whig and Democratic parties claim to be to-day. On March 1, 1784, Virginia ceded to the confederation all its lands lying northwest of the Ohio River. Jefferson, Chase of Maryland, and Howell of Rhode Island, as a committee on that and territory thereafter *to be ceded*, reported that no slavery should exist after the year 1800. Had this report been adopted, not only the Northwest, but Kentucky, Tennessee, Alabama, and Mississippi also would have been free; but it required the assent of nine States to ratify it. North Carolina was divided, and thus its vote was lost; and Delaware, Georgia, and New Jersey refused to vote. In point of fact, as it was, it was assented to by six States. Three years later, on a square vote to exclude slavery from the Northwest, only one vote, and that from New York, was against it. And yet, thirty-seven years later, five thousand citizens of Illinois out of a voting mass of less than twelve thousand, deliberately, after a long and heated contest, voted to introduce slavery in Illinois; and, to-day, a large party in the free State of Illinois are willing to vote to fasten the shackles of slavery on the fair domain of Kansas, notwithstanding it received the dowry of freedom long before its birth as a political community. I repeat, therefore, the question: Is it not plain in what direction we are tending? [*Sensation.*] In the colonial time, Mason, Pendleton, and Jefferson were as hostile to slavery in Virginia as Otis, Ames, and the Adamses were in Massachusetts; and Virginia made as earnest an effort to get rid of it as old Massachusetts did. But circumstances were against them and they failed; but not that the good will of its leading men was lacking. Yet within less than fifty years Virginia changed its tune, and made Negro-breeding

into a free State; and I should like to know the difference - should like for any one to point out the difference - between *our* making a free State of Missouri and *their* making a slave State of Kansas. [*Great applause.*] There ain't one bit of difference, except that our way would be a great mercy to humanity. But I have never said - and the Whig party has never said - and those who oppose the Nebraska bill do not as a body say, that they have any intention of interfering with slavery in the slave States. Our platform says just the contrary. We allow slavery to exist in the slave States - not because slavery is right or good, but from the necessities of our Union. We grant a fugitive slave law because it is so "nominated in the bond"; because our fathers so stipulated - had to - and we are bound to carry out this agreement. But they did not agree to introduce slavery in regions where it did not previously exist. On the contrary, they said by their example and teachings that they did not deem it expedient - did not consider it right - to do so; and it is wise and right to do just as they did about it [*Voices: "Good!"*], and that is what we propose - not to interfere with slavery where it exists (we have never tried to do it), and to give them a reasonable and efficient fugitive slave law. [*A voice: "No!"*] I say YES! [*Applause.*] It was part of the bargain, and I'm for living up to it; but I go not further; I'm not bound to do more, and I won't agree any further. [*Great applause.*]

We, here in Illinois, should feel especially proud of the provision of the Missouri Compromise excluding slavery from what is now Kansas; for an Illinois man, Jesse B. Thomas, was its father. Henry Clay, who is credited with the authorship of the Compromise in general terms, did not even vote for that provision, but only advocated the ultimate admission by a second compromise; and Thomas was, beyond all controversy, the real author of the "slavery restriction" branch of the Compromise. To show the generosity of the Northern members toward the Southern side; on a test vote to exclude slavery from Missouri, ninety voted not to exclude, and eighty-seven to exclude, every vote from the slave States being ranged with the former and fourteen votes from the free States, of whom seven were from New England alone; while on a vote to exclude slavery from what is now Kansas, the vote was one hundred and thirty-four *for*, to forty-two *against*. The scheme, as a whole, was, of course, a Southern triumph. It is idle to contend otherwise, as is now being done by the Nebraskaites; it was so shown by the votes and quite as emphatically by the expressions of representative men. Mr. Lowndes of South Carolina was never known to commit a political mistake; his was the great judgment of that section; and he declared that this measure "would restore tranquillity to the country - a result demanded by every consideration of discretion, of moderation, of wisdom, and of virtue." When the measure came before President Monroe for his approval, he put to each member of his cabinet this question: "Has Congress the constitutional power to prohibit slavery in a territory?" And John C. Calhoun and William H. Crawford from the South, equally with John Quincy Adams, Benjamin Rush, and Smith Thompson from the North, alike answered, *"Yes!"* without qualification or equivocation; and this measure, of so great consequence to the South, was passed; and Missouri was, by means of it, finally enabled to knock at the door of the Republic for an open passage to its brood of slaves. And, in spite of this, Freedom's share is about to be taken by violence - by the force of misrepresentative votes, not called for by the popular will. What name can I, in common decency, give to this wicked transaction? [*Sensation.*]

But even then the contest was not over; for when the Missouri constitution came before Congress for its approval, it forbade any free Negro or mulatto from entering the

State. In short, our Illinois "black laws" were hidden away in their constitution [*Laughter*], and the controversy was thus revived. Then it was that Mr. Clay's talents shone out conspicuously, and the controversy that shook the Union to its foundation was finally settled to the satisfaction of the conservative parties on both sides of the line, though not to the extremists on either, and Missouri was admitted by the small majority of six in the lower House. How great a majority, do you think, would have been given had Kansas also been secured for slavery? [*A voice: "A majority the other way."*] "A majority the other way," is answered. Do you think it would have been safe for a Northern man to have confronted his constituents after having voted to consign both Missouri and Kansas to hopeless slavery? And yet this man Douglas, who misrepresents his constituents, and who has exerted his highest talents in that direction, will be carried in triumph through the State, and hailed with honor while applauding that act. [*Three groans for "Dug!"*] And this shows whither we are tending. This thing of slavery is more powerful than its supporters - even than the high priests that minister at its altar. It debauches even our greatest men. It gathers strength, like a rolling snow-ball, by its own infamy. Monstrous crimes are committed in its name by persons collectively which they would not dare to commit as individuals. Its aggressions and encroachments almost surpass belief. In a despotism, one might not wonder to see slavery advance steadily and remorselessly into new dominions; but is it not wonderful, is it not even alarming, to see its steady advance in a land dedicated to the proposition that "all men are created equal"? [*Sensation.*]

It yields nothing itself; it keeps all it has, and gets all it can besides. It really came dangerously near securing Illinois in 1824; it did get Missouri in 1821. The first proposition was to admit what is now Arkansas *and* Missouri as one slave State. But the territory was divided, and Arkansas came in, without serious question, as a slave State; and afterward Missouri, not as a *free* State, as would have been equitable, but as a slave State also. Then we had Florida and Texas admitted with slavery; and now Kansas is about to be forced into the dismal procession. [*Sensation.*] And so it is wherever you look. We have not forgotten - it is but six years since - how dangerously near California came to being a slave State. Texas is a slave State, and four other slave States may be carved from its vast domain. And yet, in the year 1829, slavery was abolished throughout that vast region by a royal decree of the then sovereign of Mexico. Will you please tell me by what *right* slavery exists in Texas to-day? By the same right as, and no higher or greater than, slavery is seeking dominion in Kansas; by political force - peaceful, if that will suffice; by the torch (as in Kansas) and the bludgeon (as in the Senate chamber), if required. And so history repeats itself; and even as slavery has kept its course by craft, intimidation, and violence in the past, so it will persist, in my judgment, until met and dominated by the will of a people bent on its restriction.

We have, this very afternoon, heard bitter denunciations of Brooks in Washington, and Titus, Stringfellow, Atchison, Jones and Shannon in Kansas - the battleground of slavery. I certainly am not going to advocate or shield them; but they and their acts are but the necessary outcome of the Nebraska law. We should reserve our highest censure for the authors of the mischief, and not for the catspaws which they use. I believe it was Shakespeare who said, "Where the offence lies, there let the axe fall"; and, in my opinion, this man Douglas and the Northern men in Congress who advocate "Nebraska" are more guilty than a thousand Joneses and Stringfellows, with all their murderous practices, can be. [*Applause.*]

We have made a good beginning here to-day. As our Methodist friends would say, "I feel it is good to be here." While extremists may find some fault with the moderation of our platform, they should recollect that "the battle is not always to the strong, nor the race to the swift." In grave emergencies, moderation is generally safer than radicalism; and as this struggle is likely to be long and earnest, we must not, by our action, repel any who are in sympathy with us in the main, but rather win all that we can to our standard. We must not belittle nor overlook the facts of our condition - that we are new and comparatively weak, while our enemies are entrenched and relatively strong. They have the administration and political power; and, right or wrong, at present they have the numbers. Our friends who urge an appeal to arms with so much force and eloquence, should recollect that the government is arrayed against us, and that the numbers are now arrayed against us as well; or, to state it nearer to the truth, they are not yet expressly and affirmatively for us; and we should repel friends rather than gain them by anything savouring of revolutionary methods. As it now stands, we must appeal to the sober sense and patriotism of the people. We will make converts day by day; we will grow strong by calmness and moderation; we will grow strong by the violence and injustice of our adversaries. And, unless truth be a mockery and justice a hollow lie, we will be in the majority after a while, and then the revolution which we will accomplish will be none the less radical from being the result of pacific measures. The battle of freedom is to be fought out on principle. Slavery is a violation of the eternal right. We have temporized with it from the necessities of our conditions; but *as sure as God reigns and school children read,* **THAT BLACK FOUL LIE CAN NEVER BE CONSECRATED INTO GOD'S HALLOWED TRUTH!** [*Immense applause lasting some time.*] One of our greatest difficulties is, that men who *know* that slavery is a detestable crime and ruinous to the nation, are compelled, by our peculiar condition and other circumstances, to advocate it concretely, though damning it in the raw. Henry Clay was a brilliant example of this tendency; others of our purest statesmen are compelled to do so; and thus slavery secures actual support from those who detest it at heart. Yet Henry Clay perfected and forced through the Compromise which secured to slavery a great State as well as a political advantage. Not that he hated slavery less, but that he loved the whole Union more. As long as slavery profited by his great Compromise, the hosts of pro-slavery could not sufficiently cover him with praise; but now that this Compromise stands in their way -

> "... they never mention him,
> His name is never heard:
> Their lips are now forbid to speak
> That once familiar word."

They have slaughtered one of his most cherished measures, and his ghost would arise to rebuke them. [*Great applause.*]

Now, let us harmonize, my friends, and appeal to the moderation and patriotism of the people; to their sober second thought; to the awakened public conscience. The repeal of the sacred Missouri Compromise has installed the weapons of violence: the bludgeon, the incendiary torch, the death-dealing rifle, the bristling cannon - the weapons of kingcraft, of the inquisition, of ignorance, of barbarism, of oppression. We see its fruits in the dying bed of the heroic Sumner; in the ruins of the "Free State" hotel; in the smoking embers of the *Herald of Freedom;* in the free-State Governor of Kansas chained to a stake on freedom's soil like a horse-thief, for the crime of freedom. [*Applause.*] We see it in Christian statesmen, and Christian newspapers, and Christian pulpits, applauding *the cowardly act of a low bully,* **WHO CRAWLED UPON HIS VICTIM BEHIND HIS BACK AND DEALT THE DEADLY BLOW.** [*Sensation and applause.*] We note our political demoralization in the catch-words that are coming into such common use; on the one hand, "freedom-shriekers," and sometimes "freedom-screechers" [*Laughter*]; and, on the other hand, "border ruffians," and that fully deserved. And the significance of catch-words cannot pass unheeded, for they constitute a sign of the times. Everything in this world "jibes" in with everything else, and all the fruits of this Nebraska bill are like the poisoned source from which they come. I will not say that we may not sooner or later be compelled to meet force by force; but the time has not yet come, and if we are true to ourselves, may never come. Do not mistake that the ballot is stronger than the bullet. Therefore let the legions of slavery use bullets; but let us wait patiently till November, and fire ballots at them in return; and by that peaceful policy, I believe we shall ultimately win. [*Applause.*]

It was by that policy that here in Illinois the early fathers fought the good fight and gained the victory. In 1824 the free men of our State, led by Governor Coles (who was a native of Maryland and President Madison's private secretary), determined that those beautiful groves should never re-echo the dirge of one who has no title to himself. By their resolute determination, the winds that sweep across our broad prairies shall never cool the parched brow, nor shall the unfettered streams that bring joy and gladness to our free soil water the tired feet, of a *slave;* but so long as those heavenly breezes and sparkling streams bless the land, or the groves and their fragrance or their memory remain, the humanity to which they minister **SHALL BE FOREVER FREE!** [*Great applause.*] Palmer, Yates, Williams, Browning, and some more in this convention came from Kentucky to Illinois (instead of going to Missouri), not only to better their conditions, but also to get away from slavery. They have said so to me, and it is understood among us Kentuckians that we don't like it one bit. Now, can we, mindful of the blessings of liberty which the early men of Illinois left to us, refuse a like privilege to the free men who seek to plant Freedom's banner on our Western outposts? [*"No! No!"*] Should we not stand by our neighbors who seek to better their conditions in Kansas and Nebraska! [*"Yes! Yes!"*] Can we as Christian men, and strong and free ourselves, wield the sledge or hold the iron which is to manacle anew an already oppressed race? [*"No! No!"*] "Woe unto them," it is written, "that decree unrighteous decrees and that write grievousness which they have prescribed." Can we afford to sin any more deeply against human liberty? [*"No! No!"*]

One great trouble in the matter is, that slavery is an insidious and crafty power, and gains equally by open violence of the brutal as well as by sly management of the peaceful. Even after the ordinance of 1787, the settlers in Indiana and Illinois (it was all one government then) tried to get Congress to allow slavery temporarily, and petitions to that end were sent from Kaskaskia, and General Harrison, the Governor, urged it from Vincennes, the capital. If that had succeeded, good-by [*sic*] to liberty here. But John Randolph of Virginia made a vigorous report against it; and although they persevered so well as to get three favorable reports for it, yet the United States Senate, with the aid of some slave States, finally *squelched* it for good. [*Applause.*] And that is why this hall is to-day a temple for free men instead of a Negro livery stable. [*Great applause and laughter.*] Once let slavery get planted in a locality, by ever so weak or doubtful a title, and in ever so small numbers, and it is like the Canada thistle or Bermuda grass - you can't root it out. You yourself may detest slavery; but your neighbor has five or six slaves, and he is an excellent neighbor, or your son has married his daughter, and they beg you to help save their property, and you vote against your interest and principles to accommodate a neighbor, hoping that your vote will be on the losing side. And others do the same; and in those ways slavery gets a sure foothold. And when that is done the whole mighty Union - the force of the nation - is committed to its support. And that very process is working in Kansas to-day. And you must recollect that the slave property is worth a billion of dollars ($1,000,000,000); while free-State men must work for sentiment alone. Then there are "Blue Lodges" - as they call them - everywhere doing their secret and deadly work.

It is a very strange thing, and not solvable by any moral law that I know of, that if a man loses his horse, the whole country will turn out to help hang the thief; but if a man but a shade or two darker than I am is himself stolen, the same crowd will hang one who aids in restoring him to liberty. Such are the inconsistencies of slavery, where a horse is more sacred than a man; and the essence of *squatter* or popular sovereignty - I don't care how you call it - is that if one man chooses to make a slave of another, no third man shall be allowed to object. And if you can do this in free Kansas, and it is allowed to stand, the next thing you will see is ship loads of Negroes from Africa at the wharf at Charleston; for one thing is as truly lawful as the other; and these are the bastard notions we have got to stamp out, else they will stamp us out. [*Sensation and applause.*]

Two years ago, at Springfield, Judge Douglas avowed that Illinois came into the Union as a slave State, and that slavery was weeded out by the operation of his great, patent, everlasting principle of "popular sovereignty." [*Laughter.*] Well, now, that argument must be answered, for it has a little grain of truth at the bottom. I do not mean that it is true in essence, as he would have us believe. It could not be essentially true if the Ordinance of '87 was valid. But, in point of fact, there were some degraded beings called slaves in Kaskaskia and the other French settlements when our first State constitution was adopted; that is a fact, and I don't deny it. Slaves were brought here as early as 1720, and were kept here in spite of the Ordinance of 1787 against it. But slavery did not thrive here. On the contrary, under the influence of the Ordinance, the number *decreased* fifty-one from 1810 to 1820; while under the influence of *squatter* sovereignty, right across the river in Missouri, they *increased* seven thousand two hundred and eleven in the same time; and slavery finally faded out in Illinois, under the influence of the law of freedom, while it grew stronger and stronger in Missouri, under the law or practice of "popular sovereignty." In point of fact there were but one hundred and seventeen slaves in Illinois one year after its admission, or one to every four hundred and seventy of its population; or, to state it in another way, if Illinois was a slave State in 1820, so were New York and New Jersey much greater slave States from having had greater numbers, slavery having been established there in very early times. But there is this vital difference between all these States and the Judge's Kansas experiment: that they sought to disestablish slavery which had been already established, while the Judge seeks, so far as he can, to disestablish freedom, which had been established there by the Missouri Compromise. [*Several voices: "Good! Good!"*]

The Union is undergoing a fearful strain; but it is a stout old ship, and has weathered many a hard blow, and "the stars in their courses," aye, an invisible power, greater than the puny efforts of men, will fight for us. But we ourselves must not decline the burden of responsibility, nor take counsel of unworthy passions. Whatever duty urges us to do or to omit, must be done or omitted; and the recklessness with which our adversaries break the laws, or counsel their violation, should afford no example for us. Therefore, let us revere the Declaration of Independence; let us continue to obey the Constitution and the laws; let us keep step to the music of the Union. Let us draw a cordon, so to speak, around the slave States, and the hateful institution, like a reptile poisoning itself, will perish by its own infamy. [*Applause.*]

But we cannot be free men if this is, by our national choice, to be a land of slavery. Those who deny freedom to others, deserve it not for themselves; and, under the rule of God, cannot long retain it. [*Loud applause.*]

Did you ever, my friends, seriously reflect upon the speed with which we are tending downwards? Within the memory of men now present the leading statesmen of Virginia could make genuine, red-hot abolitionist speeches in old Virginia; and, as I have said, now even in "free Kansas" it is a crime to declare that it is free Kansas. The very sentiments that I and others have just uttered, would entitle us, and each of us, to the ignominy and seclusion of a dungeon; and yet I suppose that, like Paul, we were "free born." But if this thing is allowed to continue, it will be but one step further to impress the same rule in Illinois. [*Sensation.*]

The conclusion of all is, that we must restore the Missouri Compromise. We must highly resolve that *Kansas* **SHALL** *be free!* [*Great applause.*] We must reinstate the birthday promise of the Republic; we must reaffirm the Declaration of Independence; we must make good in essence as well as in form Madison's avowal that "the word *slave* ought not to appear in the Constitution"; and we must even go further, and decree that only local law, and not that time-honored instrument, shall shelter a slaveholder. We must make this a land of liberty in fact, as it is in name. But in seeking to attain these results - so indispensable if the liberty which is our pride and boast shall endure - we will be loyal to the Constitution and to the "flag of our Union," and no matter what our grievance - even though Kansas shall come in as a slave State; and not matter what theirs - even if we shall restore the Compromise - **WE WILL SAY TO THE SOUTHERN DISUNIONISTS, WE WON'T GO OUT OF THE UNION, AND YOU SHAN'T!!!** [*This was the climax; the audience rose to its feet* en masse, *applauded, stamped, waved handkerchiefs, threw hats in the air, and ran riot for several minutes. The arch-enchanter who wrought this transformation looked, meanwhile, like the personification of political justice.*]

But let us, meanwhile, appeal to the sense and patriotism of the people, and not to their prejudices; let us spread the floods of enthusiasm here aroused all over these vast prairies, so suggestive of freedom. Let us commence by placing in the Governor's chair at Springfield the gallant soldier Colonel Bissell, who stood for the honor of our State alike on the plains and amidst the chaparral of Mexico, and on the floor of Congress, while he defied the Southern Hotspur; and this act will have a greater moral effect than all the border ruffians can accomplish in all their raids on Kansas. There is both a power and a magic in popular opinion. To that let us now appeal; and while, in all probability, no resort to force will be needed, our moderation and forbearance will stand us in good stead when, if ever, **WE MUST MAKE AN APPEAL TO BATTLE AND TO THE GOD OF HOSTS!!** [*Immense applause and a rush for the orator.*]

THE DRED SCOTT DECISION
SPRINGFIELD, ILLINOIS
June 26, 1857

Fellow-Citizens: I am here to-night, partly by the invitation of some of you, and partly by my own inclination. Two weeks ago Judge Douglas spoke here on the several subjects of Kansas, the Dred Scott decision, and Utah. I listened to the speech at the time, and have read the report of it since. It was intended to controvert opinions which I think just, and to assail (politically, not personally,) those men who, in common with me, entertain those opinions. For this reason I wished then, and still wish, to make some answer to it, which I now take the opportunity of doing.

I begin with Utah. If it prove to be true, as is probable, that the people of Utah are in open rebellion to the United States, then Judge Douglas is in favor of repealing their territorial organization, and attaching them to the adjoining States for judicial purposes. I say, too, if they are in rebellion, they ought to be somehow coerced to obedience; and I am not now prepared to admit or deny that the Judge's mode of coercing them is not as good as any. The Republicans can fall in with it without taking back anything they have ever said. To be sure, it would be a considerable backing down by Judge Douglas from his much-vaunted doctrine of self-government for the territories; but this is only additional proof of what was very plain from the beginning, that that doctrine was a mere deceitful pretense for the benefit of slavery. Those who could not see that much in the Nebraska act itself, which forced Governors, and Secretaries, and Judges on the people of the territories, without their choice or consent, could not be made to see, though one should rise from the dead to testify.

But in all this, it is very plain the Judge evades the only question the Republicans have ever pressed upon the Democracy in regard to Utah. That question the Judge well knows to be this: "If the people of Utah shall peacefully form a State Constitution tolerating polygamy, will the Democracy admit them into the Union?" There is nothing in the United States Constitution or law against polygamy; and why is it not a part of the Judge's "sacred right of self-government" for that people to have it, or rather to *keep* it, if they choose? These questions, so far as I know, the Judge never answers. It might involve the Democracy to answer them either way, and they go unanswered.

As to Kansas. The substance of the Judge's speech on Kansas is an effort to put the free State men in the wrong for not voting at the election of delegates to the Constitutional Convention. He says: "*There is every reason to hope and believe that the law will be fairly interpreted and impartially executed, so as to insure to every bona fide inhabitant the free and quiet exercise of the elective franchise.*"

It appears extraordinary that Judge Douglas should make such a statement. He knows that, by the law, no one can vote who has not been registered; and he knows that the free State men place their refusal to vote on the ground that but few of them have been registered. It is *possible* this is not true, but Judge Douglas knows it is asserted to be true in letters, newspapers, and public speeches, and borne by every mail, and blown by every breeze to the eyes and ears of the world. He knows it is boldly declared that the people of many whole counties, and many whole neighborhoods in others, are left unregistered; yet, he does not venture to contradict the declaration, nor to point out how they *can* vote without being registered; but he just slips along, not seeming to know there is any such question of fact, and complacently declares: "There is every reason to hope and believe that the law will be fairly and impartially executed, so as to insure to every *bona fide* inhabitant the free and quiet exercise of the elective franchise."

I readily agree that if all had a chance to vote, they ought to have voted. If, on the contrary, as they allege, and Judge Douglas ventures not to particularly contradict, few only of the free State men had a chance to vote, they were perfectly right in staying from the polls in a body.

By the way since the Judge spoke, the Kansas election has come off. The Judge expressed his confidence that all the Democrats in Kansas would do their duty - including "free state Democrats" of course. The returns received here as yet are very incomplete; but so far as they go, they indicate that only about one sixth of the registered voters, have really voted; and this too, when not more, perhaps, than one half of the rightful voters have been registered, thus showing the thing to have been altogether the most exquisite farce ever enacted. I am watching with considerable interest, to ascertain what figure "the free-state Democrats" cut in the concern. Of course they voted - all democrats do their duty - and of course they did not vote for slave-state candidates. We soon shall know how many delegates *they* elected, how many candidates they had, pledged for a free state; and how many votes were cast for them.

Allow me to barely whisper my suspicion that there were no such things in Kansas as "free state Democrats" - that they were altogether mythical, good only to figure in newspapers and speeches in the free states. If there should prove to be one real living free state Democrat in Kansas, I suggest that it might be well to catch him, and stuff and preserve his skin, as an interesting specimen of that soon-to-be-extinct variety of the genus, Democrat.

And now as to the Dred Scott decision. That decision declares two propositions - first, that a negro cannot sue in the U.S. Courts, and secondly, that Congress cannot prohibit slavery in the Territories. It was made by a divided court - dividing differently on the different points. Judge Douglas does not discuss the merits of the decision; and, in that respect, I shall follow his example, believing I could no more improve on McLean and Curtis, than he could on Taney.

He denounces all who question the correctness of that decision, as offering violent resistance to it. But who resists it? Who has, in spite of the decision, declared Dred Scott free, and resisted the authority of his master over him?

Judicial decisions have two uses - first, to absolutely determine the case decided; and secondly, to indicate to the public how other similar cases will be decided when they arise. For the latter use, they are called "precedents" and "authorities."

We believe, as much as Judge Douglas, (perhaps more) in obedience to, and respect for, the judicial department of government. We think its decisions on Constitutional questions, when fully settled, should control, not only the particular cases decided, but the general policy of the country, subject to be disturbed only by amendments of the Constitution as provided in that instrument itself. More than this would be revolution. But we think the Dred Scott decision is erroneous. We know the court that made it, has often overruled its own decisions, and we shall do what we can to have it to overrule this. We offer no *resistance* to it.

Judicial decisions are of greater or less authority as precedents, according to circumstances. That this should be so, accords both with common sense, and the customary understanding of the legal profession.

If this important decision had been made by the unanimous concurrence of the judges, and without any apparent partisan bias, and in accordance with legal public expectation, and with the steady practice of the departments throughout our history, and had been in no part, based on assumed historical facts which are not really true; or, if wanting in some of these, it has been before the court more than once, and had there been affirmed and reaffirmed through a course of years, it then might be, perhaps would be, factious, nay, even revolutionary, not to acquiesce in it as a precedent.

But when, as it is true we find it wanting in all these claims to the public confidence, it is not resistance, it is not factious, it is not even disrespectful, to treat it as not having yet quite established a settled doctrine for the country. But Judge Douglas considers this view awful. Hear him:

> "The courts are the tribunals prescribed by the Constitution and created by the authority of the people to determine, expound and enforce the

law. Hence, whoever resists the final decision of
the highest judicial tribunal, aims a deadly blow
to our whole Republican system of government -
a blow, which if successful would place all our
rights and liberties at the mercy of passion,
anarchy and violence, I repeat, therefore, that if
resistance to the decisions of the Supreme Court
of the United States, in a matter like the points
decided in the Dred Scott case, clearly within
their jurisdiction as defined by the Constitution,
shall be forced upon the country as a political issue, it will become a distinct and naked issue between the friends and enemies of the Constitution - the friends and the enemies of the supremacy of the laws."

Why, this same Supreme Court once decided a national
bank to be constitutional; but General Jackson, as President of the United States, disregarded the decision, and
vetoed a bill for a re-charter, partly on constitutional
ground, declaring that each public functionary must support the Constitution, "*as he understands it.*" But hear the
General's own words. Here they are, taken from his veto
message:

"It is maintained by the advocates of the bank,
that its constitutionality, in all its features, ought
to be considered as settled by precedent, and by
the decision of the Supreme Court. To this conclusion I cannot assent. Mere precedent is a dangerous source of authority, and should not be regarded as deciding questions of constitutional
power, except where the acquiescence of the people and the States can be considered as well settled. So far from this being the case on this sub-

ject, an argument against the bank might be based on precedent. One Congress in 1791, decided in favor of a bank; another in 1811, decided against it. One Congress in 1815 decided against a bank; another in 1816 decided in its favor. Prior to the present Congress, therefore the precedents drawn from that source were equal. If we resort to the States, the expressions of legislative, judicial and executive opinions against the bank have been probably to those in its favor as four to one. There is nothing in precedent, therefore, which if its authority were admitted, ought to weigh in favor of the act before me."

I drop the quotations merely to remark that all there ever was, in the way of precedent up to the Dred Scott decision, on the points therein decided, had been against that decision. But hear General Jackson further -

"If the opinion of the Supreme Court covered the whole ground of this act, it ought not to control the co-ordinate authorities of this Government. The Congress, the executive and the court, must each for itself be guided by its own opinion of the Constitution. Each public officer, who takes an oath to support the Constitution, swears that he will support it as he understand it, and not as it is understood by others."

Again and again have I heard Judge Douglas denounce that bank decision, and applaud General Jackson for disregarding it. It would be interesting for him to look over his recent speech, and see how exactly his fierce philippics against us for resisting Supreme Court decisions, fall upon his own head. It will call to his mind a long and fierce political war in this country, upon an issue which, in his own language, and, of course, in his own changeless estimation, was "a distinct and naked issue between the friends and the enemies of the Constitution," and in which war he fought in the ranks of the enemies of the Constitution.

I have said, in substance, that the Dred Scott decision was, in part; based on assumed historical facts which were not really true; and I ought not to leave the subject without giving some reasons for saying this; I therefore give an instance or two, which I think fully sustain me. Chief Justice Taney, in delivering the opinion of the majority of the Court, insists at great length that negroes were no part of the people who made, or for whom was made, the Declaration of Independence, or the Constitution of the United States.

On the contrary, Judge Curtis, in his dissenting opinion, shows that in five of the then thirteen states, to wit, New Hampshire, Massachusetts, New York, New Jersey and North Carolina, free negroes were voters, and, in proportion to their numbers, had the same part in making the Constitution that the white people had. He shows this with so much particularity as to leave no doubt of its truth; and, as a sort of conclusion on that point, holds the following language:

"The Constitution was ordained and established by the people of the United States, through the action, in each State, of those persons who were qualified by its laws to act thereon in behalf of themselves and all other citizens of the State. In some of the States, as we have seen, colored persons were among those qualified by law to act on the subject. These colored persons were not only included in the body of 'the people of the United States,' by whom the Constitution was ordained and established; but in at least five of the States they had the power to act, and, doubtless, did act, by their suffrages, upon the question of its adoption."

Again, Chief Justice Taney says: "It is difficult, at this day, to realize the state of public opinion in relation to that unfortunate race, which prevailed in the civilized and enlightened portions of the world at the time of the Declaration of Independence, and when the Constitution of the United States was framed and adopted." And again, after quoting from the Declaration, he says: "The general words above quoted would seem to include the whole human family, and if they were used in a similar instrument at this day, would be so understood."

In these the Chief Justice does not directly assert, but plainly assumes, as a fact, that the public estimate of the black man is more favorable *now* than it was in the days of the Revolution. This assumption is a mistake. In some trifling particulars, the condition of that race has been ameliorated; but, as a whole, in this country, the change between then and now is decidedly the other way; and their ultimate destiny has never appeared so hopeless as in the last three or four years. In two of the five States - New Jersey and North Carolina - that then gave the free negro the right of voting, the right has since been taken away; and in a third - New York - it has been greatly abridged; while is has not been extended, so far as I know, to a single additional State, though the number of the States has more than doubled. In those days, as I understand, masters could, at their own pleasure, emancipate their slaves; but since then, such legal restraints have been made upon emancipation, as to amount almost to prohibition. In those days, Legislatures held the unquestioned power to abolish slavery in their respective States, but now it is becoming quite fashionable for State Constitutions to withhold that power from the Legislatures. In those days, by common consent, the spread of the black man's bondage to new countries was prohibited; but now, Congress decides that it *will* not continue the prohibition, and the Supreme Court decides that it *could* not if it would. In those days, our Declaration of Independence was held sacred by all, and thought to include all; but now, to aid in making the bondage of the negro universal and eternal, it is assailed, and sneered at, and construed, and hawked at, and torn, till, if its framers could rise from their graves, they could not at all recognize it. All the powers of earth seem rapidly combining against him. Mammon is after him; ambition follows, and philosophy follows, and the Theology of the day is fast joining the cry. They have him in his prison house; they have searched his person, and left no prying instrument with him. One after another they have closed the heavy iron doors upon him, and now they have him, as it were, bolted in with a lock of a hundred keys, which can never be unlocked without the concurrence of every key; the keys in the hands of a hundred different men, and they scattered to a hundred different and distant places; and they stand musing as to what invention, in all the dominions of mind and matter, can be produced to make the impossibility of his escape more complete than it is.

It is grossly incorrect to say or assume, that the public estimate of the negro is more favorable now than it was at the origin of the government.

Three years and a half ago, Judge Douglas brought forward his famous Nebraska bill. The country was at once in a blaze. He scorned all opposition, and carried it through Congress. Since then he has seen himself superseded in a Presidential nomination, by one indorsing the general doctrine of his measure, but at the same time standing clear of the odium of its untimely agitation, and its gross breach of national faith; and he has seen that successful rival constitutionally elected, not by the strength of friends, but by the division of adversaries, being in a popular minority of nearly four hundred thousand votes. He has seen his chief aids in his own State, Shields and Richardson, politically speaking, successively tried, convicted, and executed, for an offense not their own, but his. And now he sees his own case, standing next on the docket for trial.

There is a natural disgust in the minds of nearly all white people, to the idea of an indiscriminate amalgamation of the white and black races; and Judge Douglas evidently is basing his chief hope upon the chances of his being able to appropriate the benefit of this disgust to himself. If he can, by much drumming and repeating, fasten the odium of that idea upon his adversaries, he thinks he can struggle through the storm. He therefore clings to this hope, as a drowning man to the last plank. He makes an occasion for lugging it in from the opposition to the Dred Scott decision. He finds the Republicans insisting that the Declaration of Independence includes ALL men, black as well as white; and forthwith he boldly denies that is includes negroes at all, and proceeds to argue gravely that all who contend it does, do so only because they want to vote, and eat, and sleep, and marry with negroes! He will have it that they cannot be consistent else. Now I protest against that counterfeit logic which concludes that, because I do not want a black woman for a *slave* I must necessarily want her for a *wife.* I need not have her for either, I can just leave her alone. In some respects she certainly is not my equal; but in her natural right to eat the bread she earns with her own hands without asking leave of any one else, she is my equal, and the equal of all others.

Chief Justice Taney, in his opinion in the Dred Scott case, admits that the language of the Declaration is broad enough to include the whole human family, but he and Judge Douglas argue that the authors of that instrument did not intend to include negroes, by the fact that they did not at once, actually place them on an equality with the whites. Now this grave argument comes to just nothing at all, by the other fact, that they did not at once, *or ever afterwards,* actually place all white people on an equality with one another. And this is the staple argument of both the Chief Justice and the Senator, for doing this obvious violence to the plain, unmistakable language of the Declaration. I think the authors of that notable instrument intended to include *all* men, but they did not intend to declare all men equal *in all respects.* They did not mean to say all were equal in color, size, intellect, moral developments, or social capacity. They defined with tolerable distinctness, in what respects they did consider all men created equal - equal in "certain inalienable rights, among which are life, liberty, and the pursuit of happiness." This they said, and this meant. They did not mean to assert the obvious untruth, that all were then actually enjoying that equality, nor yet, that they were about to confer it immediately upon them. In fact they had no power to confer such a boon. They meant simply to declare the *right,* so that the *enforcement* of it might follow as fast as circumstances should permit. They meant to set up a standard maxim for free society, which could be familiar to all, and revered by all; constantly looked to, constantly labored for, and even though never perfectly attained, constantly approximated, and thereby constantly spreading and deepening its influence, and augmenting the happiness and value of life to all people of all colors everywhere. The assertion that "all men are created equal" was of no practical use in effecting our separation from Great Britain; and it was placed in the Declaration, not for that, but for future use. Its authors meant it to be, thank God, it is now proving itself, a stumbling block to those who in after times might seek to turn a free people back into the hateful paths of despotism. They knew the proneness of prosperity to breed tyrants, and they meant when such should reappear in this fair land and commence their vocation they should find left for them at least one hard nut to crack.

I have now briefly expressed my view of the *meaning* and *objects* of that part of the Declaration of Independence which declares that "all men are created equal." Now let us hear Judge Douglas's view of the same subject, as I find it in the printed report of his late speech. Here it is:

"No man can vindicate the character, motives and conduct of the signers of the Declaration of Independence, except upon the hypothesis that they referred to the white race alone, and not to the African, when they declared all men to have been created equal - that they were speaking of British subjects on this continent being equal to British subjects born and residing in Great Britain - that they were entitled to the same inalienable rights, and among them were enumerated life, liberty and the pursuit of happiness. The Declaration was adopted for the purpose of justifying the colonists in the eyes of the civilized world in with-

drawing their allegiance from the British crown,
and dissolving their connection with the mother
country."

My good friends, read that carefully over some leisure
hour, and ponder well upon it - see what a mere wreck -
mangled ruin - it makes of our once glorious Declaration.

"They were speaking of British subjects on this continent
being equal to British subjects born and residing in Great
Britain!" Why, according to this, not only negroes but
white people outside of Great Britain and America are not
spoken of in that instrument. The English, Irish and
Scotch, along with white Americans, were included to be
sure, but the French, Germans and other white people of
the world are all gone to pot along with the Judge's inferior races.

I had thought the Declaration promised something better
than the condition of British subjects; but no, it only
meant that we should be *equal* to them in their own oppressed and *unequal* condition. According to that, it gave
no promise that having kicked off the King and Lords of
Great Britain, we should not at once be saddled with a
King and Lords of our own.

I had thought the Declaration contemplated the progres-
sive improvement in the condition of all men everywhere;
but no, it merely "was adopted for the purpose of justifying the colonists in the eyes of the civilized world in withdrawing their allegiance from the British crown, and dissolving their connection with the mother country." Why,
that object having been effected some eighty years ago,
the Declaration is of no practical use now - mere rubbish -

old wadding left to rot on the battle-field after the victory is won.

I understand you are preparing to celebrate the "Fourth," to-morrow week. What for? The doings of that day had no reference to the present; and quite half of you are not even descendants of those who were referred to at that day. But I suppose you will celebrate; and will even go so far as to read the Declaration. Suppose after you read it once in the old fashioned way, you read it once more with Judge Douglas' version. It will then run thus: "We hold these truths to be self-evident that all British subjects who were on this continent eighty-one years ago, were created equal to all British subjects born and *then* residing in Great Britain."

And now I appeal to all - to Democrats as well as other - are you really willing that the Declaration shall be thus frittered away? - thus left no more at most, than an interesting memorial of the dead past? thus shorn of its vitality, and practical value; and left without the *germ* or even the *suggestion* of the individual rights of man in it?

But Judge Douglas is especially horrified at the thought of the mixing of blood by the white and black races: agreed for once - a thousand times agreed. There are white men enough to marry all the white women, and black men enough to marry all the black women; and so let them be married. On this point we fully agree with the Judge; and when he shall show that his policy is better adapted to prevent amalgamation than ours we shall drop ours, and adopt his. Let us see. In 1850 there were in the United States 405,751 mulattoes. Very few of these are the offspring of whites and *free* blacks; nearly all have sprung from black *slaves* and white masters. A separation of the races is the only perfect preventive of amalgamation; but as an immediate separation is impossible the next best thing is to *keep* them apart *where* they are not already together. If white and black people never get together in Kansas, they will never mix blood in Kansas. That is at least one self-evident truth. A few free colored persons may get into the free States, in any event; but their number is too insignificant to amount to much in the way of mixing blood. In 1850 there were in the free States, 56,649 mulattoes; but for the most part they were not born there - they came from the slave States, ready made up. In the same year the slave States had 348,874 mulattoes, all of home production. The proportion of free mulattoes to free blacks - the only colored classes in the free states - is much greater in the slave than in the free states. It is worthy to note too, that among the free states those which make the colored man the nearest to equal the white, have proportionably the fewest mulattoes, the least of amalgamation. In New Hampshire, the State which goes farthest toward equality between the races, there are just 184 mulattoes, while there are in Virginia - how many do you think? - 79,775, being 23,126 more than in all the free States together.

These statistics show that slavery is the greatest source of amalgamation; and next to it, not the elevation, but the degradation of the free blacks. Yet Judge Douglas dreads the slightest restraints on the spread of slavery, and the slightest human recognition of the negro, as tending horribly to amalgamation.

The very Dred Scott case affords a strong test as to which party most favors amalgamation, the Republicans or the dear Union-saving Democracy. Dred Scott, his wife and two daughters were all involved in the suit. We desired the court to have held that they were citizens so far at least as to entitle them to a hearing as to whether they were free or not; and then, also, that they were in fact and in law really free. Could we have had our way, the chances of these black girls ever mixing their blood with that of white people, would have been diminished at least to the extent that it could not have been without their consent. But Judge Douglas is delighted to have them decided to be slaves, and not human enough to have a hearing, even if they were free, and thus left subject to the forced concubinage of their masters, and liable to become the mothers of mulattoes in spite of themselves - the very state of case that produces nine tenths of all the mulattoes - all the mixing of blood in the nation.

Of course, I state this case as an illustration only, not meaning to say or intimate that the master of Dred Scott and his family, or any more than a percentage of masters generally, are inclined to exercise this particular power which they hold over their female slaves.

I have said that the separation of the races is the only perfect preventive of amalgamation. I have no right to say all the members of the Republican party are in favor of this, nor to say that as a party they are in favor of it. There is nothing in their platform directly on the subject. But I can say a very large proportion of its members are for it, and that the chief plank in their platform - opposition to the spread of slavery - is most favorable to that separation.

Such separation, if ever effected at all, must be effected by colonization; and no political party, as such, is now doing anything directly for colonization. Party operations at present only favor or retard colonization incidentally.

The enterprise is a difficult one; but "where there is a will there is a way," and what colonization needs most is a hearty will. Will springs from the two elements of moral sense and self-interest. Let us be brought to believe it is morally right, and at the same time, favorable to, or at least, not against, our interest, to transfer the African to his native clime, and we shall find a way to do it, however great the task may be. The children of Israel, to such numbers as to include four hundred thousand fighting men, went out of Egyptian bondage in a body.

How differently the respective courses of the Democratic and Republican parties incidentally bear on the question of forming a will - a public sentiment - for colonization, is easy to see. The Republicans inculcate, with whatever of ability they can, that the negro is a man, that his bondage is cruelly wrong, and that the field of his oppression ought not to be enlarged. The Democrats deny his manhood; deny, or dwarf to insignificance, the wrong of his bondage; so far as possible, crush all sympathy for him, and cultivate and excite hatred and disgust against him; compliment themselves as Union-savers for doing so; and call the indefinite outspreading of his bondage "a sacred right of self-government."

The plainest print cannot be read through a gold eagle; and it will be ever hard to find many men who will send a slave to Liberia, and pay his passage, while they can send him to a new country, Kansas, for instance, and sell him for fifteen hundred dollars, and the rise.

A HOUSE DIVIDED AGAINST ITSELF
SPRINGFIELD, ILLINOIS
June 16, 1858

Gentlemen: If we could first know where we are, and whither we are tending, we could better judge what to do, and how to do it.

We are now far into the fifth year, since a policy was initiated, with the avowed object, and confident promise, of putting an end to slavery agitation. Under the operation of that policy, that agitation has not only not ceased, but has constantly augmented. In my opinion, it will not cease, until a crisis shall have been reached, and passed -

"A house divided against itself cannot stand."

I believe this government cannot endure, permanently half *slave* and half *free.*

I do not expect the Union to be dissolved - I do not expect the house to fall - but I do expect it will cease to be divided.

It will become all one thing, or all the other.

Either the opponents of slavery, will arrest the further spread of it, and place it where the public mind shall rest in the belief that it is in course of ultimate extinction; or its advocates will push it forward, till it shall become alike lawful in all the States, old as well as new - North as well as South.

Have we no tendency to the latter condition?

Let any one who doubts, carefully contemplate that now almost complete legal combination - piece of *machinery*, so to speak - compounded of the Nebraska doctrine, and the Dred Scott decision. Let him consider not only what work the machinery is adapted to do, and how well adapted; but also, let him study the history of its construction, and trace, if he can, or rather *fail*, if he can, to trace the evidences of design, and concert of action, among its chief bosses, from the beginning.

The new year 1854, found slavery excluded from more than half the States by State Constitutions, and from most of the national territory by congressional prohibition.

Four days later commenced the struggle, which ended in repealing that congressional prohibition. This opened all the national territory to slavery; and was the first point gained.

But, so far, Congress only, had acted; and an indorsement by the people, real or apparent, was indispensable, to save the point already gained, and give chance for more.

This necessity had not been overlooked; but had been provided for, as well as might be, in the notable argument of "squatter sovereignty," otherwise called "*sacred right of self government*," which latter phrase, though expressive of the only rightful basis of any government, was so perverted in this attempted use of it as to amount to just this: That if any *one* man, choose to enslave *another*, no *third* man shall be allowed to object.

That argument was incorporated into the Nebraska bill itself, in the language which follows: *"It being the true intent and meaning of this act not to legislate slavery into any Territory or State, nor to exclude it therefrom; but to leave the people thereof perfectly free to form and regulate their domestic institutions in their own way, subject only to the Constitution of the United States."*

Then opened the roar of loose declamation in favor of "Squatter Sovereignty," and "Sacred right of self government."

"But," said opposition members, "let us be more specific - let us amend the bill so as to expressly declare that the people of the Territory *may* exclude slavery." "Not we," said the friends of the measure; and down they voted the amendment.

While the Nebraska bill was passing through Congress, a law case, involving the question of a negro's freedom, by reason of his owner having voluntarily taken him first into a free State and then a territory covered by the congressional prohibition, and held him as a slave for a long time in each, was passing through the U.S. Circuit Court for the District of Missouri; and both Nebraska bill and law suit were brought to a decision in the same month of May, 1854. The negro's name was "Dred Scott," which name now designates the decision finally made in the case.

Before the then next Presidential election, the law case came to, and was argued in the Supreme Court of the United States; but the decision of it was deferred until after the election. Still, before the election, Senator Trumbull, on the floor of the Senate, requests the leading advocate of the Nebraska bill to state his opinion whether the people of a territory can constitutionally exclude slavery from their limits; and the latter answers, "That is a question for the Supreme Court."

The election came. Mr. Buchanan was elected, and the indorsement, such as it was, secured. That was the second point gained. The indorsement, however, fell short of a clear popular majority by nearly four hundred thousand votes, and so, perhaps, was not over-whelmingly reliable and satisfactory. The outgoing President, in his last annual message, as impressively as possible echoed back upon the people the weight and authority of the indorsement.

The Supreme Court met again; did not announce their decision, but ordered a re-argument.

The Presidential inauguration came, and still no decision of the court; but the incoming President, in his inaugural address, fervently exhorted the people to abide by the forthcoming decision, whatever it might be.

Then, in a few days, came the decision.

The reputed author of the Nebraska bill finds an early occasion to make a speech at this capitol indorsing the Dred Scott Decision, and vehemently denouncing all opposition to it.

The new President, too, seizes the early occasion of the Silliman letter to indorse and strongly construe that decision, and to express his astonishment that any different view had ever been entertained.

At length a squabble springs up between the President and the author of the Nebraska bill, on the mere question of fact, whether the Lecompton Constitution was or was not, in any just sense, made by the people of Kansas; and in that quarrel the latter declares that all he wants is a fair vote for the people, and that he cares not whether slavery be voted down or voted up. I do not understand his declaration that he cares not whether slavery be voted down or voted up, to be intended by him other than as an apt definition of the policy he would impress upon the public mind - the principle for which he declares he has suffered much, and is ready to suffer to the end.

And well may he cling to that principle. If he has any parental feeling, well may he cling to it. That principle, is the only shred left of his original Nebraska doctrine. Under the Dred Scott decision, "squatter sovereignty" squatted out of existence, tumbled down like temporary scaffolding - like the mold at the foundry served through one blast and fell back into loose sand - helped to carry an election, and then was kicked to the winds. His late joint struggle with the Republicans, against the Lecompton Constitution, involves nothing of the original Nebraska doctrine. That struggle was made on a point, the right of a people to make their own constitution, upon which he and the Republicans have never differed.

The several points of the Dred Scott decision, in connection with Senator Douglas's "care not" policy, constitute the piece of machinery, in its present state of advancement.

The working points of that machinery are:

First, that no negro slave, imported as such from Africa, and no descendant of such slave can ever be a citizen of any State, in the sense of that term as used in the Constitution of the United States.

This point is made in order to deprive the negro, in every possible event, of the benefit of that provision of the United States Constitution, which declares that - "the citizens of each State shall be entitled to all privileges and immunities of citizens in the several states."

Secondly, that "subject to the Constitution of the United States," neither Congress nor a Territorial Legislature can exclude slavery from any United States Territory. The point is made in order that individual men may fill up the territories with slaves, without danger of losing them as property, and thus enhance the chances of permanency to the institution through all the future.

Thirdly, that whether the holding a negro in actual slavery in a free State, makes him free, as against the holder, the United States courts will not decide, but will leave to be decided by the courts of any slave State the negro may be forced into by the master. This point is made, not to be pressed immediately; but, if acquiesced in for a while, and apparently indorsed by the people at an election, then to sustain the logical conclusion that what Dred Scott's master might lawfully do with Dred Scott, in the free State of Illinois, every other master may lawfully do with any other one or one thousand slaves, in Illinois, or in any other free State.

Auxiliary to all this, and working hand in hand with it, the Nebraska doctrine, or what is left of it, is to educate and mould public opinion, at least Northern public opinion, to not care whether slavery is voted down or voted up.

This shows exactly where we now are; and partially also, whither we are tending.

It will throw additional light on the latter, to go back, and run the mind over the string of historical facts already stated. Several things will now appear less dark and mysterious than they did *when* they were transpiring. The people were to be left "perfectly free" "subject only to the Constitution." What the Constitution had to do with it, outsiders could not then see. Plainly enough now, it was an exactly fitted nitch for the Dred Scott decision to afterward come in, and declare that perfect freedom of the people, to be just no freedom at all.

Why was the amendment, expressly declaring the right of the people to exclude slavery, voted down? Plainly enough now, the adoption of it, would have spoiled the nitch for the Dred Scott decision. Why was the court decision held up? Why even a Senator's individual opinion withheld, till after the Presidential election? Plainly enough now, the speaking out then would have damaged the "perfectly free" argument upon which the election was to be carried.

Why the outgoing President's felicitation on the indorsement? Why the delay of a reargument? Why the incoming President's advance exhortation in favor of the decision?

These things look like the cautious patting and petting of a spirited horse, preparatory to mounting him, when it is dreaded that he may give the rider a fall.

And why the hasty after indorsements of the decision by the President and others?

We cannot absolutely know that all these exact adaptations are the result of preconcert. But when we see a lot
of framed timbers, different portions of which we know
have been gotten out at different times and places and by
different workmen - Stephen, Franklin, Roger, and James,
for instance - and we see these timbers joined together,
and see they exactly make the frame of a house or a mill,
all the tenons and mortises exactly fitting, and all the
lengths and proportions of the different pieces exactly
adapted to their respective places, and not a piece too
many or too few - not omitting even scaffolding - or, if a
single piece be lacking, we see the place in the frame exactly fitted and prepared to yet bring such piece in - in
such a case, we find it impossible not to believe that Stephen and Franklin and Roger and James all understood
one another from the beginning, and all worked upon a
common plan or draft drawn up before the first lick was
struck.

It should not be overlooked that, by the Nebraska bill, the
people of a State as well as Territory, were to be left
"perfectly free" "subject only to the Constitution." Why
mention a State? They were legislating for territories, and
not for or about States. Certainly the people of a State
are and ought to be subject to the Constitution of the
United States; but why is mention of this lugged into this
merely territorial law? Why are the people of a territory
and the people of a state therein lumped together, and
their relation to the Constitution therein treated as being
precisely the same?

While the opinion of the Court, by Chief Justice Taney, in
the Dred Scott case, and the separate opinions of all the
concurring Judges, expressly declare that the Constitution
of the United States neither permits Congress nor a terri-

torial legislature to exclude slavery from any United States territory, they all omit to declare whether or not the same Constitution permits a state, or the people of a state, to exclude it.

Possibly, this is a mere omission; but who can be quite sure, if McLean or Curtis had sought to get into the opinion a declaration of unlimited power in the people of a state to exclude slavery from their limits, just as Chase and Mace sought to get such declaration, in behalf of the people of a territory, into the Nebraska bill - I ask, who can be quite sure that it would not have been voted down, in the one case, as it had been in the other?

The nearest approach to the point of declaring the power of a State over slavery, is made by Judge Nelson. He approaches it more than once, using the precise idea, and almost the language too, of the Nebraska act. On one occasion his exact language is, "except in cases where the power is restrained by the Constitution of the United States, the law of the State is supreme over the subject of slavery within its jurisdiction."

In what cases the power of the states is so restrained by the U.S. Constitution is left an open question, precisely as the same question, as to the restraint on the power of the territories was left open in the Nebraska act. Put that and that together, and we have another nice little nitch, which we may, ere long, see filled with another Supreme Court decision, declaring that the Constitution of the United States does not permit a state to exclude slavery from its limits.

And this may especially be expected if the doctrine of "care not whether slavery be voted down or voted up," shall gain upon the public mind sufficiently to give promise that such a decision can be maintained when made.

Such a decision is all that slavery now lacks of being alike lawful in all the States.

Welcome or unwelcome, such decision *is* probably coming, and will soon be upon us, unless the power of the present political dynasty shall be met and overthrown. We shall lie down pleasantly dreaming that the people of Missouri are on the verge of making their State free; and we shall awake to the reality, instead, that the Supreme Court has made Illinois a slave State.

To meet and overthrow the power of that dynasty, is the work now before all those who would prevent that consummation.

This is what we have to do.

But how can we best do it?

There are those who denounce us openly to their own friends, and yet whisper us softly, that Senator Douglas is the aptest instrument there is, with which to effect that object. They do not tell us, nor has he told us, that he wishes any such object to be effected. They wish us to infer all, from the facts that he now has a little quarrel with the present head of the dynasty; and that he has regularly voted with us, on a single point, upon which, he and we, have never differed.

They remind us that he is a great man, and that the largest of us are very small ones. Let this be granted. But "a living dog is better that a dead lion." Judge Douglas, if not a dead lion for this work, is at least a caged and toothless one. How can he oppose the advances of slavery? He don't care anything about it. His avowed mission is impressing the "public heart" to care nothing about it.

A leading Douglas Democratic newspaper thinks Douglas' superior talent will be needed to resist the revival of the African slave trade.

Does Douglas believe an effort to revive that trade is approaching? He has not said so. Does he really think so? But if it is, how can he resist it? For years he has labored to prove it a sacred right of white men to take negro slaves into the new territories. Can he possibly show that it is less a sacred right to buy them where they can be bought cheapest? And, unquestionably they can be bought cheaper in Africa than in Virginia.

He has done all in his power to reduce the whole question of slavery to one of a mere right of property; and as such, how can he oppose the foreign slave trade - how can he refuse, that trade in that "property" shall be "perfectly free" - unless he does it as a protection to the home production? And as the home producers will probably not ask the protection, he will be wholly without a ground of opposition. Senator Douglas holds, we know, that a man may rightfully be wiser to-day than he was yesterday - that he may rightfully change when he finds himself wrong. But, can we for that reason, run ahead, and infer that he will make any particular change, of which he, himself, has given no intimation? Can we safely base our action upon any such vague inference?

Now, as ever, I wish to not misrepresent Judge Douglas' position, question his motives, or do aught that can be personally offensive to him.

Whenever, if ever, he and we can come together on principle so that our great cause may have assistance from his great ability, I hope to have interposed no adventitious obstacle.

But clearly, he is not now with us - he does not pretend to be - he does not promise to ever be.

Our cause, then, must be intrusted to, and conducted by its own undoubted friends - those whose hands are free, whose hearts are in the work - who do care for the result.

Two years ago the Republicans of the nation mustered over thirteen hundred thousand strong. We did this under the single impulse of resistance to a common danger, with every external circumstance against us. Of strange, discordant, and even hostile elements, we gathered from the four winds, and formed and fought the battle through, under the constant hot fire of a disciplined, proud, and pampered enemy.

Did we brave all then to falter now? - now - when that same enemy is wavering, dissevered, and belligerent? The result is not doubtful. We shall not fail - if we stand firm, we shall not fail.

Wise counsels may accelerate or mistakes delay it, but sooner or later the victory is sure to come!

THE SECOND
LINCOLN-DOUGLAS DEBATE
FREEPORT, ILLINOIS
August 27, 1858

Ladies and Gentlemen: On Saturday last, Judge Douglas and myself first met in public discussion. He spoke one hour, I an hour and a half, and he replied for half an hour. The order is now reversed. I am to speak an hour, he an hour and a half, and then I am to reply for half an hour. I propose to devote myself during the first hour to the scope of what was brought within the range of his half-hour speech at Ottawa. Of course there was brought within the scope of that half-hour's speech something of his own opening speech. In the course of that opening argument Judge Douglas proposed to me seven distinct interrogatories. In my speech of an hour and a half, I attended to some other parts of his speech, and incidentally, as I thought, answered one of the interrogatories then. I then distinctly intimated to him that I would answer the rest of his interrogatories on condition only that he should agree to answer as many for me. He made no intimation at the time of the proposition, nor did he in his reply allude at all to that suggestion of mine. I do him no injustice in saying that he occupied at least half of his reply in dealing with me as though I had refused to answer his interrogatories. I now propose that I will answer any of the interrogatories, upon condition that he will answer questions from me not exceeding the same number. I give him an opportunity to respond. The Judge remains silent. I now say that I will answer his interrogatories, whether he answers mine or not; and that after I have done so, I shall propound mine to him.

I have supposed myself, since the organization of the Republican party at Bloomington, in May, 1856, bound as a party man by the platforms of the party then and since. If in any interrogatories which I shall answer I go beyond the scope of what is within these platforms, it will be perceived that no one is responsible but myself. Having said this much, I will take up the judge's interrogatories as I find them printed in the Chicago "Times," and answer them *seriatim.* In order that there may be no mistake about it, I have copied the interrogatories in writing, and also my answers to them. The first one of these interrogatories is in these words:

Question 1: "I desire to know whether Lincoln today stands as he did in 1854, in favor of the unconditional repeal of the fugitive-slave law?"

Answer. I do not now, nor ever did, stand in favor of the unconditional repeal of the fugitive-slave law.

Question 2. "I desire him to answer whether he stands pledged to-day as he did in 1854, against the admission of any more slave States into the Union, even if the people want them?"

Answer. I do not now, nor ever did, stand pledged against the admission of any more slave States into the Union.

Question 3. "I want to know whether he stands pledged against the admission of a new State into the Union with such a constitution as the people of that State may see fit to make?"

Answer. I do not stand pledged against the admission of a new State into the Union with such a constitution as the people of that State may see fit to make.

Question 4. "I want to know whether he stands to-day pledged to the abolition of slavery in the District of Columbia?"

Answer. I do not stand to-day pledged to the abolition of slavery in the District of Columbia.

Question 5. "I desire him to answer whether he stands pledged to the prohibition of the slave-trade between the different States?"

Answer. I do not stand pledged to the prohibition of the slave-trade between the different States.

Question 6. "I desire to know whether he stands pledged to prohibit slavery in all the Territories of the United States, North as well as South of the Missouri Compromise line?"

Answer. I am impliedly, if not expressly, pledged to a belief in the right and duty of Congress to prohibit slavery in all the United States Territories.

Question 7. "I desire him to answer whether he is opposed to the acquisition of any new territory unless slavery is first prohibited therein?"

Answer. I am not generally opposed to honest acquisition of territory; and, in any given case, I would or would not oppose such acquisition, accordingly as I might think such acquisition would or would not aggravate the slavery question among ourselves.

Now, my friends, it will be perceived upon an examination of these questions and answers, that so far I have only answered that I was not pledged to this, that, or the other. The Judge has not framed his interrogatories to ask me anything more than this, and I have answered in strict accordance with the interrogatories, and have answered truly that I am not pledged at all upon any of the points to which I have answered. But I am not disposed to hang upon the exact form of his interrogatory. I am really disposed to take up at least some of these questions, and state what I really think upon them.

As to the first one, in regard to the fugitive-slave law, I have never hesitated to say, and I do not now hesitate to say, that I think, under the Constitution of the United States, the people of the Southern States are entitled to a congressional fugitive-slave law. Having said that, I have had nothing to say in regard to the existing fugitive-slave law, further than that I think it should have been framed so as to be free from some of the objections that pertain to it, without lessening its efficiency. And inasmuch as we are not now in an agitation in regard to an alteration or modification of that law, I would not be the man to introduce it as a new subject of agitation upon the general question of slavery.

In regard to the other question, of whether I am pledged to the admission of any more slave States into the Union, I state to you very frankly that I would be exceedingly sorry ever to be put in a position of having to pass upon that question. I should be exceedingly glad to know that there would never be another slave State admitted into the Union; but I must add, that if slavery shall be kept out of the Territories during the territorial existence of any one given Territory, and then the people shall, having a fair chance and a clear field, when they come to adopt the Constitution, do such an extraordinary thing as to adopt a slave constitution, uninfluenced by the actual presence of the institution among them, I see no alternative, if we own the country, but to admit them into the Union.

The third interrogatory is answered by the answer to the second, it being, as I conceive, the same as the second.

The fourth one is in regard to the abolition of slavery in the District of Columbia. In relation to that, I have my mind very distinctly made up. I should be exceedingly glad to see slavery abolished in the District of Columbia. I believe that Congress possesses the constitutional power to abolish it. Yet as a member of Congress, I should not with my present views be in favor of endeavoring to abolish slavery in the District of Columbia unless it would be upon these conditions: First, that the abolition should be gradual; second, that it should be on a vote of the majority of qualified voters in the District; and third, that compensation should be made to unwilling owners. With these three conditions, I confess I would be exceedingly glad to see Congress abolish slavery in the District of Columbia, and, in the language of Henry Clay, "sweep from our capital that foul blot upon our nation."

In regard to the fifth interrogatory, I must say here that as to the question of the abolition of the slave-trade between the different States, I can truly answer, as I have, that I am pledged to nothing about it. It is a subject to which I have not given that mature consideration that would make me feel authorized to state a position so as to hold myself entirely bound by it. In other words, that question has never been prominently enough before me to induce me to investigate whether we really have the constitutional power to do it. I could investigate it if I had sufficient time to bring myself to a conclusion upon that subject, but I have not done so, and I say so frankly to you here and to Judge Douglas. I must say, however, that if I should be of opinion that Congress does possess the constitutional power to abolish the slave-trade among the different States, I should still not be in favor of the exercise of that power unless upon some conservative principle as I conceive it, akin to what I have said in relation to the abolition of slavery in the District of Columbia.

My answer as to whether I desire that slavery should be prohibited in all the Territories of the United States is full and explicit within itself, and cannot be made clearer by any comments of mine. So I suppose in regard to the question whether I am opposed to the acquisition of any more territory unless slavery is first prohibited therein, my answer is such that I could add nothing by way of illustration, or making myself better understood, than the answer which I have placed in writing.

Now in all this the Judge has me, and he has me on the record. I suppose he had flattered himself that I was really entertaining one set of opinions for one place and another set for another place - that I was afraid to say at one place what I uttered at another. What I am saying here I suppose I say to a vast audience as strongly tending to Abolitionism as any audience in the State of Illinois, and I believe I am saying that which, if it would be offensive to any persons and render them enemies to myself, would be offensive to persons in this audience.

I now proceed to propound to the Judge the interrogatories so far as I have framed them. I will bring forward a new instalment when I get them ready. I will bring them forward now, only reaching to number four.

The first one is:

Question 1. If the people of Kansas shall, by means entirely unobjectionable in all other respects, adopt a State constitution, and ask admission into the Union under it, before they have the requisite number of inhabitants according to the English bill - some ninety-three thousand - will you vote to admit them?

Question 2. Can the people of a United States Territory, in any lawful way, against the wish of any citizen of the United States, exclude slavery from its limits prior to the formation of a State constitution?

Question 3. If the Supreme Court of the United States shall decide that States cannot exclude slavery from their limits, are you in favor of acquiescing in, adopting, and following such decision as a rule of political action?

Question 4. Are you in favor of acquiring additional territory, in disregard of how such acquisition may affect the nation on the slavery question?

As introductory to these interrogatories which Judge Douglas propounded to me at Ottawa, he read a set of resolutions which he said Judge Trumbull and myself had participated in adopting, in the first Republican State convention, held at Springfield, in October, 1854. He insisted that I and Judge Trumbull, and perhaps the entire Republican party, were responsible for the doctrines contained

in the set of resolutions which he read, and I understand
that it was from that set of resolutions that he deduced
the interrogatories which he propounded to me, using
these resolutions as a sort of authority for propounding
those questions to me. Now I say here to-day that I do not
answer his interrogatories because of their springing at all
from that set of resolutions which he read. I answered
them because Judge Douglas thought fit to ask them. I do
not now, nor ever did, recognize any responsibility upon
myself in that set of resolutions. When I replied to him
on that occasion; I assured him that I never had anything
to do with them. I repeat here to-day, that I never in any
possible form had anything to do with that set of resolutions. It turns out, I believe, that those resolutions were
never passed at any convention held in Springfield. It
turns out that they were never passed at any convention
or any public meeting that I had any part in. I believe it
turns out, in addition to all this, that there was not, in the
fall of 1854, any convention holding a session in Springfield calling itself a Republican State convention; yet it is
true there was a convention, or assemblage of men calling
themselves a convention, at Springfield, that did pass some
resolutions. But so little did I really know of the proceedings of that convention, or what set of resolutions they
had passed, though having a general knowledge that there
had been such an assemblage of men there, that when
Judge Douglas read the resolutions, I really did not know
but that they had been the resolutions passed then and
there. I did not question that they were the resolutions
adopted. For I could not bring myself to suppose that
Judge Douglas could say what he did upon this subject,
without knowing that it was true. I contented myself, on
that occasion, with denying, as I truly could, all connection
with them, not denying or affirming whether they were
passed at Springfield. Now it turns out that he had got

hold of some resolutions passed at some convention or public meeting in Kane County. I wish to say here, that I don't conceive that in any fair and just mind this discovery relieves me at all. I had just as much to do with the convention in Kane County as that at Springfield. I am just as much responsible for the resolutions at Kane County as those at Springfield, the amount of the responsibility being exactly nothing in either case; no more than there would be in regard to a set of resolutions passed in the moon.

I allude to this extraordinary matter in this canvass for some further purpose than anything yet advanced. Judge Douglas did not make his statement upon that occasion as matters that he believed to be true, but he stated them roundly as being true, in such form as to pledge his veracity for their truth. When the whole matter turns out as it does, and when we consider who Judge Douglas is - that he is a distinguished senator of the United States; that he has served nearly twelve years as such; that his character is not at all limited as an ordinary senator of the United States, but that his name has become of world-wide renown - it is most extraordinary that he should so far forget all the suggestions of justice to an adversary, or of prudence to himself, as to venture upon the assertion of that which the slightest investigation would have shown him to be wholly false. I can only account for his having done so upon the supposition that that evil genius which has attended him through his life, giving to him an apparent astonishing prosperity, such as to lead very many good men to doubt there being any advantage in virtue over vice - I say I can only account for it on the supposition that that evil genius has at last made up its mind to forsake him.

And I may add that another extraordinary feature of the Judge's conduct in this canvass - made more extraordinary by this incident - is, that he is in the habit, in almost all the speeches he makes, of charging falsehood upon his adversaries, myself and others. I now ask whether he is able to find in anything that Judge Trumbull, for instance, has said, or in anything that I have said, a justification at all compared with what we have, in this instance, for that sort of vulgarity.

I have been in the habit of charging as a matter of belief on my part, that, in the introduction of the Nebraska bill into Congress, there was a conspiracy to make slavery perpetual and national. I have arranged from time to time the evidence which establishes and proves the truth of this charge. I recurred to this charge at Ottawa. I shall not now have time to dwell upon it at very great length; but inasmuch as Judge Douglas in his reply of half an hour made some points upon me in relation to it, I propose noticing a few of them.

The Judge insists that, in the first speech I made, in which I very distinctly made that charge, he thought for a good while I was in fun - that I was playful - that I was not sincere about it - and that he only grew angry and somewhat excited when he found that I insisted upon it as a matter of earnestness. He says he characterized it as a falsehood as far as I implicated his moral character in that transaction. Well, I did not know, till he presented that view, that I had implicated his moral character. He is very much in the habit, when he argues me up into a position I never thought of occupying, of very cozily saying he has no doubt Lincoln is "conscientious" in saying so. He should remember that I did not know but what he was altogether "conscientious" in that matter. I can conceive it possible for men to conspire to do a good thing, and I really find nothing in Judge Douglas's course of arguments that is contrary to or inconsistent with his belief of a conspiracy to nationalize and spread slavery as being a good and blessed thing, and so I hope he will understand that I do not at all question but that in all this matter he is entirely "conscientious."

But to draw your attention to one of the points I made in this case, beginning at the beginning. When the Nebraska bill was introduced, or a short time afterward, by an amendment, I believe, it was provided that it must be considered "the true intent and meaning of this act not to legislate slavery into any State or Territory, or to exclude it therefrom, but to leave the people thereof perfectly free to form and regulate their own domestic institutions in their own way, subject only to the Constitution of the United States." I have called his attention to the fact that when he and some others began arguing that they were giving an increased degree of liberty to the people in the Territories over and above what they formerly had on the question of slavery, a question was raised whether the law was enacted to give such unconditional liberty to the people; and to test the sincerity of this mode of argument, Mr. Chase, of Ohio, introduced an amendment, in which he made the law - if the amendment were adopted - expressly declare that the people of the Territory should have the power to exclude slavery if they saw fit. I have asked attention also to the fact that Judge Douglas, and those who acted with him, voted that amendment down, notwithstanding it expressed exactly the thing they said was the true intent and meaning of the law. I have called attention to the fact that in subsequent times a decision of the Supreme Court has been made in which it has been declared that a Territorial Legislature has no constitutional right to exclude slavery. And I have argued and said that for men who did intend that the people of the Territory should have the right to exclude slavery absolutely and unconditionally, the voting down of Chase's amendment is wholly inexplicable. It is a puzzle - a riddle. But I have said that with men who did look forward to such a decision, or who had it in contemplation that such a decision of the Supreme Court would or might be made, the voting down of that amendment would be perfectly rational and intelligible. It would keep Congress from coming in collision with the decision when it was made. Anybody can conceive that if there was an intention or expectation that such a decision was to follow, it would not be a very desirable party attitude to get into for the Supreme Court - all or nearly all its members belonging to the same party - to decide one way, when the party in Congress had decided the other way. Hence it would be very rational for men expecting such a decision to keep the niche in that law clear for it. After pointing this out, I tell Judge Douglas that it looks to me as though here was the reason why Chase's amendment was voted down. I tell him that as he did it, and knows why he did it, if it was done for a reason different from this, he knows what that reason was, and can tell us what it was. I tell him, also, it will be vastly more satisfactory to the country for him to give some other plausible, intelligible reason why it was voted down than to stand upon his dignity and call people liars. Well, on Saturday he did make his answer, and what do you think it was? He says if I had only taken upon myself to tell the whole truth about that amendment of Chase's, no explanation would have been necessary on his part - or words to that effect. Now I say here that I am quite unconscious of having suppressed anything material to the case, and I am very frank to admit if there is any sound reason other than that which appeared to me material, it is quite fair for him to present it. What reason does he propose? That when Chase came forward with his amendment expressly authorizing the people to exclude slavery from the limits of every Territory, General Cass proposed to Chase, if he (Chase) would add to his amendment that the people should have the power to introduce or exclude, they would let it go.

This is substantially all of his reply. And because Chase would not do that they voted his amendment down. Well, it turns out, I believe, upon examination, that General Cass took some part in the little running debate upon that amendment, and then ran away and did not vote on it at all. Is not that the fact? So confident, as I think, was General Cass that there was a snake somewhere about, he chose to run away from the whole thing. This is an inference I draw from the fact that though he took part in the debate his name does not appear in the ayes and noes. But does Judge Douglas's reply amount to a satisfactory answer? [*Cries of "Yes," "Yes," and "No," "No."*] There is some little difference of opinion here. But I ask attention to a few more views bearing on the question of whether it amounts to a satisfactory answer. The men who were determined that that amendment should not get into the bill, and spoil the place where the Dred Scott decision was to come in, sought an excuse to get rid of it somewhere. One of these ways - one of these excuses - was to ask Chase to add to his proposed amendment a provision that the people might introduce slavery if they wanted to. They very well knew Chase would do no such thing - that Mr. Chase was one of the men differing from them on the broad principle of his insisting that freedom was better than slavery - a man who would not consent to enact a law penned with is own hand, by which he was made to recognize slavery on the one hand and liberty on the other as precisely equal; and when they insisted on his doing this, they very well knew they insisted on that which he would not for a moment think of doing, and that they were only bluffing him. I believe - I have not, since he made his answer, had a chance to examine the journals or "Congressional Globe," and therefore speak from memory - I believe the state of the bill at that time, according to parliamentary rules, was such that no member could propose an additional amendment to Chase's amendment. I rather think this is the truth - the Judge shakes his head. Very well. I would like to know then, if they wanted Chase's amendment fixed over, why somebody else could not have offered to do it? If they wanted it amended, why did they not offer the amendment? Why did they stand there taunting and quibbling at Chase? Why did they not put it in themselves? But to put it on the other ground: Suppose that there was such an amendment offered, and Chase's was an amendment to an amendment; until one is disposed of by parliamentary law, you cannot pile another on. Then all these gentlemen had to do was to vote Chase's on, and then, in the amended form in which the whole stood, add their own amendment to it if they wanted to put it in that shape. This was all they were obliged to do, and the ayes and noes show that there were thirty-six who voted it down, against ten who voted in favor of it. The thirty-six held entire sway and control. They could in some form or other have put that bill in the exact shape they wanted. If there was a rule preventing their amending it at the time, they could pass that, and then, Chase's amendment being merged, put it in the shape they wanted. They did not choose to do so, but they went into a quibble with Chase to get him to add what they knew he would not add, and because he would not, they stand upon that flimsy pretext for voting down what they argued was the meaning and intent of their own bill.

They left room thereby for this Dred Scott decision, which goes very far to make slavery national throughout the United States.

I pass one or two points I have because my time will very soon expire, but I must be allowed to say that Judge Douglas recurs again, as he did upon one or two other occasions, to the enormity of Lincoln - an insignificant individual like Lincoln - upon his *ipse dixit* [saying so himself] charging a conspiracy upon a large number of members of Congress, the Supreme Court, and two Presidents, to nationalize slavery. I want to say that, in the first place, I have made no charge of this sort upon my *ipse dixit.* I have only arrayed the evidence tending to prove it, and presented it to the understanding of others, saying what I think it proves, but giving you the means of judging whether it proves it or not. This is precisely what I have done. I have not placed it upon my *ipse dixit* at all. On this occasion, I wish to recall his attention to a piece of evidence which I brought forward at Ottawa on Saturday, showing that he had made substantially the same charge against substantially the same persons, excluding his dear self from the category. I ask him to give some attention to the evidence which I brought forward, that he himself had discovered a "fatal blow being struck" against the right of the people to exclude slavery from their limits, which fatal blow he assumed as in evidence in an article in the Washington "Union," published "by authority." I ask by whose authority? He discovers a similar or identical provision in the Lecompton constitution. Made by whom? The framers of that constitution. Advocated by whom? By all the members of the party in the nation, who advocated the introduction of Kansas into the Union under the Lecompton constitution.

I have asked his attention to the evidence that he arrayed to prove that such a fatal blow was being struck, and to the facts which he brought forward in support of that charge - being identical with the one which he thinks so villainous in me. He pointed it not at a newspaper editor merely, but at the President and his cabinet, and the members of Congress advocating the Lecompton constitution, and those framing that instrument. I must again be permitted to remind him, that although my *ipse dixit* may not be as great as his, yet it somewhat reduces the force of his calling my attention to the enormity of my making a like charge against him.

KEEPING THE FAITH
CHICAGO, ILLINOIS
March 1, 1859

I understand that you have to-day rallied around your principles, and they have again triumphed in the city of Chicago. I am exceedingly happy to meet you under such cheering auspices on this occasion - the first on which I have appeared before an audience since the campaign of last year. It is unsuitable to enter into a lengthy discourse, as is quite apparent, at a moment like this. I shall therefore detain you only a very short while.

It gives me peculiar pleasure to find an opportunity under such favorable circumstances to return my thanks for the gallant support that the Republicans of the city of Chicago and of the State gave to the cause in which we were all engaged in the late momentous struggle in Illinois. . . .

I wish now to add a word that has a bearing on the future. The Republican principle, the profound central truth that slavery is wrong and ought to be dealt with as a wrong - though we are always to remember the fact of its actual existence amongst us and faithfully observe all the constitutional guarantees - the unalterable principle never for a moment to be lost sight of, that it is a wrong and ought to be dealt with as such, cannot advance at all upon Judge Douglas's ground; that there is a portion of the country in which slavery must always exist; that he does not care whether it is voted up or voted down, as it is simply a question of dollars and cents. Whenever in any compromise, or arrangement, or combination that may promise some temporary advantage we are led upon that ground, then and there the great living principle upon which we have organized as a party is surrendered. The proposition now in our minds that this thing is wrong being once driven out and surrendered, then the institution of slavery necessarily becomes national.

One or two words more of what I did not think of when I rose. Suppose it is true that the Almighty has drawn a line across this continent, on the south side of which part of the people will hold the rest as slaves; that the Almighty ordered this; that it is right, unchangeably right, that men ought there to be held as slaves; that their fellow-men will always have the right to hold them as slaves. I ask you, this once admitted, how can you believe that it is not right for us, or for them coming here, to hold slaves on this other side of the line? Once we come to acknowledge that it is right, that it is the law of the Eternal Being for slavery to exist on one side of that line, have we any sure ground to object to slaves being held on the other side? Once admit the position that a man rightfully holds another man as property on one side of the line, and you must, when it suits his convenience to come to the other side, admit that he has the same right to hold his property there. Once admit Judge Douglas's proposition, and we must all finally give way. Although we may not bring ourselves to the idea that it is to our interest to have slaves in this Northern country, we shall soon bring ourselves to admit that while we may not want them, if any one else does, he has the moral right to have them. Step by step, south of the Judge's moral climate line in the States, in the Territories everywhere, and then in all the States - it is thus that Judge Douglas would lead us inevitably to the nationalization of slavery. Whether by his doctrine or squatter sovereignty, or by the ground taken by him in his recent speeches in Memphis and through the South - that wherever the climate makes it the interest of the inhabitants to encourage slave property they will pass a slave code - whether it is covertly nationalized by congressional legislation, or by Dred Scott decision, or by the sophistical and misleading doctrine he has last advanced, the same goal is inevitably reached by the one or the other device. It is only traveling to the same place by different roads.

It is in this direction lies all the danger that now exists to
the great Republican cause. I take it that so far as concerns forcibly establishing slavery in the Territories by
congressional legislation, or by virtue of the Dred Scott
decision, that day has passed. Our only serious danger is
that we shall be led upon this ground of Judge Douglas,
on the delusive assumption that it is a good way of whipping our opponents, when in fact it is a way that leads
straight to final surrender. The Republican party should
not dally with Judge Douglas when it knows where his
proposition and his leadership would take us, nor be disposed to listen to it because it was best somewhere else to
support somebody occupying his ground. That is no just
reason why we ought to go over to Judge Douglas, as we
were called upon to do last year. Never forget that we
have before us this whole matter of the right or wrong of
slavery in this Union, though the immediate question is as
to its spreading out into new Territories and States.

I do not wish to be misunderstood upon this subject of
slavery in this country. I suppose it may long exist; and
perhaps the best way for it to come to an end peaceably is
for it to exist for a length of time. But I say that the
spread and strengthening and perpetuation of it is an entirely different proposition. There we should in every
way resist it as a wrong, treating it as a wrong, with the
fixed idea that it must and will come to an end. If we do
not allow ourselves to be allured from the strict path of
our duty by such a device as shifting our ground and
throwing us into the rear of a leader who denies our first
principle, denies that there is an absolute wrong in the institution of slavery, then the future of the Republican
cause is safe, and victory is assured. You Republicans of
Illinois have deliberately taken your ground; you have
heard the whole subject discussed again and again; you
have stated your faith in platforms laid down in a State

convention and in a national convention; you have heard and talked over and considered it until you are now all of opinion that you are on a ground of unquestionable right. All you have to do is to keep the faith, to remain steadfast to the right, to stand by your banner. Nothing should lead you to leave your guns. Stand together, ready, with match in hand. Allow nothing to turn you to the right or to the left. Remember how long you have been in setting out on the true course; how long you have been in getting your neighbors to understand and believe as you now do. Stand by your principles, stand by your guns, and victory, complete and permanent, is sure at the last.

SLAVERY IS WRONG
CINCINNATI, OHIO
September 17, 1859

My Fellow-citizens of the State of Ohio: This is the first time in my life that I have appeared before an audience in so great a city as this. I therefore - though I am no longer a young man - make this appearance under some degree of embarrassment. But I have found that when one is embarrassed, usually the shortest way to get through with it is to quit talking or thinking about it, and go at something else.

I understand that you have had recently with you my very distinguished friend, Judge Douglas, of Illinois, and I understand, without having had an opportunity (not greatly sought, to be sure) of seeing a report of the speech that he made here, that he did me the honor to mention my humble name. I suppose that he did so for the purpose of making some objection to some sentiment at some time expressed by me. I should expect, it is true, that Judge Douglas had reminded you, or informed you, if you had never before heard it, that I had once in my life declared it as my opinion that this Government cannot "endure permanently half slave and half free; that a house divided against itself cannot stand," and, as I had expressed it, I did not expect the house to fall; that I did not expect the Union to be dissolved, but that I did expect it would cease to be divided; that it would become all one thing or all the other; that either the opposition of slavery will arrest the further spread of it, and place it where the public mind would rest in the belief that it was in the course of ultimate extinction, or the friends of slavery will push it forward until it becomes alike lawful in all the States, old or new, free as well as slave. I did, fifteen months ago, express that opinion, and upon many occasions Judge Douglas has denounced it, and has greatly, intentionally or unintentionally, misrepresented my purpose in the expression of that opinion.

I presume, without having seen a report of his speech, that he did so here. I presume that he alluded also to that opinion in different language, having been expressed at a subsequent time by Governor Seward, of New York, and that he took the two in a lump and denounced them; that he tried to point out that there was something couched in this opinion which led to the making of an entire uniformity of the local institutions of the various States of the Union, in utter disregard of the different States, which in their nature would seem to require a variety of institutions, and a variety of laws conforming to the differences in the nature of the different States.

Not only so; I presume he insisted that this was a declaration of war between the free and slave States - that it was the sounding to the onset of continual war between the different States, the slave and free States.

This charge, in this form, was made by Judge Douglas on, I believe, the 9th of July, 1858, in Chicago, in my hearing. On the next evening, I made some reply to it. I informed him that many of the inferences he drew from that expression of mine were altogether foreign to any purpose entertained by me, and in so far as he should ascribe these inferences to me, as my purpose, he was entirely mistaken; and in so far as he might argue that whatever might be my purpose, actions, conforming to my views, would lead to these results, he might argue and establish if he could; but, so far as purposes were concerned, he was totally mistaken as to me.

When I made that reply to him, I told him, on the question of declaring war between the different States of the Union, that I had not said I did not expect any peace upon this question until slavery was exterminated; that I had only said I expected peace when that institution was put where the public mind should rest in the belief that it was in course of ultimate extinction; that I believed, from the organization of our government until a very recent period of time, the institution had been placed and continued upon such a basis; that we had had comparative peace upon that question through a portion of that period of time, only because the public mind rested in that belief in regard to it, and that when we returned to that position in relation to that matter, I supposed we should again have peace as we previously had. I assured him, as I now assure you, that I neither then had, nor have, nor ever had, any purpose in any way of interfering with the institution of slavery where it exists. I believe we have no power, under the Constitution of the United States, or rather under the form of government under which we live, to interfere with the institution of slavery, or any other of the institutions of our sister States, be they free or slave States. I declared then, and I now re-declare, that I have as little inclination to interfere with the institution of slavery where it now exists, through the instrumentality of the General Government, or any other instrumentality, as I believe we have no power to do so. I accidentally used this expression: I had no purpose of entering into the slave States to disturb the institution of slavery. So, upon the first occasion that Judge Douglas got an opportunity to reply to me, he passed by the whole body of what I had said upon that subject, and seized upon the particular expression of mine, that I had no purpose of entering into the slave States to disturb the institution of slavery. "Oh, no," said he; "he [Lincoln] won't enter into the slave States to disturb the institution of slavery; he is too prudent a man to do such a thing as that; he only means that he will go on to the line between the free and slave States, and shoot over at them. This is all he means to do. He means to do them all the harm he can, to disturb them all he can, in such a way as to keep his own hide in perfect safety."

Well, now, I did not think, at that time, that that was either a very dignified or very logical argument; but so it was, and I had to get along with it as well as I could.

It has occurred to me here to-night that if I ever do shoot over the line at the people on the other side of the line, into a slave State, and propose to do so keeping my skin safe, that I have now about the best chance I shall ever have. I should not wonder if there are some Kentuckians about this audience; we are close to Kentucky; and whether that be so or not, we are on elevated ground, and by speaking distinctly I should not wonder if some of the Kentuckians would hear me on the other side of the river. For that reason I propose to address a portion of what I have to say to the Kentuckians.

I say, then, in the first place, to the Kentuckians, that I am what they call, as I understand it, a "Black Republican." I think slavery is wrong, morally and politically. I desire that it should be no further spread in these United States, and I should not object if it should gradually terminate in the whole Union. While I say this for myself, I say to you Kentuckians that I understand you differ radically with me upon this proposition; that you believe slavery is a good thing; that slavery is right; that it ought to be extended and perpetuated in this Union. Now, there being this broad difference between us, I do not pretend, in addressing myself to you Kentuckians, to attempt proselyting you; that would be a vain effort. I do not enter upon it. I only propose to try to show you that you ought to nominate for the next presidency, at Charleston, my distinguished friend, Judge Douglas. In all that there is no real difference between you and him; I understand he is as sincerely for you, and more wisely for you, than you are for yourselves. I will try to demonstrate that proposition. Understand now, I say that I believe he is as sincerely for you, and more wisely for you, than you are for yourselves.

What do you want more than anything else to make successful your views of slavery - to advance the outspread of it, and to secure and perpetuate the nationality of it? What do you want more than anything else? What is needed absolutely? What is indispensable to you? Why, if I may be allowed to answer the question, it is to retain a hold upon the North - it is to retain support and strength from the free States. If you can get this support and strength from the free States, you can succeed. If you do not get this support and this strength from the free States, you are in the minority, and you are beaten at once.

If that proposition be admitted - and it is undeniable - then the next thing I say to you is, that Douglas of all the men in this nation is the only man that affords you any hold upon the free States; that no other man can give you any strength in the free States. This being so, if you doubt the other branch of the proposition, whether he is for you - whether he is really for you, as I have expressed it - I propose asking your attention for a while to a few facts.

The issue between you and me, understand, is that I think slavery is wrong, and ought not to be outspread, and you think it is right, and ought to be extended and perpetuated. I now proceed to try to show to you that Douglas is as sincerely for you, and more wisely for you, than you are for yourselves.

In the first place, we know that in a government like this, a government of the people, where the voice of all the men of the country, substantially, enters into the administration of the government, what lies at the bottom of all of it is public opinion. I lay down the proposition that Judge Douglas is not only the man that promises you in advance a hold upon the North, and support in the North, but that he constantly molds public opinion to your ends; that in every possible way he can, he molds the public opinion of the North to your ends; and if there are a few things in which he seems to be against you - a few things which he says that appear to be against you, and a few that he forbears to say which you would like to have him say - you ought to remember that the saying of the one, or the forbearing to say the other would lose his hold upon the North, and, by consequence, would lose his capacity to serve you.

Upon this subject of molding public opinion, I call your attention to the fact - for a well-established fact it is - that the Judge never says your institution of slavery is wrong: he never says it is right, to be sure, but he never says it is wrong. There is not a public man in the United States, I believe, with the exception of Senator Douglas, who has not, at some time in his life, declared his opinion whether the thing is right or wrong; but Senator Douglas never declares it is wrong. He leaves himself at perfect liberty to do all in your favor which he would be hindered from doing if he were to declare the thing to be wrong. On the contrary, he takes all the chances that he has for inveigling the sentiment of the North, opposed to slavery, into your support, by never saying it is right. This you ought to set down to his credit. You ought to give him full credit for this much, little though it be in comparison to the whole which he does for you.

Some other things I will ask your attention to. He said upon the floor of the United States Senate, and he has repeated it, as I understand, a great many times, that he does not care whether slavery is "voted up or voted down."

This again shows you, or ought to show you, if you would reason upon it, that he does not believe it to be wrong; for a man may say, when he sees nothing wrong in a thing, that he does not care whether it be voted up or voted down; but no man can logically say that he cares not whether a thing goes up or goes down which appears to him to be wrong. You therefore have a demonstration in this, that to Judge Douglas's mind your favorite institution, which you desire to have spread out and made perpetual, is no wrong.

Another thing he tells you, in a speech made at Memphis, in Tennessee, shortly after the canvass in Illinois, last year. He there distinctly told the people that there was a "line drawn by the Almighty across this continent, on the one side of which the soil must always be cultivated by slaves"; that he did not pretend to know exactly where that line was, but that there was such a line. I want to ask your attention to that proposition again - that there is one portion of this continent where the Almighty has designed the soil shall always be cultivated by slaves; that its being cultivated by slaves at that place is right; that it has the direct sympathy and authority of the Almighty. Whenever you can get these Northern audiences to adopt the opinion that slavery is right on the other side of the Ohio; whenever you can get them, in pursuance of Douglas's views, to adopt that sentiment, they will very readily make the other argument, which is perfectly logical, that that which is right on that side of the Ohio cannot be wrong on this, and that if you have that property on that side of the Ohio, under the seal and stamp of the Almighty, when by any means it escapes over here, it is wrong to have constitutions and laws "to devil" you about it. So Douglas is molding the public opinion of the North, first to say that the thing is right in your State over the Ohio River, and hence to say that that which is right there is not wrong here, and that all laws and constitutions here, recognizing it as being wrong, are themselves wrong, and ought to be repealed and abrogated. He will tell you, men of Ohio, that if you choose here to have laws against slavery, it is in conformity to the idea that your climate is not suited to it; that your climate is not suited to slave labor, and therefore you have constitutions and laws against it.

Let us attend to that argument for a little while, and see if it be sound. You do not raise sugar-cane (except the new-fashioned sugar-cane, and you won't raise that long), but they do raise it in Louisiana. You don't raise it in Ohio because you can't raise it profitably, because the climate don't suit it. They do raise it in Louisiana because there it is profitable. Now Douglas will tell you that is precisely the slavery question; that they do have slaves there because they are profitable, and you don't have them here because they are not profitable. If that is so, then it leads to dealing with the one precisely as with the other. Is there, then, anything in the constitution or laws of Ohio against raising sugar-cane? Have you found it necessary to put any such provision in your law? Surely not! No man desires to raise sugar-cane in Ohio; but if any man did desire to do so, you would say it was a tyrannical law that forbids his doing so; and whenever you shall agree with Douglas, whenever your minds are brought to adopt his argument, as surely you will have reached the conclusion that although slavery is not profitable in Ohio, if any man want it, it is wrong to him not to let him have it.

In this matter Judge Douglas is preparing the public mind for you of Kentucky, to make perpetual that good thing in your estimation, about which you and I differ.

In this connection let me ask your attention to another thing. I believe it is safe to assert that, five years ago, no living man had expressed the opinion that the negro had no share in the Declaration of Independence. Let me state that again: Five years ago no living man had expressed the opinion that the negro had no share in the Declaration of Independence. If there is in this large audience any man who ever knew of that opinion being put upon paper as much as five years ago, I will be obliged to him now, or at a subsequent time, to show it.

If that be true, I wish you then to note the next fact - that within the space of five years Senator Douglas, in the argument of this question, has got his entire party, so far as I know, without exception, to join in saying that the negro has no share in the Declaration of Independence. If there be now in all these United States one Douglas man that does not say this, I have been unable upon any occasion to scare him up. Now, if none of you said this five years ago, and all of you say it now, that is a matter that you Kentuckians ought to note. That is a vast change in the Northern public sentiment upon that question.

Of what tendency is that change? The tendency of that change is to bring the public mind to the conclusion that when men are spoken of, the negro is not meant; that when negroes are spoken of, brutes alone are contemplated. That change in public sentiment has already degraded the black man, in the estimation of Douglas and his followers, from the condition of a man of some sort, and assigned him to the condition of a brute. Now you Kentuckians ought to give Douglas credit for this. That is the largest possible stride that can be made in regard to the perpetuation of your good thing of slavery.

In Kentucky, perhaps - in many of the slave States certainly - you are trying to establish the rightfulness of slavery by reference to the Bible. You are trying to show that slavery existed in the Bible times by divine ordinance. Now Douglas is wiser than you for your own benefit, upon that subject. Douglas knows that whenever you establish that slavery was right by the Bible, it will occur that that slavery was the slavery of the white man - of men without reference to color - and he knows very well that you may entertain that idea in Kentucky as much as you please, but you will never win any Northern support upon it. He makes a wiser argument for you; he makes the argument that the slavery of the black man, the slavery of the man who has a skin of a different color from your own, is right. He thereby brings to your support Northern voters who could not for a moment be brought by your own argument of the Bible-right of slavery. Will you not give him credit for that? Will you not say that in this matter he is more wisely for you than you are for yourselves?

Now, having established with his entire party this doctrine - having been entirely successful in that branch of his efforts in your behalf - he is ready for another.

At this same meeting at Memphis, he declared that in all contests between the negro and the white man, he was for the white man, but that in all questions between the negro and the crocodile he was for the negro. He did not make that declaration accidentally at Memphis. He made it a great many times in the canvass in Illinois last year (though I don't know that it was reported in any of his speeches there; but he frequently made it). I believe he repeated it at Columbus, and I should not wonder if he repeated it here. It is, then, a deliberate way of expressing himself upon that subject. It is a matter of mature deliberation with him thus to express himself upon that point of his case. It therefore requires some deliberate attention.

The first inference seems to be that if you do not enslave the negro you are wronging the white man in some way or other; and that whoever is opposed to the negro being enslaved is, in some way or other, against the white man. Is not that a falsehood? If there was a necessary conflict between the white man and the negro, I should be for the white man as much as Judge Douglas; but I say there is no such necessary conflict. I say that there is room enough for us all to be free, and that it not only does not wrong the white man that the negro should be free, but it positively wrongs the mass of the white men that the negro should be enslaved; that the mass of white men are really injured by the effects of slave-labor in the vicinity of the fields of their own labor.

Buy I do not desire to dwell upon this branch of the question more than to say that this assumption of his is false, and I do hope that that fallacy will not long prevail in the minds of intelligent white men. At all events, you ought to thank Judge Douglas for it. It is for your benefit it is made.

The other branch of it is, that in a struggle between the negro and the crocodile, he is for the negro. Well, I don't know that there is any struggle between the negro and the crocodile, either. I suppose that if a crocodile (or, as we old Ohio River boatmen used to call them, alligators) should come across a white man, he would kill him if he could, and so he would a negro. But what, at last, is this proposition? I believe that it is a sort of proposition in proportion, which may be stated thus: "As the negro is to the white man, so is the crocodile to the negro; and as the negro may rightfully treat the crocodile as a beast or reptile, so the white man may rightfully treat the negro as a beast or reptile." That is really the point of all that argument of his.

Now, my brother Kentuckians, who believe in this, you ought to thank Judge Douglas for having put that in a much more taking way than any of yourselves have done.

Again, Douglas's great principle, "popular sovereignty," as he calls it, gives you by natural consequence the revival of the slave-trade whenever you want it. If you are disposed to question this, listen awhile, consider awhile, what I shall advance in support of that proposition.

He says that it is the sacred right of the man who goes into the Territories to have slavery if he wants it. Grant that for argument's sake. Is it not the sacred right of the man who don't go there, equally to buy slaves in Africa, if he wants them? Can you point out the difference? The man who goes into the Territories of Kansas and Nebraska, or any other new Territory, with the sacred right of taking a slave there which belongs to him, would certainly have no more right to take one there than I would who own no slave, but who would desire to buy one and take him there. You will not say - you, the friends of Judge Douglas - but that the man who does not own a slave, has an equal right to buy one and take him to the Territory as the other does?

I say that Douglas's popular sovereignty, establishing his sacred right in the people, if you please, if carried to its logical conclusion, gives equally the sacred right to the people of the States or the Territories themselves to buy slaves, wherever they can buy them cheapest; and if any man can show a distinction, I should like to hear him try it. If any man can show how the people of Kansas have a better right to slaves because they want them, than the people of Georgia have to buy them in Africa, I want him to do it. I think it cannot be done. If it is "popular sovereignty" for the people to have slaves because they want them, it is popular sovereignty for them to buy them in Africa, because they desire to do so.

I know that Douglas has recently made a little effort - not seeming to notice that he had a different theory - has made an effort to get rid of that. He has written a letter, addressed to somebody, I believe, who resides in Iowa, declaring his opposition to the repeal of the laws that prohibit the African slave-trade. He bases his opposition to such repeal upon the ground that these laws are themselves one of the compromises of the Constitution of the United States. Now it would be very interesting to see Judge Douglas, or any of his friends, turn to the Constitution of the United Sates and point out that compromise, to show where there is any compromise in the Constitution, or provision in the Constitution, expressed or implied, by which the administrators of that Constitution are under any obligation to repeal the African slave-trade. I know, or at least I think I know, that the framers of that Constitution did expect that the African slave-trade would be abolished at the end of twenty years, to which time their prohibition against its being abolished extended. I think there is abundant contemporaneous history to show that the framers of the Constitution expected it to be abolished. But while they so expected, they gave nothing for that expectation, and they put no provision in the Constitution requiring it should be so abolished. The migration or importation of such persons as the States shall see fit to admit shall not be prohibited, but a certain tax might be levied upon such importation. But what was to be done after that time? The Constitution is as silent about that as it is silent, personally, about myself. There is absolutely nothing in it about that subject - there is only the expectation of the framers of the Constitution that the slave-trade would be abolished at the end of that time, and they expected it would be abolished, owing to public sentiment, before that time, and they put that provision in, in order that it should not be abolished before that time, for reasons which I suppose they thought to be sound ones, but which I will not now try to enumerate before you.

But while they expected the slave-trade would be abolished at that time, they expected that the spread of slavery into the new Territories should also be restricted. It is as easy to prove that the framers of the Constitution of the United States expected that slavery should be prohibited from extending into the new Territories, as it is to prove that it was expected that the slave-trade should be abolished. Both these things were expected. One was no more expected than the other, and one was no more a compromise of the Constitution than the other. There was nothing said in the Constitution in regard to the spread of slavery into the Territories. I grant that, but there was something very important said about it by the same generation of men in the adoption of the old Ordinance of '87, through the influence of which you here in Ohio, our neighbors in Indiana, we in Illinois, our neighbors in Michigan and Wisconsin, are happy, prosperous, teeming millions of free men. That generation of men, though not to the full extent members of the convention that framed the Constitution, were to some extent members of that convention, holding seats at the same time in one body and the other, so that if there was any compromise on either of these subjects, the strong evidence is that that compromise was in favor of the restriction of slavery from the new Territories.

But Douglas says that he is unalterably opposed to the repeal of those laws; because, in his view, it is a compromise of the Constitution. You Kentuckians, no doubt, are somewhat offended with that! You ought not to be! You ought to be patient! You ought to know that if he said less than that, he would lose the power of "lugging" the Northern States to your support. Really, what you would push him to do would take from him his entire power to serve you. And you ought to remember how long, by precedent, Judge Douglas held himself obliged to stick by compromises. You ought to remember that by the time you your-

selves think you are ready to inaugurate measures for the
revival of the African slave-trade, that sufficient time will
have arrived, by precedent, for Judge Douglas to break
through that compromise. He says now nothing more
strong than he said in 1849 when he declared in favor of
the Missouri Compromise - that precisely four years and a
quarter after he declared that compromise to be a sacred
thing, which "no ruthless hand would ever dare to touch,"
he, himself, brought forward the measure ruthlessly to destroy it. By a mere calculation of time it will only be four
years more until he is ready to take back his profession
about the sacredness of the compromise abolishing the
slave-trade. Precisely as soon as you are ready to have his
services in that direction, by fair calculation, you may be
sure of having them.

But you remember and set down to Judge Douglas's debt,
or discredit, that he, last year, said the people of Territories can, in spite of the Dred Scott decision, exclude your
slaves from those Territories; that he declared by
"unfriendly legislation" the extension of your property
into the new Territories may be cut off in the teeth of
that decision of the Supreme Court of the United States.

He assumed that position at Freeport, on the 27th of August, 1858. He said that the people of the Territories can
exclude slavery, in so many words. You ought, however, to
bear in mind that he has never said it since. You may
hunt in every speech that he has since made, and he has
never used that expression once. He has never seemed to
notice that he is stating his views differently from what
he did then; but by some sort of accident, he has always
really stated it differently. He has always since then declared that "the Constitution does not carry slavery into
the Territories of the United States beyond the power of
the people legally to control it, as other property." Now
there is a difference in the language used upon that for-

mer occasion and in this latter day. There may or may not be a difference in the meaning, but it is worth while considering whether there is not also a difference in meaning.

What is it to exclude? Why, it is to drive it out. It is in some way to put it out of the Territory. It is to force it across the line, or change its character, so that as property it is out of existence. But what is the controlling of it "as other property"? Is controlling it as other property the same thing as destroying it, or driving it away? I should think not. I should think the controlling of it as other property would be just about what you in Kentucky should want. I understanding the controlling of property means the controlling of it for the benefit of the owner of it. While I have no doubt the Supreme Court of the United States would say "God speed" to any of the territorial legislatures that should thus control slave property, they would sing quite a different tune if by the pretense of controlling it they were to undertake to pass laws which virtually excluded it, and that upon a very well known principle to all lawyers, that what a legislature cannot directly do, it cannot do by indirection; that as the legislature has not the power to drive slaves out, they have no power by indirection, by tax, or by imposing burdens in any way on that property, to effect the same end, and that any attempt to do so would be held by the Dred Scott court unconstitutional.

Douglas is not willing to stand by his first proposition that they can exclude it, because we have seen that that proposition amounts to nothing more or less than the naked absurdity that you may lawfully drive out that which has a lawful right to remain. He admitted at first that the slave might be lawfully taken into the Territories under the Constitution of the United States, and yet asserted that he might be lawfully driven out. That being the proposition, it is the absurdity I have stated. He is not willing to stand in the face of that direct, naked, and impudent absurdity; he has, therefore, modified his language into that of being "controlled as other property."

The Kentuckians don't like this in Douglas! I will tell you where it will go. He now swears by the court. He was once a leading man in Illinois to break down a court because it had made a decision he did not like. But he now not only swears by the court, the courts having got to working for you, but he denounces all men that do not swear by the courts as unpatriotic, as bad citizens. When one of these acts of unfriendly legislation shall impose such heavy burdens as to, in effect, destroy property in slaves in a Territory, and show plainly enough that there can be no mistake in the purpose of the legislature to make them so burdensome, this same Supreme Court will decide that law to be unconstitutional, and he will be ready to say for your benefit, "I swear by the court; I give it up"; and while that is going on he has been getting all his men to swear by the courts, and to give it up with him. In this again he serves you faithfully, and, as I say, more wisely than you serve yourselves.

Again, I have alluded in the beginning of these remarks to the fact that Judge Douglas has made great complaint of my having expressed the opinion that this government "cannot endure permanently half slave and half free." He has complained of Seward for using different language, and declaring that there is an "irrepressible conflict" between the principles of free and slave labor. [*A voice: "He says it is not original with Seward. That is original with Lincoln."*] I will attend to that immediately, sir. Since that time, Hickman, of Pennsylvania, expressed the same sentiment. He has never denounced Mr. Hickman. Why? There is a little chance, notwithstanding that opinion in the mouth of Hickman, that he may yet be a Douglas man. That is the difference. It is not unpatriotic to hold that opinion, if a man is a Douglas man.

But neither I, nor Seward, nor Hickman is entitled to the enviable or unenviable distinction of having first expressed that idea. That same idea was expressed by the Richmond "Enquirer" in Virginia, in 1856, quite two years before it was expressed by the first of us. And while Douglas was pluming himself that in his conflict with my humble self, last year, he had "squelched out" that fatal heresy, as he delighted to call it, and had suggested that if he only had had a chance to be in New York and meet Seward he would have "squelched" it there also, it never occurred to him to breathe a word against Pryor. I don't think that you can discover that Douglas ever talked of going to Virginia to "squelch" out that idea there. No. More than that. That same Roger A. Pryor was brought to Washington City and made the editor of the *par excellence* Douglas paper after making use of that expression which, in us, is so unpatriotic and heretical. From all this my Kentucky friends may see that this opinion is heretical in his view only when it is expressed by men suspected of a desire that the country shall all become free, and not when expressed by those fairly known to entertain the desire that the whole country shall become slave. When expressed by that class of men, it is in no wise offensive to him. In this again, my friends of Kentucky, you have Judge Douglas with you.

There is another reason why you Southern people ought to nominate Douglas at your convention at Charleston. That reason is the wonderful capacity of the man; the power he has of doing what would seem to be impossible. Let me call your attention to one of these apparently impossible things.

Douglas had three or four very distinguished men, of the most extreme antislavery views of any men in the Republican party, expressing their desire for his reelection to the Senate last year. That would, of itself, have seemed to be a little wonderful, but that wonder is heightened when we see that Wise, of Virginia, a man exactly opposed to them, a man who believes in the divine right of slavery, was also expressing his desire that Douglas should be reelected; that another man that may be said to be kindred to Wise, Mr. Breckinridge, the Vice-President, and of your own State, was also agreeing with the antislavery men in the North that Douglas ought to be reelected. Still, to heighten the wonder, a senator from Kentucky, whom I have always loved with an affection as tender and endearing as I have ever loved any man, who was opposed to the antislavery men for reasons which seemed sufficient to him, and equally opposed to Wise and Breckinridge, was writing letters into Illinois to secure the reelection of Douglas. Now that all these conflicting elements should be brought, while at daggers' points with one another, to support him, is a feat that is worthy for you to note and consider. It is quite probable that each of these classes of men thought, by the reelection of Douglas, their peculiar views would gain something: it is probable that the antislavery men thought their views would gain something; that Wise and Breckinridge thought so too, as regards their opinions; that Mr. Crittenden thought that his views would gain something, although he was opposed to both these other men. It is probable that each and all of them thought that they were using Douglas, and it is yet an unsolved problem whether he was not using them all. If he was, then it is for you to consider whether that power to perform wonders is one for you lightly to throw away.

There is one other thing that I will say to you in this relation. It is but my opinion; I give it to you without a fee. It is my opinion that it is for you to take him or be defeated; and that if you do take him you may be beaten. You will surely be beaten if you do not take him. We, the Republicans and others forming the opposition of the country, intend to "stand by our guns," to be patient and firm, and in the long run to beat you whether you take him or not. We know that before we fairly beat you, we have to beat you both together. We know that "you are all of a feather," and that we have to beat you altogether, and we expect to do it. We don't intend to be very impatient about it. We mean to be as deliberate and calm about it as it is possible to be, but as firm and resolved as it is possible for men to be. When we do as we say, beat you, you perhaps want to know what we will do with you.

I will tell you, so far as I am authorized to speak for the opposition, what we mean to do with you, we mean to treat you, as near as we possibly can, as Washington, Jefferson, and Madison treated you. We mean to leave you alone, and in no way to interfere with your institution; to abide by all and every compromise of the Constitution, and, in a word, coming back to the original proposition, to treat you, so far as degenerated men (if we have degenerated) may, according to the example of those noble fathers - Washington, Jefferson, and Madison. We mean to remember that you are as good as we; that there is no difference between us other than the difference of circumstances. We mean to recognize and bear in mind always that you have as good hearts in your bosoms as other people, or as we claim to have, and treat you accordingly. We mean to marry your girls when we have a chance - the white ones, I mean, and I have the honor to inform you that I once did have a chance in that way.

I have told you what we mean to do. I want to know, now, when that thing takes place, what do you mean to do? I often hear it intimated that you mean to divide the Union whenever a Republican or anything like it is elected President of the United States. [*A voice: "That is so."*] "That is so," one of them says; I wonder if he is a Kentuckian? [*A voice: "He is a Douglas man."*] Well, then, I want to know what you are going to do with your half of it? Are you going to split the Ohio down through, and push your half off a piece? Or are you going to keep it right alongside of us outrageous fellows? Or are you going to build up a wall some way between your country and ours, by which that movable property of yours can't come over here any more, to the danger of your losing it? Do you thing you can better yourselves on that subject by leaving us here under no obligation whatever to return those specimens of your movable property that come hither? You have divided the Union because we would not do right with you, as you think, upon that subject; when we cease to be under obligations to do anything for you, how much better off do you think you will be? Will you make war upon us and kill us all? Why, gentlemen, I think you are as gallant and as brave men as live; that you can fight as bravely in a good cause, man for man, as any other people living; that you have shown yourselves capable of this upon various occasions; but man for man, you are not better than we are, and there are not so many of you as there are of us. You will never make much of a hand at whipping us. If we were fewer in numbers than you, I think that you could whip us; if we were equal it would likely be a drawn battle; but being inferior in numbers, you will make nothing by attempting to master us.

But perhaps I have addressed myself as long, or longer, to the Kentuckians than I ought to have done, inasmuch as I have said that whatever course you take, we intend in the end to beat you. I propose to address a few remarks to our friends, by way of discussing with them the best means of keeping that promise that I have in good faith made.

It may appear a little episodical for me to mention the topic of which I shall speak now. It is a favorite proposition of Douglas's that the interference of the General Government, through the Ordinance of '87, or through any other act of the General Government, never has made, nor ever can make, a free State; that the Ordinance of '87 did not make free States of Ohio, Indiana, or Illinois; that these States are free upon his "great principle" of popular sovereignty, because the people of those several States have chosen to make them so. At Columbus, and probably here, he undertook to compliment the people that they themselves had made the State of Ohio free, and that the Ordinance of '87 was not entitled in any degree to divide the honor with him. I have no doubt that the people of the State of Ohio did make her free according to their own will and judgment; but let the facts be remembered.

In 1802, I believe, it was you who made your first constitution, with the clause prohibiting slavery, and you did it, I suppose, very nearly unanimously; but you should bear in mind that you - speaking of you as one people - that you did so unembarrassed by the actual presence of the institution amongst you; that you made it a free State, not with the embarrassment upon you of already having among you many slaves, which, if they had been here, and you had sought to make a free State, you would not know what to do with. If they had been among you, embarrassing difficulties, most probably, would have induced you to tolerate a slave Constitution instead of a free one; as, indeed, these very difficulties have constrained every people on this continent who have adopted slavery.

Pray, what was it that made you free? What kept you free? Did you not find your country free when you came to decide that Ohio should be a free State? It is important to inquire by what reason you found it so. Let us take an illustration between the States of Ohio and Kentucky.

Kentucky is separated by this river Ohio, not a mile wide. A portion of Kentucky, by reason of the course of the Ohio, is further north than this portion of Ohio in which we now stand. Kentucky is entirely covered with slavery - Ohio is entirely free from it. What made that difference? Was it climate? No! A portion of Kentucky was further north than this portion of Ohio. Was it soil? No! There is nothing in the soil of the one more favorable to slave-labor than the other. It was not climate or soil that caused one side of the line to be entirely covered with slavery and the other side free of it. What was it? Study over it. Tell us, if you can, in all the range of conjecture, if there be anything you can conceive of that made that difference, other than that there was no law of any sort keeping it out of Kentucky, while the Ordinance of '87 kept it out of Ohio. If there is any other reason than this, I confess that it is wholly beyond my power to conceive of it. This, then, I offer to combat the idea that that Ordinance has never made any State free.

I don't stop at this illustration. I come to the State of Indiana; and what I have said as between Kentucky and Ohio, I repeat as between Indiana and Kentucky; it is equally applicable. One additional argument is applicable also to Indiana. In her territorial condition she more than once petitioned Congress to abrogate the Ordinance entirely, or at least so far as to suspend its operation for a time, in order that they should exercise the "popular sovereignty" of having slaves if they wanted them. The men then controlling the General Government, imitating the men of the Revolution, refused Indiana that privilege. And so we have the evidence that Indiana supposed she could have slaves, if it were not for that Ordinance; that she besought Congress to put that barrier out of the way; that Congress refused to do so, and it all ended at last in Indiana being a free State. Tell me not then that the Ordinance of '87 had nothing to do with making Indiana a free state, when we find some men chafing against and only restrained by that barrier.

Come down again to our State of Illinois. The great Northwest Territory, including Ohio, Indiana, Illinois, Michigan, and Wisconsin, was acquired first, I believe, by the British government, in part, at least, from the French. Before the establishment of our independence, it became a part of Virginia, enabling Virginia afterward to transfer it to the General Government. There were French settlements in what is now Illinois, and at the same time there were French settlements in what is now Missouri - in the tract of country that was not purchased till about 1803. In these French settlements negro slavery had existed for many years - perhaps more than a hundred, if not as much as two hundred, years - at Kaskaskia, in Illinois, and at St. Genevieve, or Cape Girardeau, perhaps, in Missouri. The number of slaves was not very great, but there was about the same number in each place. They were there when we acquired the Territory. There was no effort made to break up the relation of master and slave, and even the Ordinance of '87 was not so enforced as to destroy that slavery in Illinois; nor did the ordinance apply to Missouri at all.

What I want to ask your attention to, at this point, is that Illinois and Missouri came into the Union about the same time, Illinois in the latter part of 1818, and Missouri, after a struggle, I believe, some time in 1820. They had been filling up with American people about the same period of time, their progress enabling them to come into the Union about the same. At the end of that ten years, in which they had been so preparing (for it was about that period of time), the number of slaves in Illinois had actually decreased; while in Missouri, beginning with very few, at the end of that ten years there were about ten thousand. This being so, and it being remembered that Missouri and

Illinois are, to a certain extent, in the same parallel of latitude - that the northern half of Missouri and the southern half of Illinois are in the same parallel of latitude - so that climate would have the same effect upon one as upon the other; and that in the soil there is no material difference so far as bears upon the question of slavery being settled upon one or the other; there being none of those natural causes to produce a difference in filling them, and yet there being a broad difference in their filling up, we are led again to inquire what was the cause of that difference.

It is most natural to say that in Missouri there was no law to keep that country from filling up with slaves, while in Illinois there was the Ordinance of '87. The Ordinance being there, slavery decreased during that ten years - the Ordinance not being in the other, it increased from a few to ten thousand. Can anybody doubt the reason of the difference?

I think all these facts most abundantly prove that my friend Judge Douglas's proposition, that the Ordinance of '87, or the national restriction of slavery, never had a tendency to make a free State, is a fallacy - a proposition without the shadow or substance of truth about it.

Douglas sometimes says that all the State (and it is part of that same proposition I have been discussing, that have become free, have become so upon his "great principle"; that the State of Illinois itself came into the Union as a slave State, and that the people, upon the "great principle" of popular sovereignty, have since made it a free State. Allow me but a little while to state to you what facts there are to justify him in saying that Illinois came into the Union as a slave State.

I have mentioned to you that there were a few old French slaves there. They numbered, I think, one or two hundred.

Besides that, there had been a territorial law for indenturing black persons. Under that law, in violation of the Ordinance of '87, but without any enforcement of the Ordinance to overthrow the system, there had been a small number of slaves introduced as indentured persons. Owing to this, the clause for the prohibition of slavery was slightly modified. Instead of running like yours, that neither slavery nor involuntary servitude, except for crime, of which the party shall have been duly convicted, should exist in the State, they said that neither slavery nor involuntary servitude should thereafter be introduced, and that the children of indentured servants should be born free; and nothing was said about the few old French slaves. Out of this fact, that the clause for prohibiting slavery was modified because of the actual presence of it, Douglas asserts again and again that Illinois came into the Union as a slave State. How far the facts sustain the conclusion that he draws, it is for intelligent and impartial men to decide. I leave it with you, with these remarks, worthy of being remembered, that that little thing, those few indentured servants being there, was of itself sufficient to modify a constitution made by a people ardently desiring to have a free constitution; showing the power of the actual presence of the institution of slavery to prevent any people, however anxious to make a free State, from making it perfectly so. I have been detaining you longer perhaps than I ought to do.

I am in some doubt whether to introduce another topic upon which I could talk awhile. [*Cries of "Go on," and "Give us it."*] It is this then - Douglas's popular sovereignty, as a principle, is simply this: If one man chooses to make a slave of another man, neither than man nor anybody else has a right to object. Apply it to government, as he seeks to apply it, and it is this: If, in a new Territory, into which a few people are beginning to enter for the purpose of making their homes, they choose to either exclude slavery from their limits, or to establish it there, however one or the other may affect the persons to be enslaved, or the infinitely greater number of persons who are afterward to inhabit that Territory, or the other members of the family of communities, of which they are but an incipient member, or the general head of the family of States as parent of all - however their action may affect one or the other of these, there is no power or right to interfere. That is Douglas's popular sovereignty applied. Now I think that there is a real popular sovereignty in the world. I think a definition of popular sovereignty, in the abstract, would be about this - that each man shall do precisely as he pleases with himself, and with all those things which exclusively concern him. Applied in government, this principle would be, that a general government shall do all those things which pertain to it, and all the local governments shall do precisely as they please in respect to those matters which exclusively concern them.

Douglas looks upon slavery as so insignificant that the people must decide that question for themselves, and yet they are not fit to decide who shall be their governor, judge, or secretary, or who shall be any of their officers. These are vast national matters, in his estimation; but the little matter in his estimation is that of planting slavery there. That is purely of local interest, which nobody should be allowed to say a word about.

Labor is the great source from which nearly all, if not all, human comforts and necessities are drawn. There is a difference in opinion about the elements of labor in society. Some men assume that there is a necessary connection between capital and labor, and that connection draws within it the whole of the labor of the community. They assume that nobody works unless capital excites them to work. They begin next to consider what is the best way. They say there are but two ways - one is to hire men and to allure them to labor by their consent; the other is to buy the men and drive them to it, and that is slavery. Having assumed that, they proceed to discuss the question of whether the laborers themselves are better off in the condition of slaves or of hired laborers, and they usually decide that they are better off in the condition of slaves.

In the first place, I say that the whole thing is a mistake. That there is a certain relation between capital and labor, I admit. That it does exist, and rightfully exists, I think is true. That men who are industrious and sober and honest in the pursuit of their own interests should after a while accumulate capital, and after that should be allowed to enjoy it in peace, and also if they should choose, when they have accumulated it, to use it to save themselves from actual labor, and hire other people to labor for them, is right. In doing so, they do not wrong the man they employ, for they find men who have not their own land to work upon, or shops to work in, and who are benefited by working for others - hired laborers, receiving their capital for it. Thus a few men that own capital hire a few others, and these establish the relation of capital and labor rightfully - a relation of which I make no complaint. But I insist that that relation, after all, does not embrace more than one-eighth of the labor of the country.

. . . . I have taken upon myself, in the name of some of you, to say that we expect upon these principles to ultimately beat them. In order to do so, I think we want and must have a national policy in regard to the institution of slavery that acknowledges and deals with that institution as being wrong. Whoever desires the prevention of the spread of slavery and the nationalization of that institution, yields all when he yields to any policy that either recognizes slavery as being right, or as being an indifferent thing. Nothing will make you successful but setting up a policy which shall treat the thing as being wrong.

When I say this, I do not mean to say that this General Government is charged with the duty of redressing or preventing all the wrongs in the world; but I do think that it is charged with preventing and redressing all wrongs which are wrongs to itself. This government is expressly charged with the duty of providing for the general welfare. We believe that the spreading out and perpetuity of the institution of slavery impairs the general welfare. We believe - nay, we know - that that is the only thing that has ever threatened the perpetuity of the Union itself. The only thing which has ever menaced the destruction of the government under which we live, is this very thing. To repress this thing, we think, is providing for the general welfare. Our friends in Kentucky differ from us. We need not make our argument for them; but we who think it is wrong in all its relations, or in some of them at least, must decide as to our own actions, and our own course, upon our own judgment.

I say that we must not interfere with the institution of slavery in the States where it exists, because the Constitution forbids it, and the general welfare does not require us to do so. We must not withhold an efficient fugitive-slave law, because the Constitution requires us, as I understand it, not to withhold such a law. But we must prevent the outspreading of the institution, because neither the Constitution nor general welfare requires us to extend it. We must prevent the revival of the African slave-trade, and the enacting by Congress of a territorial slave-code. We must prevent each of these things being done by either congresses or courts. The people of these United States are the rightful masters of both congresses and courts, not to overthrow the Constitution, but to overthrow the men who pervert the Constitution.

To do these things we must employ instrumentalities. We must hold conventions; we must adopt platforms, if we

conform to ordinary custom; we must nominate candidates; and we must carry elections. In all these things, I
think that we ought to keep in view our real purpose, and
in none do anything that stands adverse to our purpose.
If we shall adopt a platform that fails to recognize or express our purpose, or elect a man that declares himself in-
imical to our purpose, we not only take nothing by our
success, but we tacitly admit that we act upon no other
principle than a desire to have "the loaves and fishes," by
which, in the end, our apparent success is really an injury
to us.

I know that it is very desirable with me, as with everybody else, that all the elements of the Opposition shall
unite in the next presidential election, and in all future
time. I am anxious that that should be, but there are
things seriously to be considered in relation to that matter.
If the terms can be arranged, I am in favor of the union.
But suppose we shall take up some man, and put him
upon one end or the other of the ticket, who declares himself against us in regard to the prevention of the spread of
slavery, who turns up his nose and says he is tired of hearing anything more about it, who is more against us than
against the enemy - what will be the issue? Why, he will
get no slave States after all - he has tried that already until being beat is the rule for him. If we nominate him
upon that ground, he will not carry a slave State, and not
only so, but that portion of our men who are high strung
upon the principle we really fight for will not go for him,
and he won't get a single electoral vote anywhere, except,
perhaps, in the State of Maryland. There is no use in saying to us that we are stubborn and obstinate because we
won't do some such thing as this. We cannot do it. We
cannot get our men to vote it. I speak by the card, that
we cannot give the State of Illinois in such case by fifty
thousand. We would be flatter down than the "Negro Democracy" themselves have the heart to wish to see us.

After saying this much, let me say a little on the other side. There are plenty of men in the slave States that are altogether good enough for me to be either President or Vice-President, provided they will profess their sympathy with our purpose, and will place themselves on such ground that our men, upon principle, can vote for them. There are scores of them - good men in their character for intelligence, and talent, and integrity. If such a one will place himself upon the right ground, I am for his occupying one place upon the next Republican or Opposition ticket. I will heartily go for him. But unless he does so place himself, I think it is a matter of perfect nonsense to attempt to bring about a union upon any other basis; that if a union be made, the elements will scatter so that there can be no success for such a ticket, nor anything like success. The good old maxims of the Bible are applicable, and truly applicable, to human affairs, and in this, as in other things, we may say here that he who is not for us is against us; he who gathereth not with us scattereth. I should be glad to have some of the many good, and able, and noble men of the South to place themselves where we can confer upon them the high honor of an election upon one or the other end of our ticket. It would do my soul good to do that thing. It would enable us to teach them that, inasmuch as we select one of their own number to carry out our principles, we are free from the charge that we mean more than we say.

ADDRESS AT COOPER INSTITUTE
NEW YORK CITY
February 27, 1860

Mr. President and Fellow-Citizens: The facts with which I shall deal this evening are mainly old and familiar; nor is there anything new in the general use I shall make of them. If there shall be any novelty, it will be in the mode of presenting the facts, and the inferences and observations following that presentation.

In his speech last autumn, at Columbus, Ohio, as reported in "The New York Times," Senator Douglas said: "*Our fathers, when they framed the Government under which we live, understood this question just as well, and even better, than we do now.*"

I fully indorse this, and I adopt it as a text for this discourse. I so adopt it because it furnishes a precise and an agreed starting point for a discussion between Republicans and that wing of the Democracy headed by Senator Douglas. It simply leaves the inquiry: "*What was the understanding those fathers had of the question mentioned?*"

What is the frame of government under which we live?

The answer must be: "The Constitution of the United States." That Constitution consists of the original, framed in 1787, (and under which the present government first went into operation,) and twelve subsequently framed amendments, the first ten of which were framed in 1789.

Who were our fathers that framed the Constitution? I suppose the "thirty-nine" who signed the original instrument may be fairly called our fathers who framed that part of the present Government. It is almost exactly true to say they framed it, and it is altogether true to say they fairly represented the opinion and sentiment of the whole nation at that time. Their names, being familiar to nearly all, and accessible to quite all, need not be repeated.

I take these "thirty-nine," for the present, as being "our fathers who framed the Government under which we live."

What is the question which, according to the text, those fathers understood "just as well, and even better than we do now?"

It is this: Does the proper division of local from federal authority, or anything in the Constitution, forbid our *Federal Government* to control as to slavery in our *Federal Territories?*

Upon this, Senator Douglas holds the affirmative, and Republicans the negative. This affirmation and denial form an issue; and this issue - this question - is precisely what the text declares our fathers understood "better than we."

Let us now inquire whether the "thirty-nine," or any of them, ever acted upon this question; and if they did, how they acted upon it - how they expressed that better understanding?

In 1784, three years before the Constitution - the United States then owning the Northwestern Territory, and no other, the Congress of the Confederation had before them the question of prohibiting slavery in that Territory; and four of the "thirty-nine" who afterward framed the Constitution, were in that Congress and voted on that ques-

tion. Of these, Roger Sherman, Thomas Mifflin, and
Hugh Williamson voted for the prohibition, thus showing
that, in their understanding, no line dividing local from
federal authority, nor anything else, properly forbade the
Federal Government to control as to slavery in federal
territory. The other of the four - James McHenry - voted
against the prohibition, showing that, for some cause, he
thought it improper to vote for it.

In 1787, still before the Constitution, but while the Convention was in session framing it, and while the Northwestern Territory still was the only territory owned by
the United States, the same question of prohibiting slavery
in the territory again came before the Congress of the
Confederation; and two more of the "thirty-nine" who afterward signed the Constitution, were in that Congress,
and voted on the question. They were William Blount
and William Few; and they both voted for the prohibition
- thus showing that, in their understanding, no line dividing local from federal authority, nor anything else, properly forbids the Federal Government to control as to slavery in Federal territory. This time the prohibition became
a law, being part of what is now well known as the Ordinance of '87.

The question of federal control of slavery in the territories, seems not to have been directly before the Convention which framed the original Constitution; and hence it
is not recorded that the "thirty-nine," or any of them,
while engaged on that instrument, expressed any opinion
on that precise question.

In 1789, by the first Congress which sat under the Constitution, an act was passed to enforce the Ordinance of '87,
including the prohibition of slavery in the Northwestern

Territory. The bill for this act was reported by one of the "thirty-nine," Thomas Fitzsimmons, then a member of the House of Representatives from Pennsylvania. It went through all its stages without a word of opposition, and finally passed both branches without yeas and nays, which is equivalent to a unanimous passage. In this Congress there were sixteen of the thirty-nine fathers who framed the original Constitution. They were John Landgon, Nicholas Gilman, William S. Johnson, Roger Sherman, Robert Morris, Thomas Fitzsimmons, William Few, Abraham Baldwin, Rufus King, William Paterson, George Clymer, Richard Bassett, George Read, Pierce Butler, Daniel Carroll, James Madison.

This shows that, in their understanding, no line dividing local from federal authority, nor anything in the Constitution, properly forbade Congress to prohibit slavery in the federal territory; else both their fidelity to correct principle, and their oath to support the Constitution, would have constrained them to oppose the prohibition.

Again, George Washington, another of the "thirty-nine," was then President of the United States, and, as such approved and signed the bill; thus completing its validity, and thus showing that, in his understanding, no line dividing local from federal authority forbade the Federal Government to control as to slavery in federal territory.

No great while after the adoption of the original Constitution, North Carolina ceded to the Federal Government the country now constituting the State of Tennessee; and a few years later Georgia ceded that which now constitutes the States of Mississippi and Alabama. In both deeds of cession it was made a condition by the ceding States that the Federal Government should not prohibit slavery in the ceded country. Besides this, slavery was then actually in the ceded country. Under these circumstances, Congress, on taking charge of these countries, did not absolutely prohibit slavery within them. But they did interfere with it - take control of it - even there, to a certain extent. In 1798, Congress organized the Territory of Mississippi. In the act of organization, they prohibited the bringing of slaves into the Territory, from any place without the United States, by fine, and giving freedom to slaves so brought. This act passed both branches of Congress without yeas and nays.

In that Congress were three of the "thirty-nine" who framed the original Constitution. They were John Langdon, George Read and Abraham Baldwin. They all, probably, voted for it. Certainly they would have placed their opposition to it upon record, if, in their understanding, any line dividing local from federal authority, or anything in the Constitution, properly forbade the Federal Government to control as to slavery in federal territory.

In 1803, the Federal Government purchased the Louisiana country. Our former territorial acquisitions came from certain of our own States; but this Louisiana country was acquired from a foreign nation. In 1804, Congress gave a territorial organization to that part of it which now constitutes the State of Louisiana. New Orleans, lying within that part, was an old and comparatively large city. There were other considerable towns and settlements, and slavery was extensively and thoroughly intermingled with the people. Congress did not, in the Territorial Act, prohibit slavery; but they did interfere with it - take control of it - in a more marked and extensive way than they did in the case of Mississippi. The substance of the provision therein made, in relation to slaves, was:

First. That no slave should be imported into the territory from foreign parts.

Second. That no slave should be carried into it who had been imported into the United States since the first day of May, 1798.

Third. That no slave should be carried into it, except by the owner, and for his own use as a settler; the penalty in all the cases being a fine upon the violator of the law, and freedom to the slave.

This act also was passed without yeas and nays. In the Congress which passed it, there were two of the "thirty-nine." They were Abraham Baldwin and Jonathan Dayton. As stated in the case of Mississippi, it is probable they both voted for it. They would not have allowed it to pass without recording their opposition to it, if, in their understanding, it violated either the line properly dividing local from federal authority, or any provision of the Constitution.

In 1819-20, came and passed the Missouri question. Many votes were taken, by yeas and nays, in both branches of Congress, upon the various phases of the general question. Two of the "thirty-nine" - Rufus King and Charles Pinckney - were members of that Congress. Mr. King steadily voted for slavery prohibition and against all compromises, while Mr. Pinckney as steadily voted against slavery prohibition and against all compromise. By this, Mr. King showed that, in his understanding, no line dividing local from federal authority, nor anything in the Constitution, was violated by Congress prohibiting slavery in federal territory; while Mr. Pinckney, by his votes, showed that, in his understanding, there was some sufficient reason for opposing such prohibition in that case.

The cases I have mentioned are the only acts of the "thirty-nine," or of any of them, upon the direct issue, which I have been able to discover.

To enumerate the persons who thus acted, as being four in 1784, two in 1787, seventeen in 1789, three in 1798, two in 1804, and two in 1819-20 - there would be thirty of them. But this would be counting John Langdon, Roger Sherman, William Few, Rufus King, and George Read each twice, and Abraham Baldwin, three times. The true number of those of the "thirty-nine" whom I have shown to have acted upon the question, which, by the text, they understood better than we, is twenty-three, leaving sixteen not shown to have acted upon it in any way.

Here, then, we have twenty-three out of our thirty-nine fathers "who framed the government under which we live," who have, upon their official responsibility and their corporal oaths, acted upon the very question which the text affirms they "understood just as well, and even better than we do now"; and twenty-one of them - a clear majority of the whole "thirty-nine" - so acting upon it as to make them guilty of gross political impropriety and wilful perjury, if, in their understanding, any proper division between local and federal authority, or anything in the Constitution they had made themselves, and sworn to support, forbade the Federal Government to control as to slavery in the federal territory. Thus the twenty-one acted; and, as actions speak louder than words, so actions, under such responsibility, speak still louder.

Two of the twenty-three voted against Congressional prohibition of slavery in the federal territories, in the instances in which they acted upon the question. But for
what reasons they so voted is not known. They may have
done so because they thought a proper division of local
from federal authority, or some provision or principle of
the Constitution, stood in the way; or they may, without
any such question, have voted against the prohibition, on
what appeared to them to be sufficient grounds of expediency. No one who has sworn to support the Constitution
can conscientiously vote for what he understands to be an
unconstitutional measure, however expedient he may
think it; but one may and ought to vote against a measure
which he deems constitutional, if, at the same time, he
deems it inexpedient. It, therefore, would be unsafe to set
down even the two who voted against the prohibition, as
having done so because, in their understanding, any proper division of local from federal authority, or anything in
the Constitution, forbade the Federal Government to control as to slavery in federal territory.

The remaining sixteen of the "thirty-nine," so far as I have
discovered, have left no record of their understanding
upon the direct question of federal control of slavery in
the federal territories. But there is much reason to believe that their understanding upon that question would
not have appeared different from that of their twenty-
three compeers, had it been manifested at all.

For the purpose of adhering rigidly to the text, I have
purposely omitted whatever understanding may have been
manifested by any person, however distinguished, other
than the thirty-nine fathers who framed the original Constitution; and, for the same reason, I have also omitted
whatever understanding may have been manifested by any

of the "thirty-nine" even, on any other phase of the general question of slavery. If we should look into their acts and declarations on those other phases, as the foreign slave trade, and the morality and policy of slavery generally, it would appear to us that on the direct question of federal control of slavery in federal territories, the sixteen, if they had acted at all, would probably have acted just as the twenty-three did. Among that sixteen were several of the most noted anti-slavery men of those times - as Dr. Franklin, Alexander Hamilton and Gouverneur Morris - while there was not one now known to have been otherwise, unless it may be John Rutledge, of South Carolina.

The sum of the whole is, that of our thirty-nine fathers who framed the original Constitution, twenty-one - a clear majority of the whole - certainly understood that no proper division of local from federal authority, nor any part of the Constitution, forbade the Federal Government to control slavery in the federal territories; while all the rest probably had the same understanding. Such, unquestionably, was the understanding of our fathers who framed the original Constitution; and the text affirms that they understood the question "better than we."

But, so far, I have been considering the understanding of the question manifested by the framers of the original Constitution. In and by the original instrument, a mode was provided for amending it; and, as I have already stated, the present frame of "the Government under which we live" consists of that original, and twelve amendatory articles framed and adopted since. Those who now insisted that federal control of slavery in federal territories violates the Constitution, point us to the provisions which they suppose it thus violates; and, as I understand, that all fix upon provisions in these amendatory articles, and not in the original instrument. The Supreme Court, in the Dred Scott case, plant themselves upon the fifth amendment, which provides that no person shall be deprived of "life, liberty or property without due process of law"; while Senator Douglas and his peculiar adherents plant themselves upon the tenth amendment, providing that "the powers not delegated to the United States by the Constitution" "are reserved to the States respectively, or to the people."

Now, it so happens that these amendments were framed by the first Congress which sat under the Constitution - the identical Congress which passed the act already mentioned, enforcing the prohibition of slavery in the Northwestern Territory. Not only was it the same Congress, but they were the identical, same individual men who, at the same session, and at the same time within the session, had under consideration, and in progress toward maturity, these Constitutional amendments, and this act prohibiting slavery in all the territory the nation then owned. The Constitutional amendments were introduced before, and passed after the act enforcing the Ordinance of '87; so that, during the whole pendency of the act to enforce the Ordinance, the Constitutional amendments were also pending.

The seventy-six members of that Congress, including sixteen of the framers of the original Constitution, as before stated, were pre-eminently our fathers who framed that part of "the Government under which we live," which is now claimed as forbidding the Federal Government to control slavery in the federal territories.

Is it not a little presumptuous in any one at this day to affirm that the two things which that Congress deliberately framed, and carried to maturity at the same time, are absolutely inconsistent with each other? And does not such affirmation become impudently absurd when coupled with the other affirmation from the same mouth, that those who did the two things, alleged to be inconsistent, understood whether they really were inconsistent better than we - better than he who affirms that they are inconsistent?

It is surely safe to assume that the thirty-nine framers of the original Constitution, and the seventy-six members of the Congress which framed the amendments thereto, taken together, do certainly include those who may be fairly called "our fathers who framed the Government under which we live." And so assuming, I defy any man to show that any one of them ever, in his whole life, declared that, in his understanding, any proper division of local from federal authority, or any part of the Constitution, forbade the Federal Government to control as to slavery in the federal territories. I go a step further. I defy any one to show that any living man in the whole world ever did, prior to the beginning of the present century, (and I might almost say prior to the beginning of the last half of the present century,) declare that, in his understanding, any proper division of local from federal authority, or any part of the Constitution, forbade the Federal Government to control as to slavery in the federal territories. To those who now so declare, I give, not only "our fathers who framed the Government under which we live," but with them all other living men within the century in which it was framed, among whom to search, and they shall not be able to find the evidence of a single man agreeing with them.

Now, and here, let me guard a little against being misunderstood. I do not mean to say we are bound to follow implicitly in whatever our fathers did. To do so, would be to discard all the lights of current experience - to reject all progress - all improvement. What I do say is, that if we would supplant the opinions and policy of our fathers in any case, we should do so upon evidence so conclusive, and argument so clear, that even their great authority, fairly considered and weighed, cannot stand; and most surely not in a case whereof we ourselves declare they understood the question better than we.

If any man at this day sincerely believes that a proper division of local from federal authority, or any part of the Constitution, forbids the Federal Government to control as to slavery in the federal territories, he is right to say so, and to enforce his position by all truthful evidence and fair argument which he can. But he has no right to mislead others, who have less access to history, and less leisure to study it, into the false belief that "our fathers who framed the Government under which we live" were of the same opinion - thus substituting falsehood and deception for truthful evidence and fair argument. If any man at this day sincerely believes "our fathers who framed the Government under which we live," used and applied principles, in other cases, which ought to have led them to understand that a proper division of local from federal authority or some part of the Constitution, forbids the Federal Government to control as to slavery in the federal territories, he is right to say so. But he should, at the same time, brave the responsibility of declaring that, in his opinion, he understands their principles *better* than they did themselves; and especially should he not shirk that responsibility by asserting that they "understood the question just as well, and even better, than we do now."

But enough! *Let all who believe that "our fathers, who framed the Government under which we live, understood this question just as well, and even better, than we do now," speak as they spoke, and act as they acted upon it. This is all Republicans ask - all Republicans desire - in relation to slavery. As those fathers marked it, so let it be again marked, as an evil not to be extended, but to be tolerated and protected only because of and so far as its actual presence among us makes that toleration and protection a necessity. Let all the guaranties those fathers gave it, be, not grudgingly, but fully and fairly, maintained.* For this Republicans contend, and with this, so far as I know or believe, they will be content.

And now, if they would listen - as I suppose they will not - I would address a few words to the Southern people.

I would say to them - You consider yourselves a reasonable and a just people; and I consider that in the general qualities of reason and justice you are not inferior to any other people. Still, when you speak of us Republicans, you do so only to denounce us as reptiles, or, at the best, as no better than outlaws. You will grant a hearing to pirates or murderers, but nothing like it to "Black Republicans." In all your contentions with one another, each of you deems an unconditional condemnation of "Black Republicanism" as the first thing to be attended to. Indeed, such condemnation of us seems to be an indispensable prerequisite - license, so to speak - among you to be admitted or permitted to speak at all. Now, can you, or not, be prevailed upon to pause and to consider whether this is quite just to us, or even to yourselves? Bring forward your charges and specifications, and then be patient long enough to hear us deny or justify.

You say we are sectional. We deny it. That makes an issue; and the burden of proof is upon you. You produce
your proof; and what is it? Why, that our party has no
existence in your section - gets no votes in your section.
The fact is substantially true; but does it prove the issue?
If it does, then in case we should, without change of principle, begin to get votes in your section, we should thereby
cease to be sectional. You cannot escape this conclusion;
and yet, are you willing to abide by it? If you are, you
will probably soon find that we have ceased to be sectional, for we shall get votes in your section this very year.
You will then begin to discover, as the truth plainly is,
that your proof does not touch the issue. The fact that we
get no votes in your section, is a fact of your making, and
not of ours. And if there be fault in that fact, that fault
is primarily yours, and remains until you show that we repel you by some wrong principle or practice. If we do repel you by any wrong principle or practice, the fault is
ours; but this brings you to where you ought to have started - to a discussion of the right or wrong of our principle.
If our principle, put in practice, would wrong your section
for the benefit of ours, or for any other object, then our
principle, and we with it, are sectional, and are justly opposed and denounced as such. Meet us, then, on the question of whether our principle, put in practice, would
wrong your section; and so meet it as if it were possible
that something may be said on our side. Do you accept
the challenge? No! Then you really believe that the principle which "our fathers who framed the Government under which we live" thought so clearly right as to adopt it,
and indorse it again and again, upon their official oaths, is
in fact so clearly wrong as to demand your condemnation
without a moment's consideration.

Some of you delight to flaunt in our faces the warning against sectional parties given by Washington in his Farewell Address. Less than eight years before Washington gave that warning, he had, as President of the United States, approved and signed an act of Congress, enforcing the prohibition of slavery in the Northwestern Territory, which act embodied the policy of the Government upon that subject up to and at the very moment he penned that warning; and about one year after he penned it, he wrote LaFayette that he considered that prohibition a wise measure, expressing in the same connection his hope that we should at some time have a confederacy of free States.

Bearing this in mind, and seeing that sectionalism has since arisen upon this same subject, is that warning a weapon in your hands against us, or in our hands against you? Could Washington himself speak, would he cast the blame of that sectionalism upon us, who sustain his policy, or upon you who repudiate it? We respect that warning of Washington, and we commend it to you, together with his example pointing to the right application of it.

You charge that we stir up insurrections among your slaves. We deny it; and what is your proof? Harper's Ferry! John Brown!! John Brown was no Republican; and you have failed to implicate a single Republican in his Harper's Ferry enterprise. If any member of our party is guilty in that matter, you know it or you do not know it. If you do know it, you are inexcusable for not designating the man and proving the fact. If you do not know it, you are inexcusable for asserting it, and especially for persisting in the assertion after you have tried and failed to make the proof. You need not be told that persisting in a charge which one does not know to be true, is simply malicious slander.

Some of you admit that no Republican designedly aided or encouraged the Harper's Ferry affair, but still insist that our doctrines and declarations necessarily lead to such results. We do not believe it. We know we hold to no doctrine, and make no declaration, which were not held to and made by "our fathers who framed the Government under which we live." You never dealt fairly by us in relation to this affair. When it occurred, some important State elections were near at hand, and you were in evident glee with the belief that, by charging the blame upon us, you could get an advantage of us in those elections. The elections came, and your expectations were not quite fulfilled. Every Republican man knew that, as to himself at least, your charge was a slander, and he was not much inclined by it to cast his vote in your favor. Republican doctrines and declarations are accompanied with a continual protest against any interference whatever with your slaves, or with you about your slaves. Surely, this does not encourage them to revolt. True, we do, in common with "our fathers, who framed the Government under which we live," declare our belief that slavery is wrong; but the slaves do not hear us declare even this. For anything we say or do, the slaves would scarcely know there is a Republican party. I believe they would not, in fact, generally know it but for your misrepresentations of us, in their hearing. In your political contests among yourselves, each faction charges the other with sympathy with Black Republicanism; and then, to give point to the charge, defines Black Republicanism to simply be insurrection, blood and thunder among the slaves.

Slave insurrections are no more common now than they were before the Republican party was organized. What induced the Southampton Insurrection, twenty-eight years ago, in which at least three times as many lives were lost as at Harper's Ferry? You can scarcely stretch your very elastic fancy to the conclusion that Southampton was "got up by Black Republicanism." In the present state of things in the United States, I do not think a general, or even a very extensive slave insurrection is possible. The indispensable concert of action cannot be attained. The slaves have no means of rapid communication; nor can incendiary freemen, black or white, supply it. The explosive materials are everywhere in parcels; but there neither are, nor can be supplied, the indispensable connecting trains.

Much is said by Southern people about the affection of slaves for their masters and mistresses; and a part of it, at least, is true. A plot for an uprising could scarcely be devised and communicated to twenty individuals before some one of them, to save the life of a favorite master or mistress, would divulge it. This is the rule; and the slave revolution in Hayti was not an exception to it, but a case occurring under peculiar circumstances. The Gunpowder Plot of British history, though not connected with slaves, was more in point. In that case, only about twenty were admitted to the secret; and yet one of them, in his anxiety to save a friend, betrayed the plot to that friend, and, by consequence, averted the calamity. Occasional poisonings from the kitchen, and open or stealthy assassinations in the field, and local revolts extending to a score or so, will continue to occur as the natural results of slavery; but no general insurrection of slaves, as I think, can happen in this country for a long time. Whoever much fears, or much hopes for such an event, will be alike disappointed.

In the language of Mr. Jefferson, uttered many years ago, "It is still in our power to direct the process of emancipation, and deportation, peaceably, and in such slow degrees, as that the evil will wear off insensibly; and their places be, *pari passu*, filled up by free white laborers. If, on the contrary, it is left to force itself on, human nature must shudder at the prospect held up."

Mr. Jefferson did not mean to say, nor do I, that the power of emancipation is in the Federal Government. He spoke of Virginia; and, as to the power of emancipation, I speak of the slave-holding States only. The Federal Government, however, as we insist, has the power of restraining the extension of the institution - the power to insure that a slave insurrection shall never occur on any American soil which is now free from slavery.

But you will break up the Union rather than submit to a denial of your Constitutional rights.

That has a somewhat reckless sound; but it would be palliated, if not fully justified, were we proposing, by the mere force of numbers, to deprive you of some right, plainly written down in the Constitution. But we are proposing no such thing.

When you make these declarations, you have a specific and well-understood allusion to an assumed Constitutional right of yours, to take slaves into the federal territories, and to hold them there as property. But no such right is specifically written in the Constitution. That instrument is literally silent about any such right. We, on the contrary, deny that such a right has any existence in the Constitution, even by implication.

Your purpose, then, plainly stated, is that you will destroy the Government, unless you be allowed to construe and enforce the Constitution as you please, on all points in dispute between you and us. You will rule or ruin in all events.

This, plainly stated, is your language. Perhaps you will say the Supreme Court has decided the disputed Constitutional question in your favor. Not quite so. But waiving the lawyer's distinction between dictum and decision, the Court have decided the question for you in a sort of way. The Court have substantially said, it is your Constitutional right to take slaves into the federal territories, and to hold them there as property. When I say the decision was made in a sort of way, I mean it was made in a divided Court, by a bare majority of the Judges, and they not quite agreeing with one another in the reasons for making it; that it is so made as that its avowed supporters disagree with one another about its meaning, and that it was mainly based upon a mistaken statement of fact - the statement in the opinion that "the right of property in a slave is distinctly and expressly affirmed in the Constitution."

An inspection of the Constitution will show that the right of property in a slave is not "*distinctly* and *expressly* affirmed" in it. Bear in mind, the Judges do not pledge their judicial opinion that such right is *impliedly* affirmed in the Constitution; but they pledge their veracity that it is "*distinctly* and *expressly*" affirmed there - "distinctly," that is, not mingled with anything else - "expressly," that is, in words meaning just that, without the aid of any inference, and susceptible of no other meaning.

If they had only pledged their judicial opinion that such right is affirmed in the instrument by implication, it would be open to others to show that neither the word "slave" nor "slavery" is to be found in the Constitution, nor the word "property" even, in any connection with language alluding to the things slave, or slavery; and that wherever in that instrument the slave is alluded to, he is called a "person"; - and wherever his master's legal right in relation to him is alluded to, it is spoken of as "service or labor which may be due" - as a debt payable in service or labor. Also, it would be open to show, by contemporaneous history, that this mode of alluding to slaves and slavery, instead of speaking of them, was employed on purpose to exclude from the Constitution the idea that there could be property in man.

To show all this, is easy and certain.

When this obvious mistake of the Judges shall be brought to their notice, is it not reasonable to expect that they will withdraw the mistaken statement, and reconsider the conclusion based upon it?

And then it is to be remembered that "our fathers, who framed the Government under which we live" - the men who made the Constitution - decided this same Constitutional question in our favor, long ago - decided it without division among themselves, when making the decision; without division among themselves about the meaning of it after it was made, and, so far as any evidence is left, without basing it upon any mistaken statement of facts.

Under all these circumstances, do you really feel yourselves justified to break up this Government unless such a court decision as yours is, shall be at once submitted to as a conclusive and final rule of political action? But you will not abide the election of a Republican president! In that supposed event, you say, you will destroy the Union; and then, you say, the great crime of having destroyed it will be upon us! That is cool. A highwayman holds a pistol to my ear, and mutters through his teeth, "Stand and deliver, or I shall kill you, and then you will be a murderer!"

To be sure, what the robber demanded of me - my money - was my own; and I had a clear right to keep it; but it was no more my own than my vote is my own; and the threat of death to me, to extort my money, and the threat of destruction to the Union, to extort my vote, can scarcely be distinguished in principle.

A few words now to Republicans. *It is exceedingly desirable that all parts of this great Confederacy shall be at peace, and in harmony, one with another. Let us Republicans do our part to have it so. Even though much provoked, let us do nothing through passion and ill temper. Even though the Southern people will not so much as listen to us, let us calmly consider their demands, and yield to them if, in our deliberate view of our duty, we possibly can.* Judging by all they say and do, and by the subject and nature of their controversy with us, let us determine, if we can, what will satisfy them.

Will they be satisfied if the Territories be unconditionally surrendered to them? We know they will not. In all their present complaints against us, the Territories are scarcely mentioned. Invasions and insurrections are the rage now. Will it satisfy them, if, in the future, we have nothing to do with invasions and insurrections? We know it will not. We so know, because we know we never had anything to do with invasions and insurrections; and yet this total abstaining does not exempt us from the charge and the denunciation.

The question recurs, what will satisfy them? Simply this: We must not only let them alone, but we must somehow, convince them that we do let them alone. This, we know by experience, is no easy task. We have been so trying to convince them from the very beginning of our organization, but with no success. In all our platforms and speeches we have constantly protested our purpose to let them alone; but this has had no tendency to convince them. Alike unavailing to convince them, is the fact that they have never detected a man of us in any attempt to disturb them.

These natural, and apparently adequate means all failing, what will convince them? This, and this only: cease to call slavery *wrong*, and join them in calling it *right.* And this must be done thoroughly - done in *acts* as well as in *words.* Silence will not be tolerated - we must place ourselves avowedly with them. Senator Douglas's new sedition law must be enacted and enforced, suppressing all declarations that slavery is wrong, whether made in politics, in presses, in pulpits, or in private. We must arrest and return their fugitive slaves with greedy pleasure. We must pull down our Free State constitutions. The whole atmosphere must be disinfected from all taint of opposition to slavery, before they will cease to believe that all their troubles proceed from us.

I am quite aware they do not state their case precisely in this way. Most of them would probably say to us, "Let us alone, do nothing to us, and say what you please about slavery." But we do let them alone - have never disturbed them - so that, after all, it is what we say, which dissatisfies them. They will continue to accuse us of doing, until we cease saying.

I am also aware they have not, as yet, in terms, demanded the overthrow of our Free-State Constitutions. Yet those Constitutions declare the wrong of slavery, with more solemn emphasis, than do all other sayings against it; and when all these other sayings shall have been silenced, the overthrow of these Constitutions will be demanded, and nothing be left to resist the demand. It is nothing to the contrary, that they do not demand the whole of this just now. Demanding what they do, and for the reason they do, they can voluntarily stop nowhere short of this consummation. Holding, as they do, that slavery is morally right, and socially elevating, they cannot cease to demand a full national recognition of it, as a legal right, and a social blessing.

Nor can we justifiably withhold this, on any ground save our conviction that slavery is wrong. If slavery is right, all words, acts, laws, and constitutions against it, are themselves wrong, and should be silenced, and swept away. If it is right, we cannot justly object to its nationality - its universality; if it is wrong, they cannot justly insist upon its extension - its enlargement. All they ask, we could readily grant, if we thought slavery right; all we ask, they could as readily grant, if they thought it wrong. Their thinking it right, and our thinking it wrong, is the precise fact upon which depends the whole controversy. Thinking it right, as they do, they are not to blame for desiring its full recognition, as being right; but, thinking it wrong, as we do, can we yield to them? Can we cast our votes with their view, and against our own? In view of our moral, social, and political responsibilities, can we do this?

Wrong as we think slavery is, we can yet afford to let it alone where it is, because that much is due to the necessity arising from its actual presence in the nation; but can we,

while our votes will prevent it, allow it to spread into the
National Territories, and to overrun us here in these Free
States? If our sense of duty forbids this, then let us stand
by our duty, fearlessly and effectively. Let us be diverted
by none of those sophistical contrivances wherewith we
are so industriously plied and belabored - contrivances
such as groping for some middle ground between the right
and the wrong, vain as the search for a man who should
be neither a living man nor a dead man - such as a policy
of "don't care" on a question about which all true men do
care - such as Union appeals beseeching true Union men
to yield to Disunionists, reversing the divine rule, and calling, not the sinners, but the righteous to repentance - such
as invocations to Washington, imploring men to unsay
what Washington said, and undo what Washington did.

Neither let us be slandered from our duty by false accusa-
tions against us, nor frightened from it by menaces of destruction to the Government nor of dungeons to ourselves.
*Let us have faith that Right makes Might, and in that
faith, let us, to the end, dare to do our duty as we understand it.*

THE QUESTION OF SLAVERY
NEW HAVEN, CONNECTICUT
March 6, 1860

If the Republican party of this nation shall ever have the national house intrusted to its keeping, it will be the duty of that party to attend to all the affairs of national housekeeping. Whatever matters of importance may come up, whatever difficulties may arise, in the way of its administration of the government, that party will then have to attend to: it will then be compelled to attend to other questions besides this question which now assumes an overwhelming importance - the question of slavery. It is true that in the organization of the Republican party this question of slavery was more important than any other; indeed, so much more important has it become that no other national question can even get a hearing just at present. The old question of tariff - a matter that will remain one of the chief affairs of national housekeeping to all time; the question of the management of financial affairs; the question of the disposition of the public domain; how shall it be managed for the purpose of getting it well settled, and of making there the homes of a free and happy people - these will remain open and require attention for a great while yet, and these questions will have to be attended to by whatever party has the control of the government. Yet just now they cannot even obtain a hearing, and I do not purpose to detain you upon these topics, or what sort of hearing they should have when opportunity shall come. For whether we will or not, the question of slavery is the question, the all-absorbing topic, of the day. It is true that all of us - and by that I mean not the Republican party alone, but the whole American people here and elsewhere - all of us wish this question settled; wish it out of the way. It stands in the way and prevents the adjustment and the giving of necessary attention to other questions of national housekeeping. The people of the whole nation agree that this question ought to be settled, and yet it is not settled; and the reason is that they are not yet agreed how it shall be settled. All wish it done, but some wish one way and some another, and some a third, or fourth, or fifth; different bodies are pulling in different directions, and none of them having a decided majority are able to accomplish the common object.

In the beginning of the year 1854, a new policy was inaugurated with the avowed object and confident promise that it would entirely and forever put an end to the slavery agitation. It was again and again declared that under this policy, when once successfully established, the country would be forever rid of this whole question. Yet under the operation of that policy this agitation has not only not ceased, but it has been constantly augmented. And this, too, although from the day of its introduction its friends, who promised that it would wholly end all agitation, constantly insisted, down to the time that the Lecompton bill was introduced, that it was working admirably, and that its inevitable tendency was to remove the question forever from the politics of the country. Can you call to mind any Democratic speech, made after the repeal of the Missouri Compromise down to the time of the Lecompton bill, in which it was not predicted that the slavery agitation was just at an end; that "the Abolition excitement was played out," "the Kansas question was dead," "they have made the most they can out of this question and it is now forever settled"? But since the Lecompton bill, no Democrat within my experience has ever pretended that he could see the end. That cry has been dropped. They themselves do not pretend now that the agitation of this subject has come to an end yet. The truth is that this question is one of national importance, and we cannot help dealing with it; we must do something about it, whether we will or not. We cannot avoid it; the subject is one we cannot avoid considering; we can no more avoid it than a man can live without eating. It is upon us; it attaches to the body politic as much and as closely as the natural wants attach to our natural bodies. Now I think it important that this matter should be taken up in earnest and really settled. And one way to bring about a true settlement of the question is to understand its true magnitude.

There have been many efforts to settle it. Again and again it has been fondly hoped that it was settled, but every time it breaks out afresh, and more violently than ever. It was settled, our fathers hoped, by the Missouri Compromise, but it did not stay settled. Then the Compromises of 1850 were declared to be a full and final settlement of the question. The two great parties, each in national convention, adopted resolutions declaring that the settlement made by the Compromise of 1850 was a finality - that it would last forever. Yet how long before it was unsettled again? It broke out again in 1854, and blazed higher and raged more furiously than ever before, and the agitation has not rested since.

These repeated settlements must have some fault about them. There must be some inadequacy in their very nature to the purpose for which they were designed. We can only speculate us to where that fault - that inadequacy is, but we may perhaps profit by past experience.

I think that one of the causes of these repeated failures is that our best and greatest men have greatly underestimated the size of this question. They have constantly brought forward small cures for great sores - plasters too small to cover the wound. That is one reason that all settlements have proved so temporary, so evanescent.

Look at the magnitude of this subject. One sixth of our population, in round numbers - not quite one sixth, and yet more than a seventh - about one sixth of the whole population of the United States, are slaves. The owners of these slaves consider them property. The effect upon the minds of the owners is that of property, and nothing else; it induces them to insist upon all that will favorably affect its value as property, to demand laws and institutions and a public policy that shall increase and secure its value, and make it durable, lasting, and universal. The effect on the minds of the owners is to persuade them that there is no wrong in it. The slaveholder does not like to be considered a mean fellow for holding that species of property, and hence he has to struggle within himself, and sets about arguing himself into the belief that slavery is right. The property influences his mind. The dissenting minister who argued some theological point with one of the established church was always met by the reply, "I can't see it so." He opened the Bible and pointed him to a passage, but the orthodox minister replied, "I can't see it so." Then he showed him a single word - "Can you see that?" "Yes, I see it," was the reply. The dissenter laid a guinea over the word, and asked, "Do you see it now?" So here. Whether the owners of this species of property do really see it as it is, it is not for me to say; but if they do, they see it as it is through two billions of dollars, and that is a pretty thick coating. Certain it is that they do not see it as we see it. Certain it is that this two thousand million of dollars invested in this species of property is all so concentrated that the mind can grasp it at once. This immense pecuniary interest has its influence upon their minds.

But here in Connecticut and at the North slavery does not exist, and we see it through no such medium. To us it appears natural to think that slaves are human beings; men, not property; that some of the things, at least, stated about men in the Declaration of Independence apply to them as well as to us. I say we think, most of us, that this charter of freedom applies to the slave as well as to ourselves; that the class of arguments put forward to batter down that idea are also calculated to break down the very idea of free government, even for white men, and to undermine the very foundations of free society. We think slavery a great moral wrong, and while we do not claim the right to touch it where it exists, we wish to treat it as a wrong in the Territories, where our votes will reach it. We think that a respect for ourselves, a regard for future generations and for the God that made us, require that we put down this wrong where our votes will properly reach it. We think that species of labor an injury to free white men - in short, we think slavery a great moral, social, and political evil, tolerable only because, and so far as, its actual existence makes it necessary to tolerate it, and that beyond that it ought to be treated as a wrong.

Now these two ideas - the property idea that slavery is right and the idea that it is wrong - come into collision, and do actually produce that irrepressible conflict which Mr. Seward has been so roundly abused for mentioning. The two ideas conflict, and must forever conflict.

Again, in its political aspect does anything in any way endanger the perpetuity of this Union but that single thing - slavery? Many of our adversaries are anxious to claim that they are specially devoted to the Union, and take pains to charge upon us hostility to the Union. Now we claim that we are the only true Union men, and we put to them this one proposition: What ever endangered this Union save and except slavery? Did any other thing ever cause a moment's fear? All men must agree that this thing alone has ever endangered the perpetuity of the Union. But if it was threatened by any other influence, would not all men say that the best thing that could be done, if we could not or ought not to destroy it, would be at least to keep it from growing any larger? Can any man believe that the way to save the Union is to extend and increase the only thing that threatens the Union, and to suffer it to grow bigger and bigger?

Whenever this question shall be settled, it must be settled on some philosophical basis. No policy that does not rest upon philosophical public opinion can be permanently maintained. And hence there are but two policies in regard to slavery that can be at all maintained. The first, based on the property view that slavery is right, conforms to that idea throughout, and demands that we shall do everything for it that we ought to do if it were right. We must sweep away all opposition, for opposition to the right is wrong; we must agree that slavery is right, and we must adopt the idea that property has persuaded the owner to believe, that slavery is morally right and socially elevating. This gives a philosophical basis for a permanent policy of encouragement.

The other policy is one that squares with the idea that slavery is wrong, and it consists in doing everything that we ought to do if it is wrong. Now I don't wish to be misunderstood, nor to leave a gap down to be misrepresented, even. I don't mean that we ought to attack it were it ex-

ists. To me it seems that if we were to form a government anew, in view of the actual presence of slavery we
should find it necessary to frame just such a government
as our fathers did: giving to the slaveholder the entire
control where the system was established, while we possess the power to restrain it from going outside those limits. From the necessities of the case we should be compelled to form just such a government as our blessed fathers gave us; and surely if they have so made it, that adds
another reason why we should let slavery alone where it
exists.

If I saw a venomous snake crawling in the road, any man
would say I might seize the nearest stick and kill it; but if
I found that snake in bed with my children, that would be
another question. I might hurt the children more than the
snake, and it might bite them. Much more, if I found it in
bed with my neighbor's children, and I had bound myself
by a solemn compact not to meddle with his children under any circumstances, it would become me to let that particular mode of getting rid of the gentleman alone. But if
there was a bed newly made up, to which the children
were to be taken, and it was proposed to take a batch of
young snakes and put them there with them, I take it no
man would say there was any question how I ought to decide!

That is just the case. The new Territories are the newly
made bed to which our children are to go, and it lies with
the nation to say whether they shall have snakes mixed up
with them or not. It does not seem as if there could be
much hesitation what our policy should be.

Now I have spoken of a policy based on the idea that slavery is wrong, and a policy based upon the idea that it is

right. But an effort has been made for a policy that shall treat it as neither right nor wrong. It is based upon utter indifference. Its leading advocate has said: "I don't care whether it be voted up or down." "It is merely a matter of dollars and cents." "The Almighty has drawn a line across this continent, on one side of which all soil must forever be cultivated by slave labor, and on the other by free." "When the struggle is between the white man and the negro, I am for the white man; when it is between the negro and the crocodile, I am for the negro." Its central idea is indifference. It holds that it makes no more difference to us whether the Territories become free or slave States, than whether my neighbor stocks his farm with horned cattle or puts it into tobacco. All recognize this policy, the plausible sugar-coated name of which is "popular sovereignty."

That saying, "In the struggle between the white man and the negro," etc., which, I know, came from the same source as this policy - that saying marks another step. There is a falsehood wrapped up in that statement. "In the struggle between the white man and the negro," assumes that there is a struggle, in which either the white man must enslave the negro or the negro must enslave the white. There is no such struggle. It is merely an ingenious falsehood to degrade and brutalize the negro. Let each let the other alone, and there is no struggle about it. If it was like two wrecked seamen on a narrow plank, where each must push the other off or drown himself, I would push the negro off - or a white man either; but it is not: the plank is large enough for both. This good earth is plenty broad enough for white man and negro both, and there is no need of either pushing the other off.

So that saying, "In the struggle between the negro and the crocodile," etc., is made up from the idea that down where the crocodile inhabits, a white man can't labor; it must be nothing else but crocodile or negro; if the negro does not, the crocodile must possess the earth; in that case he declares for the negro. The meaning of the whole is just this: As a white man is to a negro, so is a negro to a crocodile; and as the negro may rightfully treat the crocodile, so may the white man rightfully treat the negro. This very dear phrase coined by its author, and so dear that he deliberately repeats it in many speeches, has a tendency to still further brutalize the negro, and to bring public opinion to the point of utter indifference whether men so brutalized are enslaved or not. When that time shall come, if ever, I think that policy to which I refer may prevail. But I hope the good free men of this country will never allow it to come, and until then the policy can never be maintained.

Now, consider the effect of this policy. We in the States are not to care whether freedom or slavery gets the better, but the people in the Territories may care. They are to decide, and they may think what they please; it is a matter of dollars and cents! But are not the people of the Territories detailed from the States? If this feeling of indifference - this absence of moral sense about the question - prevails in the States, will it not be carried into the Territories? Will not every man say, "I don't care; it is nothing to me"? If any one comes that wants slavery, must they not say, "I don't care whether freedom or slavery be voted up or voted down"? It results at last in nationalizing the institution of slavery. Even if fairly carried out, that policy is just as certain to nationalize slavery as the doctrine of Jeff Davis himself. These are only two roads to the same goal, and "popular sovereignty" is just as sure, and almost as short, as the other.

What we want, and we all want, is to have with us the men who think slavery wrong. But those who say they hate slavery, and are opposed to it, but yet act with the Democratic party - where are they? Let us apply a few tests. You say that you think slavery a wrong, but you renounce all attempts to restrain it. Is there anything else that you think wrong, that you are not willing to deal with as a wrong? Why are you so careful, so tender of this one wrong and no other? You will not let us do a single thing as if it was wrong; there is no place where you will allow it to be even called wrong. We must not call it wrong in the free States, because it is not there, and we must not call it wrong in the slave States, because it is there; we must not call it wrong in politics, because that is bringing morality into politics, and we must not call it wrong in the pulpit, because that is bringing politics into religion; we must not bring it into the tract society, or other societies, because those are such unsuitable places, and there is no single place, according to you, where this wrong thing can properly be called wrong.

Perhaps you will plead that if the people of slave States should of themselves set on foot an effort for emancipation, you would wish them success and bid them Godspeed. Let us test that! In 1858 the Emancipation party of Missouri, with Frank Blair at their head, tried to get up a movement for that purpose; and, having started a party, contested the State. Blair was beaten, apparently if not truly, and when the news came to Connecticut, you, who knew that Frank Blair was taking hold of this thing by the right end, and doing the only thing that you say can properly be done to remove this wrong - did you bow your heads in sorrow because of that defeat? Do you, any of you, know one single Democrat that showed sorrow over that result? Not one! On the contrary, every man threw up his hat, and hallooed at the top of his lungs, "Hooray for Democracy!"

Now gentlemen, the Republicans desire to place this great question of slavery on the very basis on which our fathers placed it, and no other. It is easy to demonstrate that "our fathers who framed this government under which we live" looked on slavery as wrong, and so framed it and everything about it as to square with the idea that it was wrong, so far as the necessities arising from its existence permitted. In forming the Constitution they found the slave-trade existing, capital invested in it, fields depending upon it for labor, and the whole system resting upon the importation of slave labor. They therefore did not prohibit the slave-trade at once, but they gave the power to prohibit it after twenty years. Why was this? What other foreign trade did they treat in that way? Would they have done this if they had not thought slavery wrong?

Another thing was done by some of the same men who framed the Constitution, and afterward adopted as their own act by the first Congress held under that Constitution, of which many of the framers were members - they prohibited the spread of slavery in the Territories. Thus the same men, the framers of the Constitution, cut off the supply and prohibited the spread of slavery; and both acts show conclusively that they considered that the thing was wrong.

If additional proof is wanting, it can be found in the phraseology of the Constitution. When men are framing a supreme law and chart of government to secure blessings and prosperity to untold generations yet to come, they use language as short and direct and plain as can be found to express their meaning. In all matters but this of slavery the framers of the Constitution used the very clearest, shortest, and most direct language. But the Constitution alludes to slavery three times without mentioning it once! The language used becomes ambiguous, roundabout, and mystical. They speak of the "immigration of persons," and mean the importation of slaves, but do not say so. In establishing a basis of representation they say "all other persons," when they mean to say slaves. Why did they not use the shortest phrase? In providing for the return of fugitives they say "persons held to service or labor." If they had said "slaves," it would have been plainer and less liable to misconstruction. Why didn't they do it? We cannot doubt that it was done on purpose. Only one reason is possible, and that is supplied us by one of the framers of the Constitution - and it is not possible for man to conceive of any other. They expected and desired that the system would come to an end, and meant that when it did the Constitution should not show that there ever had been a slave in this good free country of ours.

I will dwell on that no longer. I see the signs of the approaching triumph of the Republicans in the bearing of their political adversaries. A great deal of this war with us nowadays is mere bushwhacking. At the battle of Waterloo, when Napoleon's cavalry had charged again and again upon the unbroken squares of British infantry, at last they were giving up the attempt, and going off in disorder, when some of the officers, in mere vexation and complete despair, fired their pistols at those solid squares. The Democrats are in that sort of extreme desperation; it is nothing else. I will take up a few of these arguments.

There is "the irrepressible conflict." How they rail at Seward for that saying! They repeat it constantly; and although the proof has been thrust under their noses again and again that almost every good man since the formation of our government has uttered that same sentiment, from General Washington, who "trusted that we should yet have a confederacy of free States," with Jefferson, Jay, Monroe, down to the latest days, yet they refuse to notice that at all, and persist in railing at Seward for saying it. Even Roger A. Pryor, editor of the Richmond "Enquirer," uttered the same sentiment in almost the same language, and yet so little offense did it give the Democrats that he was sent for to Washington to edit the "States" - the Douglas organ there, while Douglas goes into hydrophobia and spasms of rage because Seward dared to repeat it. That is what I call bushwhacking - a sort of argument that they must know any child can see through.

Another is John Brown! You stir up insurrections; you invade the South! John Brown! Harper's Ferry! Why, John Brown was not a Republican! You have never implicated a single Republican in that Harper's Ferry enterprise. We tell you if any member of the Republican party is guilty in that matter, you know it or you do not know it. If you do know it, you are inexcusable not to designate the man and prove the fact. If you do not know it, you are inexcusable to assert it, and especially to persist in the assertion after you have tried and failed to make the proof. You need not be told that persisting in a charge which one does not know to be true is simple malicious slander. Some of you admit that no Republican designedly aided or encouraged the Harper's Ferry affair; but still insist that our doctrines and declarations necessarily lead to such results. We do not believe it. We know we hold to no doctrines and make no declarations which were not held to and made by our fathers who framed the government under which we live, and we cannot see how declarations that were patriotic when they made them are villainous when we make them. You never dealt fairly by us in relation to that affair - and I will say frankly that I know of nothing in your character that should lead us to suppose that you would. You had just been soundly thrashed in elections in several States, and others were soon to come. You rejoiced at the occasion, and only were troubled that there were not three times as many killed in the affair. You were in evident glee; there was no sorrow for the killed nor for the peace of Virginia disturbed; you were rejoicing that by charging Republicans with this thing you might get an advantage of us in New York and the other States. You pulled that string as tightly as you could, but your very generous and worthy expectations were not quite fulfilled. Each Republican knew that the charge was a slander as to himself at least, and was not inclined by it to cast his vote in your favor. It was mere bushwhacking, because you had nothing else to do. You are still on that track, and I say, Go on! If you think you can slander a woman into loving you, or a man into voting for you, try it till you are satisfied.

FAREWELL ADDRESS
SPRINGFIELD, ILLINOIS
February 11, 1861

My Friends:

No one, not in my situation, can appreciate my feeling of sadness at this parting. To this place, and the kindness of these people, I owe everything. Here I have lived a quarter of a century, and have passed from a young to an old man. Here my children have been born, and one is buried.

I now leave, not knowing when or whether ever I may return, with a task before me greater than that which rested upon Washington. Without the assistance of that Divine Being who ever attended him, I cannot succeed. With that assistance, I cannot fail. Trusting in Him who can go with me, and remain with you, and be everywhere for good, let us confidently hope that all will yet be well. To His care commending you, as I hope in your prayers you will commend me, I bid you an affectionate farewell.

ADDRESS AT INDEPENDENCE HALL
PHILADELPHIA, PENNSYLVANIA
February 22, 1861

I am filled with deep emotion at finding myself standing
in this place, where were collected together the wisdom,
the patriotism, the devotion to principle, from which
sprang the institutions under which we live. You have
kindly suggested to me that in my hands is the task of restoring peace to our distracted country. I can say in return, sir, that all the political sentiments I entertain have
been drawn, so far as I have been able to draw them, from
the sentiments which originated in and were given to the
world from this Hall. I have never had a feeling, politically, that did not spring from the sentiments embodied in
the Declaration of Independence. I have often pondered
over the dangers which were incurred by the men who assembled here and framed and adopted that Declaration. I
have pondered over the toils that were endured by the officers and soldiers of the army who achieved that independence. I have often inquired of myself what great
principle or idea it was that kept this Confederacy so long
together. It was not the mere matter of separation of the
colonies from the motherland, but that sentiment in the
Declaration of Independence which gave liberty not alone
to the people of this country, but hope to all the world,
for all future time. It was that which gave promise that
in due time the weights would be lifted from the shoulders of all men, and that all should have an equal chance.
This is the sentiment embodied in the Declaration of Independence. Now, my friends, can this country be saved on
that basis? If it can, I will consider myself one of the
happiest men in the world if I can help to save it. If it
cannot be saved upon that principle, it will be truly awful.

But if this country cannot be saved without giving up that principle, I was about to say I would rather be assassinated on this spot than surrender it. Now, in my view of the present aspect of affairs, there is no need of bloodshed and war. There is no necessity for it. I am not in favor of such a course; and I may say in advance that there will be no bloodshed unless it is forced upon the government. The government will not use force, unless force is used against it.

My friends, this is wholly an unprepared speech. I did not expect to be called on to say a word when I came here. I supposed I was merely to do something toward raising a flag. I may, therefore, have said something indiscreet. But I have said nothing but what I am willing to live by, and, if it be the pleasure of Almighty God, to die by.

FIRST INAUGURAL ADDRESS
WASHINGTON, DC
March 4, 1861

Fellow-Citizens of the United States: In compliance with a custom as old as the government itself, I appear before you to address you briefly, and to take, in your presence, the oath prescribed by the Constitution of the United States, to be taken by the President "before he enters on the execution of his office."

I do not consider it necessary at present for me to discuss those matters of administration about which there is no special anxiety or excitement.

Apprehension seems to exist among the people of the Southern States, that by the accession of a Republican Administration, their property, and their peace, and personal security, are to be endangered. There has never been any reasonable cause for such apprehension. Indeed, the most ample evidence to the contrary has all the while existed, and been open to their inspection. It is found in nearly all the published speeches of him who now addresses you. I do but quote from one of those speeches when I declare that "I have no purpose, directly or indirectly, to interfere with the institution of slavery in the States where it exists. I believe I have no lawful right to do so, and I have no inclination to do so." Those who nominated and elected me did so with full knowledge that I had made this, and many similar declarations, and had never recanted them. And more than this, they placed in the platform, for my acceptance, and as a law to themselves, and to me, the clear and emphatic resolution which I now read:

"*Resolved*, That the maintenance inviolate of the rights of the States, and especially the right of each State to order and control its own domestic institutions according to its own judgment exclusively, is essential to that balance of power on which the perfection and endurance of our political fabric depend; and we denounce the lawless invasion by armed force of the soil of any State or Territory, no matter under what pretext, as among the gravest of crimes."

I now reiterate these sentiments: and in doing so, I only press upon the public attention the most conclusive evidence of which the case is susceptible, that the property, peace and security of no section are to be in any wise endangered by the now incoming Administration. I add too, that all the protection which, consistently with the Constitution and the laws, can be given, will be cheerfully given to all the States when lawfully demanded, for whatever cause - as cheerfully to one section as to another.

There is much controversy about the delivering up of fugitives from service or labor. The clause I now read is as plainly written in the Constitution as any other of its provisions:

"No person held to service or labor in one State, under the laws thereof, escaping into another, shall, in consequence of any law or regulation therein, be discharged from such service or labor, but shall be delivered up on claim of the party to whom such service or labor may be due."

It is scarcely questioned that this provision was intended by those who made it, for the reclaiming of what we call fugitive slaves; and the intention of the law-giver is the law. All members of Congress swear their support to the whole Constitution - to this provision as much as to any other. To the proposition, then, that slaves whose cases come within the terms of this clause, "shall be delivered up," their oaths are unanimous. Now, if they would make the effort in good temper, could they not, with nearly equal unanimity, frame and pass a law, by means of which to keep good that unanimous oath?

There is some difference of opinion whether this clause should be enforced by national or by state authority; but surely that difference is not a very material one. If the slave is to be surrendered, it can be of but little consequence to him, or to others, by which authority it is done. And should any one, in any case, be content that his oath shall go unkept, on a merely unsubstantial controversy as to *how* it shall be kept?

Again, in any law upon this subject, ought not all the safeguards of liberty known in civilized and humane jurisprudence to be introduced, so that a free man be not, in any case, surrendered as a slave? And might it not be well, at the same time to provide by law for the enforcement of that clause in the Constitution which guarantees that "the citizens of each State shall be entitled to all privileges and immunities of citizens in the several States?"

I take the official oath to-day, with no mental reservations, and with no purpose to construe the Constitution or laws, by any hypercritical rules. And while I do not choose now to specify particular acts of Congress as proper to be enforced, I do suggest that it will be much safer for all, both in official and private stations, to conform to, and abide by, all those acts which stand unrepealed, than to violate any of them, trusting to find impunity in having them held to be unconstitutional.

It is seventy-two years since the first inauguration of a President under our national Constitution. During that period fifteen different and greatly distinguished citizens, have, in succession, administered the executive branch of the government. They have conducted it through many perils; and, generally, with great success. Yet, with all this scope of precedent, I now enter upon the same task for the brief constitutional term of four years, under great and peculiar difficulty. A disruption of the Federal Union, heretofore only menaced, is now formidably attempted.

I hold, that in contemplation of universal law, and of the Constitution, the Union of these States is perpetual. Perpetuity is implied, if not expressed, in the fundamental law of all national governments. It is safe to assert that no government proper, ever had a provision in its organic law for its own termination. Continue to execute all the express provisions of our national Constitution, and the Union will endure forever - it being impossible to destroy it, except by some action not provided for in the instrument itself.

Again, if the United States be not a government proper, but an association of States in the nature of contract merely, can it, as a contract, be peaceably unmade, by less than all the parties who made it? One party to a contract may violate it - break it, so to speak; but does it not require all to lawfully rescind it?

Descending from these general principles, we find the proposition that, in legal contemplation, the Union is perpetual, confirmed by the history of the Union itself. The Union is much older than the Constitution. It was formed in fact, by the Articles of Association in 1774. It was matured and continued by the Declaration of Independence in 1776. It was further matured and the faith of all the then thirteen States expressly plighted and engaged that it should be perpetual, by the Articles of Confederation in 1778. And finally, in 1787, one of the declared objects for ordaining and establishing the Constitution, was "*to form a more perfect Union.*"

But if the destruction of the Union, by one, or by a part only, of the States, be lawfully possible, the Union is *less* perfect than before the Constitution, having lost the vital element of perpetuity.

It follows from these views that no State, upon its own mere motion, can lawfully get out of the Union - that *resolves* and *ordinances* to that effect are legally void, and that acts of violence, within any State or States, against the authority of the United States, are insurrectionary or revolutionary, according to circumstances.

I therefore consider that in view of the Constitution and the laws, the Union is unbroken; and to the extent of my ability I shall take care, as the Constitution itself expressly enjoins upon me, that the laws of the Union be faithfully executed in all the States. Doing this I deem to be only a simple duty on my part; and I shall perform it, so far as practicable, unless my rightful masters, the American people, shall withhold the requisite means, or, in some authoritative manner, direct the contrary. I trust this will not be regarded as a menace, but only as the declared purpose of the Union that it will constitutionally defend and maintain itself.

In doing this there needs to be no bloodshed or violence; and there shall be none, unless it be forced upon the national authority. The power confided to me will be used to hold, occupy, and possess the property and places belonging to the government, and to collect the duties and imposts; but beyond what may be necessary for these objects, there will be no invasion - no using of force against or among the people anywhere. Where hostility to the United States, in any interior locality, shall be so great and so universal, as to prevent competent resident citizens from holding the Federal offices, there will be no attempt to force obnoxious strangers among the people for that object. While the strict legal right may exist in the government to enforce the exercise of these offices, the attempt to do so would be so irritating, and so nearly impracticable with all, that I deem it better to forego, for the time, the uses of such offices.

The mails, unless repelled, will continue to be furnished in all parts of the Union. So far as possible, the people everywhere shall have that sense of perfect security which is most favorable to calm thought and reflection. The course here indicated will be followed, unless current events and experience shall show a modification or change to be proper; and in every case and exigency my best discretion will be exercised according to circumstances actually existing, and with a view and a hope of a peaceful solution of the national troubles, and the restoration of fraternal sympathies and affections.

That there are persons in one section or another who seek to destroy the Union at all events, and are glad of any pretext to do it, I will neither affirm or deny; but if there be such, I need address no word to them. To those, however, who really love the Union, may I not speak?

Before entering upon so grave a matter as the destruction of our national fabric, with all its benefits, its memories and its hopes, would it not be wise to ascertain precisely why we do it? Will you hazard so desperate a step, while there is any possibility that any portion of the ills you fly from have no real existence? Will you, while the certain ills you fly to, are greater than all the real ones you fly from? Will you risk the commission of so fearful a mistake?

All profess to be content in the Union, if all constitutional rights can be maintained. Is it true, then, that any right, plainly written in the Constitution, has been denied? I think not. Happily the human mind is so constituted, that no party can reach to the audacity of doing this. Think, if you can, of a single instance in which a plainly written provision of the Constitution has ever been denied. If, by the mere force of numbers, a majority should deprive a minority of any clearly written constitutional right, it might, in a moral point of view, justify revolution - certainly would, if such a right were a vital one. But such is not our case. All the vital rights of minorities, and of individuals, are so plainly assured to them, by affirmations and negations, guarantees and prohibitions, in the Constitution, that controversies never arise concerning them. But no organic law can ever be framed with a provision specifically applicable to every question which may occur in practical administration. No foresight can anticipate, nor any document of reasonable length contain express provisions for all possible questions. Shall fugitives from labor be surrendered by national or by State authority? The Constitution does not expressly say. *May* Congress prohibit slavery in the territories? The Constitution does not expressly say. *Must* Congress protect slavery in the territories? The Constitution does not expressly say.

From questions of this class spring all our constitutional controversies, and we divide upon them into majorities and minorities. If the minority will not acquiesce, the majority must, or the government must cease. There is no other alternative; for continuing the government, is acquiescence on one side or the other. If a minority, in such case, will secede rather than acquiesce, they make a precedent which, in turn, will divide and ruin them; for a minority of their own will secede from them whenever a majority refuses to be controlled by such minority. For instance, why may not any portion of a new confederacy, a year or two hence, arbitrarily secede again, precisely as portions of the present Union now claim to secede from it? All who cherish disunion sentiments, are now being educated to the exact temper of doing this.

Is there such perfect identity of interests among the States to compose a new Union, as to produce harmony only, and prevent renewed secession?

Plainly, the central idea of secession, is the essence of anarchy. A majority, held in restraint by constitutional checks and limitations, and always changing easily with deliberate changes of popular opinions and sentiments, is the only true sovereign of a free people. Whoever rejects it, does, of necessity, fly to anarchy or to despotism. Unanimity is impossible; the rule of a minority, as a permanent arrangement, is wholly inadmissible; so that, rejecting the majority principle, anarchy or despotism in some form is all that is left.

I do not forget the position assumed by some, that constitutional questions are to be decided by the Supreme Court; nor do I deny that such decisions must be binding in any case, upon the parties to a suit, as to the object of that suit, while they are also entitled to very high respect and consideration in all parallel cases by all other departments of the government. And while it is obviously possible that such decision may be erroneous in any given case, still the evil effect following it, being limited to that particular case, with the chance that it may be over-ruled, and never become a precedent for other cases, can better be borne than could the evils of a different practice. At the same time, the candid citizen must confess that if the policy of the government upon vital questions, affecting the whole people, is to be irrevocably fixed by decisions of the Supreme Court, the instant they are made, in ordinary litigation between parties, in personal actions, the people will have ceased to be their own rulers, having to that extent practically resigned their government into the hands of that eminent tribunal. Nor is there in this view any assault upon the court or the judges. It is a duty from which they may not shrink, to decide cases properly brought before them; and it is no fault of theirs if others seek to turn their decisions to political purposes.

One section of our country believes slavery is *right*, and ought to be extended, while the other believes it is *wrong*, and ought not to be extended. This is the only substantial dispute. The fugitive slave clause of the Constitution, and the law for the suppression of the foreign slave trade, are each as well enforced, perhaps, as any law can ever be in a community where the moral sense of the people imperfectly supports the law itself. The great body of the people abide by the dry legal obligation in both cases, and a few break over in each. This, I think, cannot be perfectly cured; and it would be worse in both cases *after* the separation of the sections, than before. The foreign slave trade, now imperfectly suppressed, would be ultimately revived without restriction, in one section; while fugitive slaves, now only partially surrendered, would not be surrendered at all, by the other.

Physically speaking, we cannot separate. We cannot remove our respective sections from each other, nor build an impassable wall between them. A husband and wife may be divorced, and go out of the presence, and beyond the reach of each other; but the different parts of our country cannot do this. They cannot but remain face to face; and intercourse, either amicable or hostile, must continue between them. Is it possible, then, to make that intercourse more advantageous or more satisfactory, *after* separation than *before?* Can aliens make treaties easier than friends can make laws? Can treaties be more faithfully enforced between aliens than laws can among friends? Suppose you go to war, you cannot fight always; and when, after much loss on both sides, and no gain on either, you cease fighting, the identical old questions, as to terms of intercourse, are again upon you.

This country, with its institutions, belongs to the people who inhabit it. Whenever they shall grow weary of the existing government, they can exercise their *constitutional* right of amending it, or their *revolutionary* right to dismember or overthrow it. I cannot be ignorant of the fact that many worthy and patriotic citizens are desirous of having the national Constitution amended. While I make no recommendation of amendments, I fully recognize the rightful authority of the people over the whole subject to be exercised in either of the modes prescribed in the instrument itself; and I should under existing circumstances favor rather than oppose a fair opportunity being afforded the people to act upon it.

I will venture to add that to me the Convention mode seems preferable, in that it allows amendments to originate with the people themselves, instead of only permitting them to take or reject propositions, originated by others, not especially chosen for the purpose, and which might not be precisely such as they would wish to either accept or refuse.

I understand a proposed amendment to the Constitution, which amendment, however, I have not seen, has passed Congress, to the effect that the federal government shall never interfere with the domestic institutions of the States, including that of persons held to service. To avoid misconstruction of what I have said, I depart from my purpose not to speak of particular amendments, so far as to say that holding such a provision to now be implied constitutional law, I have no objection to its being made express and irrevocable.

The Chief Magistrate derives all his authority from the people, and they have conferred none upon him to fix terms for the separation of the States. The people themselves can do this also if they choose; but the executive, as such, has nothing to do with it. His duty is to administer the present government, as it came to his hands, and to transmit it, unimpaired by him, to his successor.

Why should there not be a patient confidence in the ultimate justice of the people? Is there any better or equal hope, in the world? In our present differences, is either party without faith of being in the right? If the Almighty Ruler of nations, with his eternal truth and justice, be on your side of the North or on yours of the South, that truth, and that justice, will surely prevail, by the judgment of this great tribunal, the American people.

By the frame of the government under which we live, this same people have wisely given their public servants but little power for mischief; and have, with equal wisdom provided for the return of that little to their own hands at very short intervals. While the people retain their virtue and vigilance, no administration, by any extreme of wickedness or folly, can very seriously injure the government in the short space of four years.

My countrymen, one and all, think calmly and *well*, upon this whole subject. Nothing valuable can be lost by taking time. If there be an object to *hurry* any of you, in hot haste, to a step which you would never take *deliberately*, that object will be frustrated by taking time; but no good object can be frustrated by it. Such of you as are now dissatisfied, still have the old Constitution unimpaired, and, on the sensitive point, the laws of your own framing under it; while the new administration will have no immediate power, if it would, to change either. If it were admitted that you who are dissatisfied, hold the right side in the dispute, there still is no single good reason for precipitate action. Intelligence, patriotism, Christianity, and a firm reliance on Him, who has never yet forsaken this favored land, are still competent to adjust, in the best way, all our present difficulty.

In *your* hands, my dissatisfied fellow countrymen, and not in *mine*, is the momentous issue of civil war. The government will not assail *you*. You can have no conflict, without being yourselves the aggressors. *You* have no oath registered in Heaven to destroy the government, while *I* shall have the most solemn one to "preserve, protect and defend" it.

I am loath to close. We are not enemies, but friends. We must not be enemies. Though passion may have strained, it must not break our bonds of affection. The mystic chords of memory, stretching from every battle-field, and patriot grave, to every living heart and hearth-stone, all over this broad land, will yet swell the chorus of the Union, when again touched, as surely they will be, by the better angels of our nature.

CONFEDERATE SECESSION
WASHINGTON, DC
July 4, 1861

Fellow-citizens of the Senate and House of Representatives: Having been convened on an extraordinary occasion, as authorized by the Constitution, your attention is not called to any ordinary subject of legislation.

At the beginning of the present presidential term, four months ago, the functions of the Federal Government were found to be generally suspended within the several States of South Carolina, Georgia, Alabama, Mississippi, Louisiana, and Florida, excepting only those of the Post-office Department.

Within these States all the forts, arsenals, dock-yards, customhouses, and the like, including the movable and stationary property in and about them, had been seized, and were held in open hostility to this government, excepting only Forts Pickens, Taylor, and Jefferson, on and near the Florida coast, and Fort Sumter, in Charleston Harbor, South Carolina. The forts thus seized had been put in improved condition, new ones had been built, and armed forces had been organized and were organizing, all avowedly with the same hostile purpose.

The forts remaining in the possession of the Federal Government in and near these States were either besieged or menaced by warlike preparations, and especially Fort Sumter was nearly surrounded by well-protected hostile batteries, with guns equal in quality to the best of its own, and outnumbering the latter as perhaps ten to one. A disproportionate share of the Federal muskets and rifles had somehow found their way into these States, and had been seized to be used against the government. Accumulations of the public revenue lying within them had been seized for the same object. The navy was scattered in distant seas, leaving but a very small part of it within the immediate reach of the government. Officers of the Federal army and navy had resigned in great numbers; and of those resigning a large proportion had taken up arms against the government. Simultaneously, and in connection with all this, the purpose to sever the Federal Union was openly avowed. In accordance with this purpose, an ordinance had been adopted in each of these States, declaring the States respectively to be separated from the National Union. A formula for instituting a combined government of these States had been promulgated; and this illegal organization, in the character of Confederate States, was already invoking recognition, aid, and intervention from foreign powers.

Finding this condition of things, and believing it to be an imperative duty upon the incoming executive to prevent, if possible, the consummation of such attempt to destroy the Federal Union, a choice of means to that end became indispensable. This choice was made and was declared in the Inaugural Address. The policy chosen looked to the exhaustion of all peaceful measures before a resort to any stronger ones. It sought only to hold the public places and property not already wrested from the government, and to collect the revenue, relying for the rest on time, discussion, and the ballot-box. It promised a continuance of the mails, at government expense, to the very people who were resisting the government; and it gave repeated pledges against any disturbance to any of the people, or any of their rights. Of all that which a President might constitutionally and justifiably do in such a case, every-

thing was forborne without which it was believed possible
to keep the government on foot.

On the 5th of March (the present incumbent's first full
day in office), a letter of Major Anderson, commanding at
Fort Sumter, written on the 28th of February and received at the War Department on the 4th of March, was
by that department placed in his hands. This letter expressed the professional opinion of the writer that rein-
forcements could not be thrown into that fort within the
time for his relief, rendered necessary by the limited supply of provisions, and with a view of holding possession
of the same, with a force of less than twenty thousand
good and well-disciplined men. This opinion was concurred in by all the officers of his command, and their
memoranda on the subject were made inclosures of Major
Anderson's letter. The whole was immediately laid before
Lieutenant-General Scott, who at once concurred with
Major Anderson in opinion. On reflection, however, he
took full time, consulting with other officers, both of the
army and the navy, and at the end of four days came re-
luctantly but decidedly to the same conclusion as before.
He also stated at the same time that no such sufficient
force was then at the control of the government, or could
be raised and brought to the ground within the time when
the provisions in the fort would be exhausted. In a purely
military point of view, this reduced the duty of the administration in the case to the mere matter of getting the
garrison safely out of the fort.

It was believed, however, that to so abandon that position,
under the circumstances, would be utterly ruinous; that
the necessity under which it was to be done would not be
fully understood; that by many it would be construed as a
part of a voluntary policy; that at home it would discour-

age the friends of the Union, embolden its adversaries, and go far to insure to the latter a recognition abroad; that, in fact, it would be our national destruction consummated. This could not be allowed. Starvation was not yet upon the garrison, and ere it would be reached Fort Pickens might be reinforced. This last would be a clear indication of policy, and would better enable the country to accept the evacuation of Fort Sumter as a military necessity. An order was at once directed to be sent for the landing of the troops from the steamship *Brooklyn* into Fort Pickens. This order could not go by land, but must take the longer and slower route by sea. The first return news from the order was received just one week before the fall of Fort Sumter. The news itself was that the officer commanding the *Sabine*, to which vessel the troops had been transferred from the *Brooklyn*, acting upon some *quasi* armistice of the late administration (and of the existence of which the present administration, up to the time the order was despatched, had only too vague and uncertain rumors to fix attention), had refused to land the troops. To now reinforce Fort Pickens before a crisis would be reached at Fort Sumter was impossible - rendered so by the near exhaustion of provisions in the latter-named fort. In precaution against such a conjuncture, the government had, a few days before, commenced preparing an expedition as well adapted as might be to relieve Fort Sumter, which expedition was intended to be ultimately used, or not, according to circumstances. The strongest anticipated case for using it was now presented, and it was resolved to send it forward. As had been intended in this contingency, it was also resolved to notify the Governor of South Carolina that he might expect an attempt would be made to provision the fort; and that, if the attempt should not be resisted, there would be no effort to throw in men, arms, or ammunition, without further notice, or in case of an attack upon the fort. This notice was accordingly given; whereupon the fort was attacked and bombarded to its fall, without even awaiting the arrival of the provisioning expedition.

It is thus seen that the assault upon the reduction of Fort Sumter was in no sense a matter of self-defense on the part of the assailants. They well knew that the garrison in the fort could by no possibility commit aggression upon them. They knew - they were expressly notified - that the giving of bread to the few brave and hungry men of the garrison was all which would on that occasion be attempted, unless themselves, by resisting so much, should provoke more. They knew that this government desired to keep the garrison in the fort, not to assail them, but merely to maintain visible possession, and thus to preserve the Union from actual and immediate dissolution - trusting, as hereinbefore stated, to time, discussion, and the ballot-box for final adjustment; and they assailed and reduced the fort for precisely the reverse object - to drive out the visible authority of the Federal Union, and thus force it to immediate dissolution. That this was their object the executive well understood; and having said to them in the inaugural address, "You can have no conflict without being yourselves the aggressors," he took pains not only to keep this declaration good, but also to keep the case so free from the power of ingenious sophistry that the world should not be able to misunderstand it. By the affair at Fort Sumter, with its surrounding circumstances, that point was reached. Then and thereby the assailants of the government began the conflict of arms, without a gun in sight or in expectancy to return their fire, save only the few in the fort sent to that harbor years before for their own protection, and still ready to give that protection in whatever was lawful. In this act, discarding all else, they have forced upon the country the distinct issue, "immediate dissolution or blood."

And this issue embraces more than the fate of these United States. It presents to the whole family of man the question whether a constitutional republic or democracy - a government of the people by the same people - can or cannot maintain its territorial integrity against its own domestic foes. It presents the question whether discontented individuals, too few in numbers to control administration according to organic law in any case, can always, upon the pretenses made in this case, or on any other pretenses, or arbitrarily without any pretense, break up their government, and thus practically put an end to free government upon the earth. It forces us to ask: "Is there, in all republics, this inherent and fatal weakness?" "Must a government, of necessity, be too strong for the liberties of its own people, or too weak to maintain its own existence?"

So viewing the issue, no choice was left but to call out the war power of the government; and so to resist force employed for its destruction, by force for its preservation.

The call was made, and the response of the country was most gratifying, surpassing in unanimity and spirit the most sanguine expectation. Yet none of the States commonly called slave States, except Delaware, gave a regiment through regular State organization. A few regiments have been organized within some others of those States by individual enterprise, and received into the government service. Of course the seceded States, so called (and to which Texas has been joined about the time of the inauguration), gave no troops to the cause of the Union. The border States, so called, were not uniform in their action, some of them being almost for the Union, while in others - as Virginia, North Carolina, Tennessee, and Arkansas - the Union sentiment was nearly repressed and silenced. The course taken in Virginia was the most remarkable - perhaps the most important. A convention elected by the people of that State to consider this very question of disrupting the Federal Union was in session at the capital of Virginia when Fort Sumter fell. To this body the people had chosen a large majority of professed Union men. Almost immediately after the fall of Sumter, many members of that majority went over to the original disunion minority, and with them adopted an ordinance for withdrawing the State from the Union. Whether this change was wrought by their great approval of the assault upon Sumter, or their great resentment at the government's resistance to that assault, is not definitely known. Although they submitted the ordinance for ratification to a vote of the people, to be taken on a day then somewhat more that a month distant, the convention and the legislature (which was also in session at the same time and place), with leading men of the State not members of either, immediately commenced acting as if the State were already out of the Union. They pushed military preparations vigorously forward all over the State. They seized the United States armory at Harper's Ferry, and the navy-yard at Gosport, near Norfolk. They received - perhaps invited - into their State large bodies of troops, with their warlike appointments, from the so-called seceded States. They formally entered into a treaty of temporary alliance and co-operation with the so-called "Confederate States," and sent members to their congress at Montgomery. And, finally, they permitted the insurrectionary government to be transferred to their capital at Richmond.

The people of Virginia have thus allowed this giant insurrection to make its nest within her borders; and this government has no choice left but to deal with it where it finds it. And it has the less regret as the loyal citizens have, in due form, claimed its protection. Those loyal citizens this government is bound to recognize and protect, as being Virginia.

In the border States, so called - in fact, the Middle States - there are those who favor a policy which they call "armed neutrality"; that is, an arming of those States to prevent the Union forces passing one way, or the disunion the other, over their soil. This would be disunion completed. Figuratively speaking, it would be the building of an impassable wall along the line of separation - and yet not quite an impassable one, for under the guise of neutrality it would tie the hands of Union men and freely pass supplies from among them to the insurrectionists, which it could not do as an open enemy. At a stroke it would take all the trouble off the hands of secession, except only what proceeds from the external blockade. It would do for the disunionists that which, of all things, they most desire - feed them well, and give them disunion without a struggle of their own. It recognizes no fidelity to the Constitution, no obligation to maintain the Union; and while very many who have favored it are doubtless loyal citizens, it is nevertheless, very injurious in effect.

Recurring to the action of the government, it may be stated that at first a call was made for 75,000 militia; and, rapidly following this, a proclamation was issued for closing the ports of the insurrectionary districts by proceedings in the nature of blockade. So far all was believed to be strictly legal. At this point the insurrectionists announced their purpose to enter upon the practice of privateering.

Other calls were made for volunteers to serve for three years, unless sooner discharged, and also for large additions to the regular army and navy. These measures, whether strictly legal or not, were ventured upon, under what appeared to be a popular demand and a public necessity; trusting then, as now, that Congress would readily ratify them. It is believed that nothing has been done beyond the constitutional competency of Congress.

Soon after the first call for militia, it was considered a duty to authorize the commanding general in proper cases, according to his discretion, to suspend the privilege of the writ of *habeas corpus*, or, in other words, to arrest and detain, without resort to the ordinary processes and forms of law, such individuals as he might deem dangerous to the public safety. This authority has purposely been exercised but very sparingly. Nevertheless, the legality and propriety of what has been done under it are questioned, and the attention of the country has been called to the proposition that one who has sworn to "take care that the laws be faithfully executed" should not himself violate them. Of course some consideration was given to the questions of power and propriety before this matter was acted upon. The whole of the laws which were required to be faithfully executed were being resisted and failing of execution in nearly one-third of the States. Must they be allowed to finally fail of execution, even had it been perfectly clear that by the use of the means necessary to their execution some single law, made in such extreme tenderness of the citizen's liberty that, practically, it relieves more of the guilty than of the innocent, should to a very limited extent be violated? To state the question more directly, are all the laws but one to go unexecuted, and the government itself go to pieces lest that one be violated? Even in such a case, would not the official oath be broken if the government should be overthrown, when it was believed that disregarding the single law would tend to preserve it? But it was not believed that this question was presented. It was not believed that any law was violated. The provision of the Constitution that "the privilege of the writ of *habeas corpus* shall not be suspended, unless when in cases of rebellion or invasion, the public safety may require it," is equivalent to a provision - is a provision - that such privilege may be suspended when, in case of rebellion or invasion, the public safety does require it. It was decided that we have a case of rebellion, and that the public safety does require the qualified suspension of the privilege of the writ which was authorized to be made. Now it is insisted that Congress, and not the executive, is vested with this power. But the Constitution itself is silent as to which or who is to exercise the power; and as the provision was plainly made for a dangerous emergency, it cannot be believed the framers of the instrument intended that in every case the danger should run its course until Congress could be called together, the very assembling of which might be prevented, as was intended in this case, by the rebellion.

No more extended argument is now offered, as an opinion at some length will probably be presented by the attorney-general. Whether there shall be any legislation upon the subject, and if any, what, is submitted entirely to the better judgment of Congress.

The forbearance of this government had been so extraordinary and so long continued as to lead some foreign nations to shape their action as if they supposed the early destruction of our National Union was probable. While this, on discovery, gave the executive some concern, he is now happy to say that the sovereignty and rights of the

United States are now everywhere practically respected by foreign powers; and a general sympathy with the country is manifested throughout the world.

The reports of the Secretaries of the Treasury, War, and the Navy will give the information in detail deemed necessary and convenient for your deliberation and action; while the executive and all the departments will stand ready to supply omissions, or to communicate new facts considered important for you to know.

It is now recommended that you give the legal means for making this contest a short and decisive one: that you place at the control of the government for the work at least four hundred thousand men and $400,000,000. That number of men is about one tenth of those of proper ages within the regions where, apparently, all are willing to engage; and the sum is less than a twenty-third part of the money value owned by the men who seem ready to devote the whole. A debt of $600,000,000 now is a less sum per head than was the debt of our Revolution when we came out of that struggle; and the money value in the country now bears even a greater proportion to what it was then than does the population. Surely each man has as strong a motive now to preserve our liberties as each had then to establish them.

A right result at this time will be worth more to the world then ten times the men and ten times the money. The evidence reaching us from the country leaves no doubt that the material for the work is abundant, and that it needs only the hand of legislation to give it legal sanction, and the hand of the executive to give it practical shape and efficiency. One of the greatest perplexities of the government is to avoid receiving troops faster than it can provide for them. In a word, the people will save their government if the government itself will do its part only indifferently well.

It might seem, at first thought, to be of little difference whether the present movement at the South be called "secession" or "rebellion." The movers, however, well understand the difference. At the beginning they knew they could never raise their treason to any respectable magnitude by any name which implies violation of law. They knew their people possessed as much of moral sense, as much of devotion to law and order, and as much pride in and reverence for the history and government of their common country as any other civilized and patriotic people. They knew they could make no advancement directly in the teeth of these strong and noble sentiments. Accordingly, they commenced by an insidious debauching of the public mind. They invented an ingenious sophism which, if conceded, was followed by perfectly logical steps, through all the incidents, to the complete destruction of the Union. The sophism itself is that any State of the Union may consistently with the National Constitution, and therefore lawfully and peacefully, withdraw from the Union without the consent of the Union or of any other State. The little disguise that the supposed right is to be exercised only for just cause, themselves to be the sole judges of its justice, is too thin to merit any notice.

With rebellion thus sugar-coated they have been drugging the public mind of their section for more than thirty years, and until at length they have brought many good men to a willingness to take up arms against the government the day after some assemblage of men have enacted the farcical pretense of taking their State out of the Union, who could have been brought to no such thing the day before.

This sophism derives much, perhaps the whole, of its currency from the assumption that there is some omnipotent and sacred supremacy pertaining to a State - to each State of our Federal Union. Our States have neither more nor less power than that reserved to them in the Union by the Constitution - no one of them ever having been a State out of the Union. The original ones passed into the Union even before they cast off their British colonial dependence; and the new ones each came into the Union directly from a condition of dependence, excepting Texas. And even Texas, in its temporary independence, was never designated a State. The new ones only took the designation of States on coming into the Union, while that name was first adopted for the old ones in and by the Declaration of Independence. Therein the "United Colonies" were declared to be "free and independent States"; but even then the object plainly was not to declare their independence of one another or of the Union, but directly the contrary, as their mutual pledge and their mutual action before, at the time, and afterward, abundantly show. The express plighting of faith by each and all of the original thirteen in the Articles of Confederation, two years later, that the Union shall be perpetual, is most conclusive. Having never been States either in substance or in name outside of the Union, whence this magical omnipotence of "State Rights," asserting a claim of power to lawfully destroy the Union itself? Much is said about the "sovereignty" of the States; but the word even is not in the National Constitution, nor, as is believed, in any of the State constitutions. What is "sovereignty" in the political sense of the term? Would it be far wrong to define it "a political community without a political superior"? Tested by this, no one of our States except Texas ever was a sovereignty. And even Texas gave up the character on coming into the Union; by which act she acknowledged the Constitution of the United States, and the laws and treaties of the United States made in pursuance of the Constitution, to be for her the supreme law of the land. The States have their status in the Union, and they have no other legal status. If they break from this, they can only do so against law and by revolution. The Union, and not themselves separately, procured their independence and their liberty. By conquest or purchase the Union gave each of them whatever of independence or liberty it has. The Union is older than any of the States, and, in fact, it created them as States. Originally some dependent colonies made the Union, and, in turn, the Union threw off their old dependence for them, and made them States, such as they are. Not one of them ever had a State constitution independent of the Union. Of course, it is not forgotten that all the new States framed their constitutions before they entered the Union - nevertheless, dependent upon and preparatory to coming into the Union.

Unquestionably the States have the powers and rights reserved to them in and by the National Constitution; but among these surely are not included all conceivable powers, however mischievous or destructive, but, at most, such only as were known in the world at the time as governmental powers; and certainly a power to destroy the government itself had never been known as a governmental, as a merely administrative power. This relative matter of national power and State rights, as a principle, is no other than the principle of generality and locality. Whatever concerns the whole should be confided to the whole - to the General Government; while whatever concerns only the State should be left exclusively to the State. This is all there is of original principle about it. Whether the National Constitution in defining boundaries between the two has applied the principle with exact accuracy, is not to be questioned. We are all bound by that defining, without question.

What is not combated is the position that secession is consistent with the Constitution - is lawful and peaceful. It is not contended that there is any express law for it; and nothing should ever be implied as law which leads to unjust or absurd consequences. The nation purchased with money the countries out of which several of these States were formed. It is just that they shall go off without leave and without refunding? The nation paid very large sums (in the aggregate, I believe, nearly a hundred millions) to relieve Florida of the aboriginal tribes. Is it just that she shall now be off without consent or without making any return? The nation is now in debt for money applied to the benefit of these so-called seceding States in common with the rest. Is it just either that creditors shall go unpaid or the remaining States pay the whole? A part of the present national debt was contracted to pay the old debts of Texas. Is it just that she shall leave and pay no part of this herself?

Again, if one State may secede, so may another; and when all shall have seceded, none is left to pay the debts. Is this quite just to creditors? Did we notify them of this sage view of ours when we borrowed their money? If we now recognize this doctrine by allowing the seceders to go in peace, it is difficult to see what we can do if others choose to go or to extort terms upon which they will promise to remain.

The seceders insist that our Constitution admits of secession. They have assumed to make a national constitution of their own, in which of necessity they have either discarded or retained the right of secession as they insist it exists in ours. If they have discarded it, they thereby admit that on principle it ought not to be in ours. If they have retained it by their own construction of ours, they show that to be consistent they must secede from one another whenever they shall find it the easiest way of settling their debts, or effecting any other selfish or unjust object. The principle itself is one of disintegration, and upon which no government can possibly endure.

If all the States save one should assert the power to drive that one out of the Union, it is presumed the whole class of seceder politicians would at once deny the power and denounce the act as the greatest outrage upon State rights. But suppose that precisely the same act, instead of being called "driving the one out," should be called "the seceding of the others from that one," it would be exactly what the seceders claim to do, unless, indeed, they make the point that the one, because it is a minority, may rightfully do what the others, because they are a majority, may not rightfully do. These politicians are subtle and profound on the rights of minorities. They are not partial to that power which made the Constitution and speaks from the preamble calling itself "We, the People."

It may well be questioned whether there is to-day a majority of the legally qualified voters of any State, except perhaps South Carolina, in favor of disunion. There is much reason to believe that the Union men are the majority in many, if not in every other one, of the so-called seceded States. The contrary has not been demonstrated in any one of them. It is ventured to affirm this even of Virginia and Tennessee; for the result of an election held in military camps, where the bayonets are all on one side of the question voted upon, can scarcely be considered as demonstrating popular sentiment. At such an election, all that large class who are at once for the Union and against coercion would be coerced to vote against the Union.

It may be affirmed without extravagance that the free institutions we enjoy have developed the powers and improved the condition of our whole people beyond any example in the world. Of this we now have a striking and an impressive illustration. So large an army as the government has now on foot was never before known, without a soldier in it but who has taken his place there of his own free choice. But more than this, there are many single regiments whose members, one and another, possess full practical knowledge of all the arts, sciences, professions, and whatever else, whether useful or elegant, is known in the world; and there is scarcely one from which there could not be selected a President, a cabinet, a congress, and perhaps a court, abundantly competent to administer the government itself. Nor do I say this is not true also in the army of our late friends, now adversaries in this contest; but if it is, so much better the reason why the government which has conferred such benefits on both them and us should not be broken up. Whoever in any section proposes to abandon such a government would do well to consider in deference to what principle it is that he does it - what better he is likely to get in its stead - whether the substitute will give, or be intended to give, so much of good to the people? There are some foreshadowings on this subject. Our adversaries have adopted some declarations of independence in which, unlike the good old one, penned by Jefferson, they omit the words "all men are created equal." Why? They have adopted a temporary national constitution, in the preamble of which, unlike our good old one, signed by Washington, they omit "We, the People," and substitute, "We, the deputies of the sovereign and independent States." Why? Why this deliberate pressing out of view the rights of men and the authority of the people?

This is essentially a people's contest. On the side of the Union it is a struggle for maintaining in the world that form and substance of government whose leading object is to elevate the condition of men - to lift artificial weights from all shoulders; to clear the paths of laudable pursuit for all; to afford all an unfettered start, and a fair chance in the race of life. Yielding to partial and temporary departures, from necessity, this is the leading object of the government for whose existence we contend.

I am most happy to believe that the plain people understand and appreciate this. It is worthy of note that while in this, the government's hour of trial, large numbers of those in the army and navy who have been favored with the offices have resigned and proved false to the hand which had pampered them, not one common soldier or common sailor is known to have deserted his flag.

Great honor is due to those officers who remained true, despite the example of their treacherous associates; but the greatest honor, and most important fact of all, is the unanimous firmness of the common soldiers and common sailors. To the last man, so far as known, they have successfully resisted the traitorous efforts of those whose commands, but an hour before, they obeyed as absolute law. This is the patriotic instinct of the plain people. They understand, without an argument, that the destroying of the government which was made by Washington means no good to them.

Our popular government has often been called an experiment. Two points in it our people have already settled - the successful establishing and the successful administering of it. One still remains - its successful maintenance against a formidable internal attempt to overthrow it. It is now for them to demonstrate to the world that those who can fairly carry an election can also suppress a rebellion; that ballots are the rightful and peaceful successors of bullets; and that when ballots have fairly and constitutionally decided, there can be no successful appeal back to bullets; that there can be no successful appeal, except to ballots themselves, at succeeding elections. Such will be a great lesson of peace: teaching men that what they cannot take by an election, neither can they take it by a war; teaching all the folly of being the beginners of a war.

Let there be some uneasiness in the minds of candid men as to what is to be the course of the government toward the Southern States after the rebellion shall have been suppressed, the executive deems it proper to say it will be his purpose then, as ever, to be guided by the Constitution and the laws; and that he probably will have no different understanding of the powers and duties of the Federal Government relatively to the rights of the States and the people, under the Constitution, than that expressed in the Inaugural Address.

He desires to preserve the government, that it may be administered for all as it was administered by the men who made it. Loyal citizens everywhere have the right to claim this of their government, and the government has no right to withhold or neglect it. It is not perceived that in giving it there is any coercion, any conquest, or any subjugation, in any just sense of those terms.

The Constitution provides, and all the States have accepted the provision, that "the United States shall guarantee to every State in this Union a republican form of government." But if a State may lawfully go out of the Union, having done so, it may also discard the republican form of government; so that to prevent its going out is an indispensable means to the end of maintaining the guarantee mentioned; and when an end is lawful and obligatory, the indispensable means to it are also lawful and obligatory.

It was with the deepest regret that the executive found the duty of employing the war power in defense of the government forced upon him. He could but perform this duty or surrender the existence of the government. No compromise by public servants could, in this case, be a cure; not that compromises are not often proper, but that no popular government can long survive a marked precedent that those who carry an election can only save the government from immediate destruction by giving up the main point upon which the people gave the election. The people themselves, and not their servants, can safely reverse their own deliberate decisions.

As a private citizen the executive could not have consented that these institutions shall perish; much less could he, in betrayal of so vast and so sacred a trust as the free people have confided to him. He felt that he had no moral right to shrink, nor even to count the chances of his own life in what might follow. In full view of his great responsibility he has, so far, done what he has deemed his duty. You will now, according to your own judgment, perform yours. He sincerely hopes that your views and your actions may so accord with his, as to assure all faithful citizens who have been disturbed in their rights of a certain and speedy restoration to them, under the Constitution and the laws.

And having thus chosen our course, without guile and with pure purpose, let us renew our trust in God, and go forward without fear and with manly hearts.

FIRST ANNUAL MESSAGE ON
THE STATE OF THE UNION
December 3, 1861

Fellow-citizens of the Senate and House of Representatives. In the midst of unprecedented political troubles we have cause of great gratitude to God for unusual good health and most abundant harvests.

You will not be surprised to learn that, in the peculiar exigencies of the times, our intercourse with foreign nations has been attended with profound solicitude, chiefly turning upon our own domestic affairs.

A disloyal portion of the American people have, during the whole year, been engaged in an attempt to divide and destroy the Union. A nation which endures factious domestic division is exposed to disrespect abroad; and one party, if not both, is sure, sooner or later, to invoke foreign intervention. Nations thus tempted to interfere are not always able to resist the counsels of seeming expediency and ungenerous ambition, although measures adopted under such influences seldom fail to be unfortunate and injurious to those adopting them.

The disloyal citizens of the United States who have offered the ruin of our country in return for the aid and comfort which they have invoked abroad, have received less patronage and encouragement than they probably expected. If it were just to suppose, as the insurgents have seemed to assume, that foreign nations in this case, discarding all moral, social, and treaty obligations, would act solely and selfishly for the most speedy restoration of commerce, including, especially, the acquisition of cotton, those nations appear as yet not to have seen their way to their object more directly or clearly through the destruction than through the preservation of the Union. If we could dare to believe that foreign nations are actuated by no higher principle than this, I am quite sure a sound argument could be made to show them that they can reach their aim more readily and easily by aiding to crush this rebellion than by giving encouragement to it. . . .

The Inaugural Address at the beginning of the administration, and the message to Congress at the late special session, were both mainly devoted to the domestic controversy out of which the insurrection and consequent war have sprung. Nothing now occurs to add or subtract, to or from, the principles or general purposes stated and expressed in those documents.

The last ray of hope for preserving the Union peaceably expired at the assault upon Fort Sumter; and a general review of what has occurred since may not be unprofitable. What was painfully uncertain then is much better defined and more distinct now; and the progress of events is plainly in the right direction. The insurgents confidently claimed a strong support from north of Mason and Dixon's line; and the friends of the Union were not free from apprehension on the point. This, however, was soon settled definitely, and on the right side. South of the line, noble little Delaware led off right from the first. Maryland was made to seem against the Union. Our soldiers were assaulted, bridges were burned, and railroads torn up within her limits, and we were many days, at one time, without the ability to bring a single regiment over her soil to the capital. Now her bridges and railroads are repaired and open to the government; she already gives seven regiments to the cause of the Union and none to the enemy;

and her people, at a regular election, have sustained the Union by a larger majority and a larger aggregate vote than they ever before gave to any candidate or any question. Kentucky, too, for some time in doubt, is now decidedly, and, I think, unchangeably, ranged on the side of the Union. Missouri is comparatively quite, and, I believe, cannot again be overrun by the insurrectionists. These three States of Maryland, Kentucky, and Missouri, neither of which would promise a single soldier at first, have now an aggregate of not less than forty thousand in the field for the Union, while of their citizens certainly not more than a third of that number, and they of doubtful whereabouts and doubtful existence, are in arms against it. After a somewhat bloody struggle of months, winter closes on the Union people of western Virginia, leaving them masters of their own country.

An insurgent force of about 1500, for months dominating the narrow peninsular region constituting the counties of Accomac and Northampton, and known as the eastern shore of Virginia, together with some contiguous parts of Maryland, have laid down their arms, and the people there have renewed their allegiance to and accepted the protection of the old flag. This leaves no armed insurrectionist north of the Potomac or east of the Chesapeake.

Also we have obtained a footing at each of the isolated points, on the southern coast, of Hatteras, Port Royal, Tybee Island, near Savannah, and Ship Island; and we likewise have some general accounts of popular movements in behalf of the Union in North Carolina and Tennessee.

These things demonstrate that the cause of the Union is advancing steadily and certainly southward.

Since your last adjournment Lieutenant-General Scott has retired from the head of the army. During his long life the nation has not been unmindful of his merit; yet, on calling to mind how faithfully, ably, and brilliantly he has served the country from a time far back in our history when few of the now living had been born, and thenceforward continually, I cannot but think we are still his debtors. I submit, therefore, for your consideration what further mark of recognition is due to him and to ourselves as a grateful people.

With the retirement of General Scott came the executive duty of appointing in his stead a general-in-chief of the army. It is a fortunate circumstance that neither in council nor country was there, so far as I know, any difference of opinion as to the proper person to be selected. The retiring chief repeatedly expressed his judgment in favor of General McClellan for the position, and in this the nation seemed to give a unanimous concurrence. The designation of General McClellan is, therefore, in considerable degree the selection of the country as well as of the executive, and hence there is better reason to hope there will be given him the confidence and cordial support thus by fair implication promised, and without which he cannot with so full efficiency serve the country.

It has been said that one bad general is better than two good ones; and the saying is true, if taken to mean no more than that an army is better directed by a single mind, though inferior, than by two superior ones at variance and cross-purposes with each other.

And the same is true in all joint operations wherein those engaged can have none but a common end in view, and can differ only as to the choice of means. In a storm at sea no one on board can wish the ship to sink; and yet not infrequently all go down together because too many will direct, and no single mind can be allowed to control.

It continues to develop that the insurrection is largely, if not exclusively, a war upon the first principle of popular government - the rights of the people. Conclusive evidence of this is found in the most grave and maturely considered public documents as well as in the general tone of the insurgents. In those documents we find the abridgment of the existing right of suffrage and the denial to the people of all right to participate in the selection of public officers except the legislative, boldly advocated, with labored arguments to prove that large control of the people in government is the source of all political evil. Monarchy itself is sometimes hinted at as a possible refuge from the power of the people.

In my present position I could scarcely be justified were I to omit raising a warning voice against this approach of returning despotism.

It is not needed nor fitting here that a general argument should be made in favor of popular institutions; but there is one point, with its connections, not so hackneyed as most others, to which I ask a brief attention. It is the effort to place capital on an equal footing with, if not above, labor, in the structure of government. It is assumed that labor is available only in connection with capital; that nobody labors unless somebody else, owning capital, somehow by the use of it induces him to labor. This assumed, it is next considered whether it is best that capital shall hire laborers, and thus induce them to work by their own consent, or buy them, and drive them to it without their consent. Having proceeded thus far, it is naturally concluded that all laborers are either hired laborers or what we call slaves. And, further, it is assumed that whoever is once a hired laborer is fixed in that condition for life.

Now, there is no such relation between capital and labor as assumed, nor is there any such thing as a free man being fixed for life in the condition of a hired laborer. Both these assumptions are false, and all inferences from them are groundless.

Labor is prior to, and independent of, capital. Capital is only the fruit of labor, and could never have existed if labor had not first existed. Labor is the superior of capital, and deserves much the higher consideration. Capital has its rights, which are as worthy of protection as any other rights. Nor is it denied that there is, and probably always will be, a relation between labor and capital producing mutual benefits. The error is in assuming that the whole labor of the community exists within that relation. A few men own capital, and that few avoid labor themselves, and with their capital hire or buy another few to labor for them. A large majority belong to neither class - neither work for others nor have others working for them. In most of the Southern States a majority of the whole people, of all colors, are neither slaves nor masters; while in the Northern a large majority are neither hirers nor hired. Men with their families - wives, sons, and daughters - work for themselves, on their farms, in their houses, and in their shops, taking the whole product to themselves, and asking no favors of capital on the one hand, nor of hired laborers or slaves on the other. It is not forgotten that a considerable number of persons mingle their own labor with capital - that is, they labor with their own hands and also buy or hire others to labor for them; but this is only a mixed and not a distinct class. No principle stated is disturbed by the existence of this mixed class.

Again, as has already been said, there is not, of necessity, any such thing as the free hired laborer being fixed to that condition for life. Many independent men everywhere in these States, a few years back in their lives, were hired laborers. The prudent, penniless beginner in the world labors for wages awhile, saves a surplus with which to buy tools or land for himself, then labors on his own account another while, and at length hires another new beginner to help him. This is the just and generous and prosperous system which opens the way to all - gives hope to all, and consequent energy and progress and improvement of condition to all. No men living are more worthy to be trusted than those who toil up from poverty - none less inclined to take or touch aught which they have not honestly earned. Let them beware of surrendering a political power which they already possess, and which, if surrendered, will surely be used to close the door of advancement against such as they, and to fix new disabilities and burdens upon them, till all of liberty shall be lost.

From the first taking of our national census to the last are seventy years; and we find our population at the end of the period eight times as great as it was at the beginning. The increase of those other things which men deem desirable has been even greater. We thus have, at one view, what the popular principle, applied to government, through the machinery of the States and the Union, has produced in a given time; and also what, if firmly maintained, it promises for the future. There are already among us those who, if the Union be preserved, will live to see it contain 250,000,000. The struggle of today is not altogether for today - it is for a vast future also. With a reliance on Providence all the more firm and earnest, let us proceed in the great task which events have devolved upon us.

SECOND ANNUAL MESSAGE ON
THE STATE OF THE UNION
December 1, 1862

Fellow-citizens of the Senate and House of Representatives: Since your last annual assembling another year of health and bountiful harvests has passed; and while it has not pleased the Almighty to bless us with a return of peace, we can but press on, guided by the best light he gives us, trusting that in his own good time and wise way all will yet be well.

. . . . A nation may be said to consist of its territory, its people, and its laws. The territory is the only part which is of certain durability. "One generation passeth away, and another generation cometh, but the earth abideth forever." It is of the first importance to duly consider and estimate this ever-enduring part. That portion of the earth's surface which is owned and inhabited by the people of the United States is well adapted to be the home of one national family, and it is not well adapted for two or more. Its vast extent and its variety of climate and productions are of advantage in this age for one people, whatever they might have been in former ages. Steam, telegraphs, and intelligence have brought these to be an advantageous combination for one united people.

In the inaugural address I briefly pointed out the total inadequacy of disunion as a remedy for the differences between the people of the two sections. . . .

There is no line, straight or crooked, suitable for a national boundary upon which to divide. Trace through, from

east to west, upon the line between the free and slave
country, and we shall find a little more than one third of
its length are rivers, easy to be crossed, and populated, or
soon to be populated, thickly upon both sides; while nearly all its remaining length are merely surveyors' lines,
over which people may walk back and forth without any
consciousness of their presence. No part of this line can
be made any more difficult to pass by writing it down on
paper or parchment as a national boundary. The fact of
separation, if it comes, gives up on the part of the seceding section the fugitive-slave clause along with all other
constitutional obligations upon the section seceded from,
while I should expect no treaty stipulation would be ever
made to take its place.

But there is another difficulty. The great interior region,
bounded east by the Alleghanies, north by the British dominions, west by the Rocky Mountains, and south by the
line along which the culture of corn and cotton meets, and
which includes part of Virginia, part of Tennessee, all of
Kentucky, Ohio, Indiana, Michigan, Wisconsin, Illinois,
Missouri, Kansas, Iowa, Minnesota, and the Territories of
Dakota, Nebraska, and part of Colorado, already has above
ten millions of people, and will have fifty millions within
fifty years if not prevented by any political folly or mistake. It contains more than one third of the country
owned by the United States - certainly more than one million of square miles. Once half as populous as Massachusetts already is, it would have more than seventy-five millions of people. A glance at the map shows that, territori-
ally speaking, it is the great body of the republic. The
other parts are but marginal borders to it, the magnificent
region sloping west from the Rocky Mountains to the Pacific being the deepest and also the richest in undeveloped
resources. In the production of provisions, grains, grasses,

and all which proceed from them, this great interior region is naturally one of the most important in the world.

Ascertain from the statistics the small proportion of the region which has, as yet, been brought into cultivation, and also the large and rapidly increasing amount of its products, and we shall be overwhelmed with the magnitude of the prospect presented; and yet this region has no seacoast, touches no ocean anywhere. As part of one nation, its people now find, and may forever find, their way to Europe by New York, to South America and Africa by New Orleans, and to Asia by San Francisco. But separate our common country into two nations, as designed by the present rebellion, and every man of this great interior region is thereby cut off from some one or more of these outlets - not, perhaps, by a physical barrier, but by embarrassing and onerous trade regulations.

And this is true wherever a dividing or boundary line may be fixed. Place it between the now free and slave country, or place it south of Kentucky or north of Ohio, and still the truth remains that none south of it can trade to any port or place north of it, and none north of it can trade to any port or place south of it, except upon terms dictated by a government foreign to them. These outlets, east, west, and south, are indispensable to the well-being of the people inhabiting, and to inhabit, this vast interior region. Which of the three may be the best, is no proper question. All are better than either; and all of right belong to that people and to their successors forever. True to themselves, they will not ask where a line of separation shall be, but will vow rather that there shall be no such line. Nor are the marginal regions less interested in these communications to and through them to the great outside world. They, too, and each of them, must have access to this Egypt of the West without paying toll at the crossing of any national boundary.

Our national strife springs not from our permanent part, not from the land we inhabit, not from our national homestead. There is no possible severing of this but would multiply, and not mitigate, evils among us. In all its adaptations and aptitudes it demands union and abhors separation. In fact, it would ere long force reunion, however much of blood and treasure the separation might have cost.

Our strife pertains to ourselves - to the passing generations of men; and it can without convulsion be hushed forever with the passing of one generation. . . .

I do not forget the gravity which should characterize a paper addressed to the Congress of the nation by the Chief Magistrate of the nation. Nor do I forget that some of you are my seniors, nor that many of you have more experience than I in the conduct of public affairs. Yet I trust that in view of the great responsibility resting upon me, you will perceive no want of respect to yourselves in any undue earnestness I may seem to display.

Is it doubted, then, that the plan I propose, if adopted, would shorten the war, and thus lessen its expenditure of money and of blood? Is it doubted that it would restore the national authority and national prosperity, and perpetuate both indefinitely? Is it doubted that we here - Congress and Executive - can secure its adoption? Will not the good people respond to a united and earnest appeal from us? Can we, can they, by any other means so certainly or so speedily assure these vital objects? We can succeed only by concert. It is not "Can any of us imagine better?" but, "Can we all do better?" Object whatsoever is possible, still the question occurs, "Can we do better?" The dogmas of the quiet past are inadequate to the stormy present. The occasion is piled high with difficulty, and we must rise with the occasion. As our case is new, so we must think anew and act anew. We must disenthrall ourselves, and then we shall save our country.

Fellow-citizens, we cannot escape history. We of this Congress and this administration will be remembered in spite of ourselves. No personal significance or insignificance can spare one or another of us. The fiery trial through which we pass will light us down, in honor or dishonor, to the latest generation. We say we are for the Union. The world will not forget that we say this. We know how to save the Union. The world knows we do know how to save it. We - even we here - hold the power and bear the responsibility. In giving freedom to the slave, we assure freedom to the free - honorable alike in what we give and what we preserve. We shall nobly save or meanly lose the last, best hope of earth. Other means may succeed; this could not fail. The way is plain, peaceful, generous, just - a way which, if followed, the world will forever applaud, and God must forever bless.

THE EMANCIPATION PROCLAMATION
January 1, 1863

WHEREAS, on the twenty-second day of September, in the year of our Lord one thousand eight hundred and sixty-two, a proclamation was issued by the President of the United States, containing, among other things, the following, to wit:

"That on the first day of January, in the year of our Lord one thousand eight hundred and sixty-three, all persons held as slaves within any State, or designated part of a State, the people whereof shall then be in rebellion against the United States, shall be then, thenceforward, and forever free; and the Executive Government of the United States, including the military and naval authority thereof, will recognize and maintain the freedom of such persons, and will do no act or acts to repress such persons, or any of them, in any efforts they may make for their actual freedom.

"That the Executive will, on the first day of January aforesaid, by proclamation, designate the States and parts of States, if any, in which the people thereof respectively shall then be in rebellion against the United States; and the fact that any State, or the people thereof, shall on that day be in good faith represented in the Congress of the United States by members chosen thereto at elections wherein a majority of the qualified voters of such State shall have participated, shall in the absence of strong countervailing testimony be deemed conclusive evidence that such State and the people thereof are not then in rebellion against the United States."

Now, therefore, I, Abraham Lincoln, President of the United States, by virtue of the power in me vested as commander-in-chief of the army and navy of the United States, in time of actual armed rebellion against the authority and government of the United States, and as a fit and necessary war measure for suppressing said rebellion, do, on this first day of January, in the year of our Lord one thousand eight hundred and sixty-three, and in accordance with my purpose so to do, publicly proclaimed for the full period of 100 days from the day first above mentioned, order and designate as the States and parts of States wherein the people thereof, respectively, are this day in rebellion against the United States, the following, to wit:

Arkansas, Texas, Louisiana (except the parishes of St. Bernard, Plaquemines, Jefferson, St. John, St. Charles, St. James, Ascension, Assumption, Terre Bonne, Lafourche, St. Mary, St. Martin, and Orleans, including the city of New Orleans), Mississippi, Alabama, Florida, Georgia, South Carolina, North Carolina, and Virginia (except the forty-eight counties designated as West Virginia, and also the counties of Berkeley, Accomac, Northampton, Elizabeth City, York, Princess Ann, and Norfolk, including the cities of Norfolk and Portsmouth), and which excepted parts are for the present left precisely as if this proclamation were not issued.

And by virtue of the power and for the purpose aforesaid, I do order and declare that all persons held as slaves within said designated States and parts of States are, and henceforward shall be, free; and that the Executive Government of the United States, including the military and naval authorities thereof, will recognize and maintain the freedom of said persons.

And I hereby enjoin upon the people so declared to be free to abstain from all violence, unless in necessary self-defense; and I recommend to them that, in all cases when allowed, they labor faithfully for reasonable wages.

And I further declare and make known that such persons of suitable condition will be received into the armed service of the United States to garrison forts, positions, stations, and other places, and to man vessels of all sorts in said service.

And upon this act, sincerely believed to be an act of justice, warranted by the Constitution upon military necessity, I invoke the considerate judgment of mankind and the gracious favor of Almighty God.

THE GETTYSBURG ADDRESS
NATIONAL CEMETERY
GETTYSBURG, PENNSYLVANIA
November 19, 1863

Fourscore and seven years ago our fathers brought forth on this continent a new nation, conceived in liberty, and dedicated to the proposition that all men are created equal.

Now we are engaged in a great civil war, testing whether that nation, or any nation so conceived and so dedicated, can long endure. We are met on a great battlefield of that war. We have come to dedicate a portion of that field as a final resting place for those who here gave their lives that that nation might live. It is altogether fitting and proper that we should do this.

But, in a larger sense, we can not dedicate - we can not consecrate - we can not hallow - this ground. The brave men, living and dead, who struggled here, have consecrated it far above our poor power to add or detract. The world will little note nor long remember what we say here, but it can never forget what they did here. It is for us, the living, rather, to be dedicated here to the unfinished work which they who fought here have thus far so nobly advanced. It is rather for us to be here dedicated to the great task remaining before us - that from these honored dead we take increased devotion to that cause for which they gave the last full measure of devotion - that we here highly resolve that these dead shall not have died in vain - that this nation, under God, shall have a new birth of freedom - and that government of the people, by the people, for the people, shall not perish from the earth.

THIRD ANNUAL MESSAGE ON THE STATE OF THE UNION
December 8, 1863

Fellow-citizens of the Senate and House of Representatives: Another year of health, and of sufficiently abundant harvest, has passed. For these, and especially for the improved condition of our national affairs, our renewed and profoundest gratitude to God is due.

We remain in peace and friendship with foreign powers.

The efforts of disloyal citizens of the United States to involve us in foreign wars, to aid an inexcusable insurrection, have been unavailing. Her Britannic Majesty's government, as was justly expected, have exercised their authority to prevent the departure of new hostile expeditions from British ports. The Emperor of France has, by a like proceeding, promptly vindicated the neutrality which he proclaimed at the beginning of the contest. Questions of great intricacy and importance have arisen out of the blockade, and other belligerent operations, between the government and several of the maritime powers, but they have been discussed, and, as far as was possible, accommodated, in a spirit of frankness, justice, and mutual goodwill. It is especially gratifying that our prize courts by the impartiality of their adjudications, have commanded the respect and confidence of maritime powers.

The supplemental treaty between the United States and Great Britain for the suppression of the African slave-trade, made on the 17th day of February last, has been duly ratified and carried into execution. It is believed that, so far as American ports and American citizens are concerned, that ` inhuman and odious traffic has been brought to an end.

. . . . When Congress assembled a year ago the war had already lasted nearly twenty months, and there had been many conflicts on both land and sea with varying results. The rebellion has been pressed back into reduced limits; yet the tone of public feeling and opinion, at home and abroad, was not satisfactory. With other signs, the popular elections, then just past, indicated uneasiness among ourselves, while, amid much that was cold and menacing, the kindest words coming from Europe were uttered in accents of pity that we were too blind to surrender a hopeless cause. Our commerce was suffering greatly by a few armed vessels built upon, and furnished from, foreign shores, and we were threatened with such additions from the same quarter as would sweep our trade from the sea and raise our blockade. We had failed to elicit from European governments anything hopeful upon this subject. The preliminary emancipation proclamation, issued in September, was running its assigned period to the beginning of the new year. A month later the final proclamation came, including the announcement that colored men of suitable condition would be received into the war service. The policy of emancipation, and of employing black soldiers, gave to the future a new aspect, about which hope, and fear, and doubt contended in uncertain conflict. According to our political system, as a matter of civil administration, the General Government had no lawful power to effect emancipation in any State, and for a long time it had been hoped that the rebellion could be suppressed without resorting to it as a military measure. It was all the while deemed possible that the necessity for it might come, and that if it should, the crisis of the contest would then be presented. It came, and, as was anticipated, it was

followed by dark and doubtful days. Eleven months having now passed, we are permitted to take another review.
The rebel borders are pressed still further back, and, by
the complete opening of the Mississippi, the country
dominated by the rebellion is divided into distinct parts,
with no practical communication between them. Tennessee and Arkansas have been substantially cleared of insurgent control, and influential citizens in each, owners of
slaves and advocates of slavery at the beginning of the rebellion, now declare openly for emancipation in their respective States. Of those States not included in the Emancipation Proclamation, Maryland and Missouri, neither of
which three years ago would tolerate any restraint upon
the extension of slavery into new Territories, only dispute
now as to the best mode of removing it within their own
limits.

Of those who were slaves at the beginning of the rebellion, full one hundred thousand are now in the United
States military service, about one half of which number
actually bear arms in the ranks; thus giving the double advantage of taking so much labor from the insurgent cause,
and supplying the places which otherwise must be filled
with so many white men. So far as tested, it is difficult to
say they are not as good soldiers as any. No servile insurrection, or tendency to violence or cruelty, has marked the
measures of emancipation and arming the blacks. The
measures have been much discussed in foreign countries,
and contemporary with such discussion the tone of public
sentiment there is much improved. At home the same
measures have been fully discussed, supported, criticized,
and denounced, and the annual elections following are
highly encouraging to those whose official duty it is to
bear the country through this great trial. Thus we have

the new reckoning. The crisis which threatened to divide the friends of the Union is past.

Looking now to the present and future, and with reference to a resumption of the national authority within the States wherein that authority has been suspended, I have thought fit to issue a proclamation, a copy of which is herewith transmitted. On examination of this proclamation it will appear, as is believed, that nothing is attempted beyond what is amply justified by the Constitution. True, the form of an oath is given, but no man is coerced to take it. The man is only promised a pardon in case he voluntarily takes the oath. The Constitution authorizes the executive to grant or withhold the pardon at his own absolute discretion; and this includes the power to grant on terms, as is fully established by judicial and other authorities.

It is also proffered that if, in any of the States named, a State government shall be, in the mode prescribed, set up, such government shall be recognized and guaranteed by the United States, and that under it the State shall, on the constitutional conditions, be protected against invasion and domestic violence. The constitutional obligation of the United States to guarantee to every State in the Union a republican form of government, and to protect the State in the cases stated, is explicit and full. But why tender the benefits of this provision only to a State government set up in this particular way? This section of the Constitution contemplates a case wherein the element within a State favorable to republican government in the Union may be too feeble for an opposite and hostile element external to, or even within, the State; and such are precisely the cases with which we are now dealing.

An attempt to guarantee and protect a revived State government, constructed in whole, or in preponderating part, from the very element against whose hostility and violence it is to be protected, is simply absurd. There must be a test by which to separate the opposing elements, so as to build only from the sound; and that test is a sufficiently liberal one which accepts as sound whoever will make a sworn recantation of his former unsoundness.

But if it be proper to require, as a test of admission to the political body, an oath of allegiance to the Constitution of the United States, and to the Union under it, why also to the laws and proclamations in regard to slavery? Those laws and proclamations were enacted and put forth for the purpose of aiding in the suppression of the rebellion. To give them their fullest effect, there had to be a pledge for their maintenance. In my judgment they have aided, and will further aid, the cause for which they were intended. To now abandon them would be not only to relinquish a lever of power, but would also be a cruel and an astounding breach of faith. I may add, at this point, that while I remain in my present position I shall not attempt to retract or modify the Emancipation Proclamation; nor shall I return to slavery any person who is free by the terms of that proclamation, or by any of the acts of Congress. For these and other reasons it is thought best that support of these measures shall be included in the oath; and it is believed the executive may lawfully claim it in return for pardon and restoration of forfeited rights, which he has clear constitutional power to withhold altogether, or grant upon the terms which he shall deem wisest for the public interest. It should be observed, also, that this part of the oath is subject to the modifying and abrogating power of legislation and supreme judicial decision.

The proposed acquiescence of the national executive in any reasonable temporary State arrangement for the freed people is made with the view of possibly modifying the confusion and destitution which must at best attend all classes by a total revolution of labor throughout whole States. It is hoped that the already deeply afflicted people in those States may be somewhat more ready to give up the cause of their affliction, if, to this extent, this vital matter be left to themselves; while no power of the national executive to prevent an abuse is abridged by the proposition.

The suggestion in the proclamation as to maintaining the political framework of the States on what is called reconstruction is made in the hope that it may do good without danger of harm. It will save labor, and avoid great confusion.

But why any proclamation now upon this subject? This question is beset with the conflicting views that the step might be delayed too long or be taken too soon. In some States the elements for resumption seem ready for action, but remain inactive apparently for want of a rallying-point - a plan of action. Why shall A adopt the plan of B, rather than B that of A? And if A and B should agree, how can they know but that the General Government here will reject their plan? By the proclamation a plan is presented which may be accepted by them as a rallying point, and which they are assured in advance will not be rejected here. This may bring them to act sooner than they otherwise would.

The objection to a premature presentation of a plan by the national executive consists in the danger of committals on points which could be more safely left to further de-

velopments. Care has been taken to so shape the document as to avoid embarrassments from this source. Saying
that, on certain terms, certain classes will be pardoned,
with rights restored, it is not said that other classes, or
other terms, will never be included. Saying that reconstruction will be accepted if presented in a specified way,
it is not said it will never be accepted in any other way.

The movements, by State action, for emancipation in several of the States not included in the Emancipation Proclamation, are matters of profound gratulation. And while
I do not repeat in detail what I have heretofore so earnestly urged upon this subject, my general views and feelings
remain unchanged; and I trust that Congress will omit no
fair opportunity of aiding these important steps to a great
consummation.

In the midst of other cares, however important, we must
not lose sight of the fact that the war power is still our
main reliance. To that power alone can we look, yet for a
time, to give confidence to the people in the contested regions that the insurgent power will not again overrun
them. Until that confidence shall be established, little can
be done anywhere for what is called reconstruction.
Hence our chiefest care must still be directed to the army
and navy, who have thus far borne their harder part so
nobly and well. And it may be esteemed fortunate that in
giving the greatest efficiency to these indispensable arms,
we do also honorably recognize the gallant men, from
commander to sentinel, who compose them, and to whom,
more than to others, the world must stand indebted for
the home of freedom disenthralled, regenerated, enlarged,
and perpetuated.

THE SHEEP AND THE WOLF
BALTIMORE, MARYLAND
April 18, 1864

Ladies and Gentlemen. Calling to mind that we are in Baltimore, we cannot fail to note that the world moves. Looking upon these many people assembled here to serve, as they best may, the soldiers of the Union, it occurs at once that three years ago the same soldiers could not so much as pass through Baltimore. The change from then till now is both great and gratifying. Blessings on the brave men who have wrought the change, and the fair women who strive to reward them for it!

But Baltimore suggests more than could happen within Baltimore. The change within Baltimore is part only of a far wider change. When the war began, three years ago, neither party, nor any man, expected it would last till now. Each looked for the end, in some way, long ere today. Neither did any anticipate that domestic slavery would be much affected by the war. But here we are; the war has not ended, and slavery has been much affected - how much needs not now to be recounted. So true is it that man proposes and God disposes.

But we can see the past, though we may not claim to have directed it; and seeing it, in this case, we feel more hopeful and confident for the future.

The world has never had a good definition of the word liberty, and the American people just now, are much in want of one. We all declare for liberty; but in using the same word we do not all mean the same thing. With some the word liberty may mean for each man to do as he pleases with himself, and the product of his labor; while with others the same word may mean for some men to do as they please with other men, and the product of other men's labor. Here are two, not only different, but incom-

patible things, called by the same name, liberty. And it
follows that each of the things is, by the respective parties, called by two different and incompatible names - liberty and tyranny.

The shepherd drives the wolf from the sheep's throat, for
which the sheep thanks the shepherd as his liberator,
while the wolf denounces him for the same act, as the destroyer of liberty, especially as the sheep was a black one.
Plainly, the sheep and the wolf are not agreed upon a
definition of the word liberty; and precisely the same difference prevails to-day among us human creatures, even in
the North, and all professing to love liberty. Hence we
behold the process by which thousands are daily passing
from under the yoke of bondage hailed by some as the advance of liberty, and bewailed by others as the destruction
of all liberty. Recently, as it seems, the people of Maryland have been doing something to define liberty, and
thanks to them that, in what they have done, the wolf's
dictionary has been repudiated.

It is not very becoming for one in my position to make
speeches at great length; but there is another subject upon
which I feel that I ought to say a word.

A painful rumor - true, I fear - has reached us of the massacre by the rebel forces at Fort Pillow, in the west end of
Tennessee, on the Mississippi river, of some three hundred
colored soldiers and white officers, who had just been
overpowered by their assailants. There seems to be some
anxiety in the public mind whether the government is doing its duty to the colored soldiers, and to the service, at
this point. At the beginning of the war, and for some
time, the use of colored troops was not contemplated; and
how the change of purpose was wrought I will not now
take time to explain. Upon a clear conviction of duty I
resolved to turn that element of strength to account; and I

am responsible for it to the American people, to the Christian world,' to history, and in my final account to God. Having determined to use the negro as a solider, there is no way but to give him all the protection given to any other soldier. The difficulty is not in stating the principle, but in practically applying it. It is a mistake to suppose the government is indifferent to this matter, or is not doing the best it can in regard to it. We do not to-day know that a colored soldier, or white officer commanding colored soldiers, has been massacred by the rebels when made a prisoner. We fear it - believe it, I may say - but we do not know it. To take the life of one of their prisoners on the assumption that they murder ours, when it is short of certainty that they do murder ours, might be too serious, too cruel, a mistake. We are having the Fort Pillow affair thoroughly investigated; and such investigation will probably show conclusively how the truth is. If after all that has been said it shall turn out that there has been no massacre at Fort Pillow, it will be almost safe to say there has been none, and will be none, elsewhere. If there has been the massacre of three hundred there, or even the tenth part of three hundred, it will be conclusively proved; and being so proved, the retribution shall as surely come. It will be matter of grave consideration in what exact course to apply the retribution; but in the supposed case it must come.

WAR IS TERRIBLE
PHILADELPHIA, PENNSYLVANIA
June 16, 1864

I suppose that this toast was intended to open the way for me to say something.

War, at the best, is terrible, and this war of ours, in its magnitude and in its duration, is one of the most terrible. It has deranged business, totally in many localities, and partially in all localities. It has destroyed property and ruined homes; it has produced a national debt and taxation unprecedented, at least in this country; it has carried mourning to almost every home, until it can almost be said that the "heavens are hung in black."

Yet the war continues, and several relieving coincidents have accompanied it from the very beginning which have not been known, as I understand, or have any knowledge of, in any former wars in the history of the world. The Sanitary Commission, with all its benevolent labors; the Christian Commission, with all its Christian and benevolent labors; and the various places, arrangements, so to speak, and institutions, have contributed to the comfort and relief of the soldiers. You have two of these places in this city - the Cooper Shop and Union Volunteer Refreshment Saloons. And lastly, these fairs, which, I believe, began only last August, if I mistake not, in Chicago, then at Boston, at Cincinnati, Brooklyn, New York, and Baltimore, and those at present held at St. Louis, Pittsburg, and Philadelphia. The motive and object that lie at the bottom of all these are most worthy; for, say what you will, after all, the most is due to the soldier who takes his life in his hands and goes to fight the battles of his country. In what is contributed to his comfort when he passes to and fro, and in what is contributed to him when he is sick and wounded, in whatever shape it comes, whether from the fair and tender hand of woman, or from any other source, it is much, very much. But I think that there is still that which is of as much value to him in the continual reminders he sees in the newspapers that while he is absent he is yet remembered by the loved ones at home. Another view of these various institutions, if I may so call them, is worthy of consideration, I think. They are voluntary contributions, given zealously and earnestly, on top of all the disturbances of business, of all the disorders, of all the taxation, and of all the burdens that the war has imposed upon us, giving proof that the national resources are not at all exhausted, and that the national spirit of patriotism is even firmer and stronger than at the commencement of the war.

It is a pertinent question, often asked in the mind privately, and from one to the other, when is the war to end? Surely I feel as deep an interest in this question as any other can; but I do not wish to name a day, a month, or a year, when it is to end. I do not wish to run any risk of seeing the time come without our being ready for the end, for fear of disappointment because the time had come and not the end. We accepted this war for an object, a worthy object, and the war will end when that object is attained. Under God, I hope it never will end until that time. Speaking of the present campaign, General Grant is reported to have said, "I am going through on this line if it takes all summer." This war has taken three years; it was begun or accepted upon the line of restoring the national authority over the whole national domain, and for the American people, as far as my knowledge enables me to speak, I say we are going through on this line if it takes three years more.

My friends, I did not know but that I might be called upon to say a few words before I got away from here, but I did not know it was coming just here. I have never been in the habit of making predictions in regard to the war, but I am almost tempted to make one. If I were to hazard it, it is this: That Grant is this evening, with General Meade and General Hancock, and the brave officers and soldiers with him, in a position from whence he will never be dislodged until Richmond is taken; and I have but one single proposition to put now, and perhaps I can best put it in the form of an interrogative. If I shall discover that General Grant and the noble officers and men under him can be greatly facilitated in their work by a sudden pouring forward of men and assistance, will you give them to me? Are you ready to march? [*Cries of "Yes."*] Then I say, Stand ready, for I am watching for the chance. I thank you, gentlemen.

A DAY OF THANKSGIVING
October 20, 1864

It has pleased almighty God to prolong our national life another year, defending us with his guardian care against unfriendly designs from abroad, and vouchsafing to us in his mercy many and signal victories over the enemy, who is of our own household. It has also pleased our heavenly Father to favor as well our citizens in their homes as our soldiers in their camps, and our sailors on the rivers and seas, with unusual health. He has largely augmented our free population by emancipation and by immigration, while he has opened to us new sources of wealth, and has crowned the labor of our working-men in every department of industry with abundant rewards. Moreover, he has been pleased to animate and inspire our minds and hearts with fortitude, courage, and resolution sufficient for the great trial of civil war into which we have been brought by our adherence as a nation to the cause of freedom and humanity, and to afford to us reasonable hopes of an ultimate and happy deliverance from all our dangers and afflictions.

Now, therefore, I, Abraham Lincoln, President of the United States, do hereby appoint and set apart the last Thursday of November next as a day which I desire to be observed by all my fellow-citizens, wherever they may then be, as a day of thanksgiving and praise to almighty God, the beneficent Creator and Ruler of the universe. And I do further recommend to my fellow-citizens aforesaid, that on that occasion they do reverently humble themselves in the dust, and from thence offer up penitent and fervent prayers and supplications to the great Disposer of events for a return of the inestimable blessings of peace, union, and harmony throughout the land which it has pleased him to assign as a dwelling-place for ourselves and for our posterity throughout all generations.

THE RE-ELECTION SPEECH
WASHINGTON, DC
November 10, 1864

It has long been a grave question whether any government, not too strong for the liberties of its people, can be strong enough to maintain its existence in great emergencies. On this point the present rebellion brought our republic to a severe test, and a presidential election occurring in regular course during the rebellion, added not a little to the strain.

If the loyal people united were put to the utmost of their strength by the rebellion, must they not fail when divided and partially paralyzed by a political war among themselves? But the election was a necessity. We cannot have free government without elections; and if the rebellion could force us to forego or postpone a national election, it might fairly claim to have already conquered and ruined us. The strife of the election is but human nature practically applied to the facts of the case. What has occurred in this case must ever recur in similar cases. Human nature will not change. In any future great national trial, compared with the men of this, we shall have as weak and as strong, as silly and as wise, as bad and as good. Let us, therefore, study the incidents of this as philosophy to learn wisdom from, and none of them as wrongs to be revenged. But the election, along with its incidental and undesirable strife, has done good too. It has demonstrated that a people's government can sustain a national election in the midst of a great civil war. Until now, it has not been known to the world that this was a possibility. It shows, also, how sound and how strong we still are. It shows that, even among candidates of the same party, he who is most devoted to the Union and most opposed to treason can receive most of the people's votes. It shows, also, to the extent yet known, that we have more men now than we had when the war began. Gold is good in its place, but living, brave, patriotic men are better than gold.

But the rebellion continues, and now that the election is over, may not all having a common interest reunite in a common effort to save our common country? For my own part, I have striven and shall strive to avoid placing any obstacle in the way. So long as I have been here I have not willingly planted a thorn in any man's bosom. While I am deeply sensible to the high compliment of a reelection, and duly grateful, as I trust, to almighty God for having directed my countrymen to a right conclusion, as I think, for their own good, it adds nothing to my satisfaction that any other man may be disappointed or pained by the result.

May I ask those who have not differed with me to join with me in this same spirit toward those who have? And now let me close by asking three hearty cheers for our brave soldiers and seamen and their gallant and skillful commanders.

FOURTH ANNUAL MESSAGE ON THE STATE OF THE UNION
December 6, 1864

In a great national crisis like ours, unanimity of action among those seeking a common end is very desirable - almost indispensable. And yet no approach to such unanimity is attainable unless some deference shall be paid to the will of the majority, simply because it is the will of the majority. In this case the common end is the maintenance of the Union, and among the means to secure that end, such will, through the election, is most clearly declared in favor of such constitutional amendment.

The most reliable indication of public purpose in this country is derived through our popular elections. Judging by the recent canvass and its result, the purpose of the people within the loyal States to maintain the integrity of the Union, was never more firm nor more nearly unanimous than now. The extraordinary calmness and good order with which the millions of voters met and mingled at the polls give strong assurance of this. Not only all those who supported the Union ticket, so called, but a great majority of the opposing party also, may be fairly claimed to entertain, and to be actuated by, the same purpose. It is an unanswerable argument to this effect, that no candidate for any office whatever, high or low, has ventured to seek votes on the avowal that he was for giving up the Union. There has been much impugning of motives, and much heated controversy as to the proper means and best mode of advancing the Union cause; but on the distinct issue of Union or no Union the politicians have shown their instinctive knowledge that there is no diversity among the people. In affording the people the fair opportunity of

showing one to another and to the world this firmness and
unanimity of purpose, the election has been of vast value
to the national cause.

The election has exhibited another fact, not less valuable
to be known - the fact that we do not approach exhaustion
in the most important branch of national resources - that
of living men. While it is melancholy to reflect that the
war has filled so many graves, and carried mourning to so
many hearts, it is some relief to know that compared with
the surviving, the fallen have been so few. While corps,
and divisions, and brigades, and regiments have formed,
and fought, and dwindled, and gone out of existence, a
great majority of the men who composed them are still
living. The same is true of the naval service. The election
returns prove this. So many voters could not else be
found. The States regularly holding elections, both now
and four years ago - to wit: California, Connecticut, Delaware, Illinois, Indiana, Iowa, Kentucky, Maine, Maryland,
Massachusetts, Michigan, Minnesota, Missouri, New
Hampshire, New Jersey, New York, Ohio, Oregon, Pennsylvania, Rhode Island, Vermont, West Virginia, and Wisconsin - cast 3,982,011 votes now, against 3,870,222 cast
then; showing an aggregate now of 3,982,011. To this is
to be added 33,762 cast now in the new States of Kansas
and Nevada, which States did not vote in 1860; thus swell-
ing the aggregate to 4,015,773, and the net increase during the three years and a half of war, to 145,551. A table
is appended, showing particulars. To this again should be
added the number of all soldiers in the field from Massachusetts, Rhode Island, New Jersey, Delaware, Indiana, Illinois, and California, who by the laws of those States could
not vote away from their homes, and which number cannot be less than 90,000. Nor yet is this all. The number
in organized Territories is triple now what it was four

years ago, while thousands, white and black, join us as the national arms press back the insurgent lines. So much is shown, affirmatively and negatively, by the election.

It is not material to inquire how the increase has been produced, or to show that it would have been greater but for the war, which is probably true. The important fact remains demonstrated that we have more men now than we had when the war began; that we are not exhausted, nor in process of exhaustion; that we are gaining strength, and may, if need be, maintain the contest indefinitely. This as to men. Material resources are now more complete and abundant than ever.

The national resources, then, are unexhausted, and, as we believe, inexhaustible. The public purpose to reestablish and maintain the national authority is unchanged, and, as we believe, unchangeable. The manner of continuing the effort remains to choose. On careful consideration of all the evidence accessible, it seems to me that no attempt at negotiation with the insurgent leader could result in any good. He would accept nothing short of severance of the Union - precisely what we will not and cannot give. His declarations to this effect are explicit and oft repeated. He does not attempt to deceive us. He affords us no excuse to deceive ourselves. He cannot voluntarily reaccept the Union; we cannot voluntarily yield it.

Between him and us the issue is distinct, simple, and inflexible. It is an issue which can only be tried by war, and decided by victory. If we yield, we are beaten; if the Southern people fail him, he is beaten. Either way it would be the victory and defeat following war. What is true, however, of him who heads the insurgent cause, is not necessarily true of those who follow. Although he cannot re-accept the Union, they can. Some of them, we know, already desire peace and reunion. The number of such may increase.

They can at any moment have peace simply by laying down their arms and submitting to the national authority under the Constitution. After so much the government could not, if it would, maintain war against them. The loyal people would not sustain or allow it. If questions should remain, we would adjust them by the peaceful means of legislation, conference, courts, and votes, operating only in constitutional and lawful channels. Some certain, and other possible, questions are, and would be, beyond the executive power to adjust; as, for instance, the admission of members into Congress, and whatever might require the appropriation of money. The executive power itself would be greatly diminished by the cessation of actual war. Pardons and remissions of forfeitures, however, would still be within executive control. In what spirit and temper this control would be exercised, can be fairly judged of by the past.

A year ago general pardon and amnesty, upon specified terms, were offered to all except certain designated classes, and it was at the same time made known that the excepted classes were still within contemplation of special clemency. During the year many availed themselves of the general provision, and many more would only that the signs of bad faith in some led to such precautionary measures as rendered the practical process less easy and certain. During the same time, also, special pardons have been granted to individuals of the excepted classes, and no voluntary application has been denied.

Thus, practically, the door has been for a full year open to all, except such as were not in condition to make free choice - that is, such as were in custody or under constraint. It is still so open to all; but the time may come - probably will come - when public duty shall demand that it be closed; and that in lieu more rigorous measures than heretofore shall be adopted.

In presenting the abandonment of armed resistance to the national authority on the part of the insurgents as the only indispensable condition to ending the war on the part of the government, I retract nothing heretofore said as to slavery. I repeat the declaration made a year ago, that "while I remain in my present position I shall not attempt to retract or modify the Emancipation Proclamation, nor shall I return to slavery any person who is free by the terms of that proclamation, or by any of the acts of Congress."

If the people should, by whatever mode or means, make it an executive duty to reenslave such persons, another, and not I, must be their instrument to perform it.

In stating a single condition of peace, I mean simply to say, that the war will cease on the part of the government whenever it shall have ceased on the part of those who began it.

SECOND INAUGURAL ADDRESS
WASHINGTON, DC
March 4, 1865

At this second appearing to take the oath of the presidential office, there is less occasion for an extended address than there was at the first. Then a statement, somewhat in detail, of a course to be pursued, seemed fitting and proper. Now, at the expiration of four years, during which public declarations have been constantly called forth on every point and phase of the great contest which still absorbs the attention, and engrosses the energies of the nation, little that is new could be presented. The progress of our arms, upon which all else chiefly depends, is as well known to the public as to myself; and it is, I trust, reasonably satisfactory and encouraging to all. With high hope for the future, no prediction in regard to it is ventured.

On the occasion corresponding to this four years ago, all thoughts were anxiously directed to an impending civil war. All dreaded it - all sought to avert it. While the inaugural address was being delivered from this place, devoted altogether to *saving* the Union without war, insurgent agents were in the city seeking to *destroy* it without war - seeking to dissolve the Union, and divide effects, by negotiation. Both parties deprecated war; but one of them would *make* war rather than let the nation survive; and the other would *accept* war rather than let it perish. And the war came.

One eighth of the whole population were colored slaves, not distributed generally over the Union, but localized in the Southern part of it. These slaves constituted a pecul-

iar and powerful interest. All knew that this interest was,
somehow, the cause of the war. To strengthen, perpetuate,
and extend this interest was the object for which the insurgents would rend the Union, even by war; while the
government claimed no right to do more than to restrict
the territorial enlargement of it. Neither party expected
for the war, the magnitude, or the duration, which it has
already attained. Neither anticipated that the *cause* of the
conflict might cease with, or even before, the conflict itself should cease. Each looked for an easier triumph, and
a result less fundamental and astounding. Both read the
same bible, and pray to the same God; and each invokes
His aid against the other. It may seem strange that any
men should dare to ask a just God's assistance in wringing
their bread from the sweat of other men's faces; but let us
judge not that we be not judged. The prayers of both
could not be answered; that of neither has been answered
fully. The Almighty has his own purposes. "Woe unto
the world because of offences! for it must needs be that
offences come; but woe to that man by whom the offence
cometh!" If we shall suppose that American Slavery is
one of those offences which, in the providence of God,
must needs come, but which, having continued through
His appointed time, He now wills to remove, and that He
gives to both North and South, this terrible war, as the
woe due to those by whom the offence came, shall we dis-
cern therein any departure from those divine attributes
which the believers in a Living God always ascribe to
Him? Fondly do we hope - fervently do we pray - that
this mighty scourge of war may speedily pass away. Yet,
if God wills that it continue, until all the wealth piled by
the bond-man's two hundred and fifty years of unrequited
toil shall be sunk, and until every drop of blood drawn
with the lash, shall be paid by another drawn with the
sword, as was said three thousand years ago, so still it

must be said; "the judgments of the Lord, are true and righteous altogether."

With malice toward none; with charity for all; with firmness in the right, as God gives us to see the right, let us strive on to finish the work we are in; to bind up the nation's wounds; to care for him who shall have borne the battle, and for his widow, and his orphan - to do all which may achieve and cherish a just and lasting peace, among ourselves, and with all nations.

RECONSTRUCTION OF THE UNION
THE LAST PUBLIC SPEECH
WASHINGTON, DC
April 11, 1865

We meet this evening, not in sorrow, but in gladness of
heart. The evacuation of Petersburg and Richmond, and
the surrender of the principal insurgent army, give hope
of a righteous and speedy peace whose joyous expression
can not be restrained. In the midst of this, however, He
from whom all blessings flow, must not be forgotten. A
call for a national thanksgiving is being prepared, and will
be duly promulgated. Nor must those whose harder part
gives us the cause of rejoicing, be overlooked. Their hon-
ors must not be parcelled out with others. I myself was
near the front, and had the high pleasure of transmitting
much of the good news to you; but no part of the honor,
for plan or execution, is mine. To General Grant, his
skillful officers, and brave men, all belongs. The gallant
Navy stood ready, but was not in reach to take active part.

By these recent successes the re-inauguration of the national authority - reconstruction - which has had a large
share of thought from the first, is pressed much more
closely upon our attention. It is fraught with great difficulty. Unlike a case of a war between independent nations, there is no authorized organ for us to treat with.
No one man has authority to give up the rebellion for any
other man. We simply must begin with, and mould from,
disorganized and discordant elements. Nor is it a small
additional embarrassment that we, the loyal people, differ
among ourselves as to the mode, manner, and means of reconstruction.

As a general rule, I abstain from reading the reports of attacks upon myself, wishing not to be provoked by that to which I can not properly offer an answer. In spite of this precaution, however, it comes to my knowledge that I am much censured for some supposed agency in setting up, and seeking to sustain, the new State government of Louisiana. In this I have done just so much as, and no more than, the public knows. In the Annual Message of December 1863 and accompanying Proclamation, I presented *a* plan of reconstruction (as the phrase goes) which, I promised, if adopted by any State, should be acceptable to, and sustained by, the Executive government of the nation. I distinctly stated that this was not the only plan which might possibly be acceptable; and I also distinctly protested that the Executive claimed no right to say when, or whether members should be admitted to seats in Congress from such States. The plan was, in advance, submitted to the then Cabinet, and distinctly approved by every member of it. One of them suggested that I should then, and in that connection, apply the Emancipation Proclamation to the theretofore excepted parts of Virginia and Louisiana; that I should drop the suggestion about apprenticeship for freed-people, and that I should omit the protest against my own power, in regard to the admission of members to Congress; but even he approved every part and parcel of the plan which has since been employed or touched by the action of Louisiana. The new constitution of Louisiana, declaring emancipation for the whole State, practically applies the Proclamation to the part previously excepted. It does not adopt apprenticeship for freed-people; and it is silent, as it could not well be otherwise, about the admission of members to Congress. So that, as it applies to Louisiana, every member of the Cabinet fully approved the plan. The message went to Congress, and I received many commendations of the plan, written and verbal; and not a single objection to it, from any professed emancipationist, came to my knowledge, until after the news reached Washington that the people of Louisiana had begun to move in accordance with it. From about July 1862, I had corresponded with different persons, supposed to be interested, seeking a reconstruction of a State government for Louisiana. When the message of 1863, with the plan before mentioned, reached New Orleans, General Banks wrote me that he was confident the people, with his military cooperation, would reconstruct, substantially on that plan. I wrote him, and some of them to try it; they tried it, and the result is known. Such only has been my agency in getting up the Louisiana government. As to sustaining it, my promise is out, as before stated. But, as bad promises are better broken than kept, I shall treat this as a bad promise, and break it, whenever I shall be convinced that keeping it is adverse to the public interest. But I have not yet been so convinced.

I have been shown a letter on this subject, supposed to be an able one, in which the writer expresses regret that my mind has not seemed to be definitely fixed on the question whether the seceded States, so called, are in the Union or out of it. It would perhaps, add astonishment to his regret, were he to learn that since I have found professed Union men endeavoring to make that question, I have *purposely* forborne any public expression upon it. As appears to me that question has not been, nor yet is, a practically material one, and that any discussion of it, while it thus remains practically immaterial, could have no effect other than the mischievous one of dividing our friends. As yet, whatever it may hereafter become, that question is bad, as the basis of a controversy, and good for nothing at all - a merely pernicious abstraction.

We all agree that the seceded States, so called, are out of their proper practical relation with the Union; and that the sole object of the government, civil and military, in regard to those States is to again get them into that proper practical relation. I believe it is not only possible, but in fact, easier to do this, without deciding, or even considering, whether these States have ever been out of the Union, than with it. Finding themselves safely at home, it would be utterly immaterial whether they had ever been abroad. Let us all join in doing the acts necessary to restoring the proper practical relations between these States and the Union; and each forever after, innocently indulge his own opinion whether, in doing the acts, he brought the States from without, into the Union, or only gave them proper assistance, they never having been out of it.

The amount of constituency, so to speak, on which the new Louisiana government rests, would be more satisfactory to all, if it contained fifty, thirty, or even twenty thousand, instead of only about twelve thousand, as it does. It is also unsatisfactory to some that the elective franchise is not given to the colored man. I would myself prefer that it were now conferred on the very intelligent, and on those who serve our cause as soldiers. Still the question is not whether the Louisiana government, as it stands, is quite all that is desirable. The question is, "Will it be wiser to take it as it is, and help to improve it; or to reject, and disperse it?" "Can Louisiana be brought into proper practical relation with the Union *sooner* by *sustaining,* or by *discarding* her new State government?"

Some twelve thousand voters in the heretofore slave-state of Louisiana have sworn allegiance to the Union, assumed to be the rightful political power of the State, held elections, organized a State government, adopted a free-state constitution, giving the benefit of public schools equally to black and white, and empowering the Legislature to confer the elective franchise upon the colored man. Their Legislature has already voted to ratify the constitutional amendment recently passed by Congress, abolishing slavery throughout the nation. These twelve thousand persons are thus fully committed to the Union, and to perpetual freedom in the state - committed to the very things, and nearly all the things the nation wants - and they ask the nation's recognition and its assistance to make good their committal. Now, if we reject, and spurn them, we do our utmost to disorganize and disperse them. We in effect say to the white men "You are worthless, or worse - we will neither help you, nor be helped by you." To the blacks we say "This cup of liberty which these, your old masters, hold to your lips, we will dash from you, and leave you to the chances of gathering the spilled and scattered contents in some vague and undefined when, where, and how." If this course, discouraging and paralyzing both white and black, has any tendency to bring Louisiana into proper practical relations with the Union, I have, so far, been unable to perceive it. If, on the contrary, we recognize, and sustain the new government of Louisiana, the converse of all this is made true. We encourage the hearts, and nerve the arms of the twelve thousand to adhere to their work, and argue for it, and proselyte for it, and fight for it, and feed it, and grow it, and ripen it to a complete success.

The colored man too, in seeing all united for him, is inspired with vigilance, and energy, and daring, to the same end. Grant that he desires the elective franchise, will he not attain it sooner by saving the already advanced steps toward it, than by running backward over them? Concede that the new government of Louisiana is only to what it should be as the egg is to the fowl, shall we sooner have the fowl by hatching the egg than by smashing it? Again, if we reject Louisiana, we also reject one vote in favor of the proposed amendment to the national Constitution. To meet this proposition, it has been argued that no more than three fourths of those States which have not attempted secession are necessary to validly ratify the amendment. I do not commit myself against this, further than to say that such a ratification would be questionable, and sure to be persistently questioned; while a ratification by three-fourths of all the States would be unquestioned and unquestionable.

I repeat the question. "Can Louisiana be brought into proper practical relation with the Union *sooner* by *sustaining* or by *discarding* her new State Government?"

What has been said of Louisiana will apply generally to other States. And yet so great peculiarities pertain to each state, and such important and sudden changes occur in the same state; and, withal, so new and unprecedented is the whole case, that no exclusive, and inflexible plan can safely be prescribed as to details and collaterals. Such exclusive, and inflexible plan, would surely become a new entanglement. Important principles may, and must, be inflexible.

In the present *"situation"* as the phrase goes, it may be my duty to make some new announcement to the people of the South. I am considering, and shall not fail to act, when satisfied that action will be proper.

BIBLIOGRAPHY

Alger, Horatio, Jr. *Abraham Lincoln, the Backwoods Boy.* New York, NY: J.R. Anderson & H.S. Allen, 1883.

Angle, Paul M., Editor. *Abraham Lincoln, by Some Men Who Knew Him.* Chicago: Americana House, 1950.

Angle, Paul, M., Editor. *The Lincoln Reader.* New Brunswick, NJ: Rutgers University Press, 1947.

Ayres, Alex, Editor. *The Wit and Wisdom of Abraham Lincoln.* New York, NY: NAL-Dutton, 1992.

Baringer, William. *Lincoln's Rise to Power.* Boston, MA: Little, Brown & Co., 1937.

Barton, William E. *Abraham Lincoln and His Books.* Folcroft, PA: Folcroft Library Editions, 1976.

Barton, William E. *Lincoln at Gettysburg.* Indianapolis, IN: Bobbs-Merrill Co., 1930.

Basler, Roy P. *Abraham Lincoln: His Speeches and Writings.* Cleveland, OH: World Publishing Co., 1946.

Basler, Roy P. *Lincoln.* New York, NY: Grove Press, 1962.

Basler, Roy P. *A Touchstone for Greatness: Essays, Addresses and Occasional Pieces about Abraham Lincoln.* Westport, CT: Greenwood Press, 1973.

Basler, Roy P. and Christian O. Basler, Editors. *The Collected Works of Abraham Lincoln, 1848-1865.* New Brunswick, NJ: Rutgers University Press, 1990.

Beveridge, Albert J. *Abraham Lincoln, 1809-1858.* Boston, MA: Houghton-Mifflin Co., 1928.

Bryan, George S. *The Great American Myth: The True Story of Lincoln's Murder.* New York, NY: Carrick & Evans, 1940.

Cox, Earnest S. *Lincoln's Negro Policy.* Richmond, VA: The William Byrd Press, 1938.

Crissey, Elwell. *Lincoln's Lost Speech: The Pivot of His Career.* New York, NY: Hawthorn Books, 1967.

Fehrenbacher, Don E. *The Leadership of Abraham Lincoln.* New York, NY: John Wiley & Sons, 1970.

Fehrenbacher, Don E., Editor. *Abraham Lincoln: A Documentary Portrait Through His Speeches and Writings.* Palo Alto, CA: Stanford University Press, 964.

Fehrenbacher, Don E., Editor. *Speeches & Writings of Abraham Lincoln.* New York, NY: Library of America, 1989.

Handlin, Oscar and Lilian Handlin. *Abraham Lincoln and the Union.* Boston, MA: Little, Brown & Co., 1980.

Harris, T.M. *The Assassination of Lincoln: A History of the Great Conspiracy: Trail of the Conspirators by a Military Commission.* Boston, MA: American Citizen Co., 1892.

Hay, John. *Lincoln and the Civil War in the Diaries and Letters of John Hay.* New York, NY: Dodd, Mead & Co., 1939.

Heidorf, Christian J. *Gettysburg: The One Hundred Twenty-Fifth Anniversary: What They Did Here.* Gansevoort, NY: Harlow & Taylor, 1990.

Herndon, William Henry. *Abraham Lincoln.* New York, NY: Appleton, 1892.

Herndon, William Henry. *The Hidden Lincoln.* New York, NY: Viking Press, 1938.

Herndon, William Henry. *Life of Lincoln.* Cleveland, OH: World Publishing Co., 1942.

Hill, Frederick T. *Abraham Lincoln As a Lawyer.* Albuquerque, NM: American Classical College Press, 1985.

Hill, Frederick T. *Lincoln, the Lawyer.* New York, NY: Century Co., 1906.

Holmes, Torielf. *April Tragedy.* Gaithersburg, MD: Olde Soldier Books, 1987.

Kranz, Henry B., Editor. *Abraham Lincoln: A New Portrait.* New York, NY: Putnam, 1959.

Lee, Andrew. *Lincoln.* North Pomfret, VT: Trafalgar Square, 1989.

The Lincoln Encyclopedia: The Spoken and Written Words of Abraham Lincoln Arranged for Ready Reference. Westport, CT: Greenwood Press, 1980.

Lincoln, Abraham. *Lincoln's Devotional.* Great Neck, NY: Channel Press, 1957.

Lincoln's Own Yarns and Stories. Grand Rapids, MI: Bengal Press, 1980.

Matthews, Elizabeth W. *Lincoln as a Lawyer: An Annotated Bibliography.* Carbondale, IL: Southern Illinois University Press, 1991.

McCartney, Clarence E. *Lincoln and His Generals.* Salem, NH: Ayer Co., 1970.

McCarty, Burke. *The Suppressed Truth About the Assassination of Abraham Lincoln.* Philadelphia, PA: B. McCarty, 1924.

McGinnis, Ralph Y. *Quotations from Abraham Lincoln.* Chicago, IL: Nelson-Hall, 1978.

McPherson, James M. *Abraham Lincoln and the Second American Revolution.* New York, NY: Oxford University Press, 1991.

Mearns, David C. *The Lincoln Papers.* Garden City, NY: Doubleday, 1948.

Miers, Earl S. *Lincoln Day-by-Day.* Dayton, OH: Morning side Bookshop, 1988.

Mitgang, Herbert, Editor. *Abraham Lincoln: A Press Portrait.* Athens, GA: University of Georgia Press, 1989.

Monaghan, James. *Lincoln Bibliography, 1839-1939.* Springfield, IL: Illinois State Historical Library, 1945.

Moore, Basil, Editor. *Basil Moore's Lincoln.* Mahomet, IL: Mayhaven Publishing, 1991.

Morgenthau, Hans J. and David Hein. *Essays on Lincoln's Faith and Politics.* Lanham, MD: University Press of America, 1983.

Neely, Mark E., Jr. *The Abraham Lincoln Encyclopedia.* New York, NY: McGraw-Hill Co., 1984.

Neely, Mark E., Jr. *The Fate of Liberty: Abraham Lincoln and Civil Liberties.* New York, NY: Oxford University Press, 1992.

Nichols, David A. *Lincoln and the Indians: Civil War Policy and Politics.* Columbia, MO: University of Missouri Press, 1978.

Nicolay, John George and John Hay. *Abraham Lincoln: A History.* New York, NY: Century Co., 1990.

Oates, Stephen B. *Abraham Lincoln: The Man Behind the Myths.* New York, NY: NAL-Dutton, 1985.

Oates, Stephen B. *With Malice Toward None: The Life of Abraham Lincoln.* New York, NY: NAL-Dutton, 1978.

O'Neal, Michael. *The Assassination of Abraham Lincoln: Opposing Viewpoints.* San Diego, CA: Greenhaven, 1991.

Quarles, Benjamin. *Lincoln and the Negro.* New York, NY: Oxford University Press, 1962.

Randall, J.G. and Richard N. Current. *Lincoln the President: Last Full Measure.* Urbana, IL: University of Illinois Press, 1991.

Randall, James G. *Lincoln and the South.* Westport, CT: Greenwood Press, 1980.

Rawley, James A., Editor. *Lincoln and Civil War Politics.* New York, NY: Holt, Rinehart & Winston, 1969.

Rhodehamel, John and Thomas F. Schwartz. *The Last Best Hope of Earth: Abraham Lincoln and the Promise of America.* San Marino, CA: Huntington Library, 1993.

Rice, Allen T., Editor. *Reminiscences of Abraham Lincoln.* New York, NY: Harper & Brothers, 1909.

Riddle, Donald W. *Congressman Abraham Lincoln.* Westport, CT: Greenwood Press, 1979.

Sandburg, Carl. *Abraham Lincoln.* New York, NY: Scribners, 1939.

Sandburg, Carl. *Abraham Lincoln Grows Up.* New York, NY: Harcourt, Brace, 1928.

Sandburg, Carl. *Abraham Lincoln: The Prairie Years.* New York, NY: Harcourt, Brace, Jovanovich, 1970.

Sandburg, Carl. *Abraham Lincoln: The War Years.* New York, NY: Harcourt, Brace & World, 1939.

Scripps, John L. *Life of Abraham Lincoln.* Westport, CT: Greenwood Press, 1969.

Simon, Paul. *Lincoln's Preparation for Greatness.* Urbana, IL: University of Illinois Press, 1990.

Stephenson, Nathaniel W. *Abraham Lincoln and the Union: Chronicle of the Embattled North.* New Haven, CT: Yale University Press, 1921.

Thomas, Benjamin P. *Abraham Lincoln: A Biography.* New York, NY: Random House, 1979.

Thomas, Benjamin P. *Portrait for Posterity: Lincoln and His Biographers.* Salem, NH: Ayer Co., 1972.

Thomas, John L. *Abraham Lincoln and the American Political Tradition.* Amherst, MA: University of Massachusetts Press, 1986.

Thurow, Glen E. *Abraham Lincoln and the American Political Tradition.* Albany, NY: State University of New York Press, 1976.

Tice, George. *Lincoln.* New Brunswick, NJ: Rutgers University Press, 1984.

Tidwell, William A., et al. *Come Retribution: The Confederate Secret Service and the Assassination of Lincoln.* Jackson, MS: University Press of Mississippi, 1988.

Tilley, John S. *Lincoln Takes Command.* Chapel Hill, NC: University of North Carolina Press, 1941.

Turner, Thomas R. *Beware the People Weeping: Public Opinion and the Assassination of Abraham Lincoln.* Baton Rouge, LA: Louisiana State University Press, 1991.

Warren, Louis. *Lincoln's Youth: Indiana Years 1816-1830.* Urbana, IL: University of Illinois Press, 1993.

Wilbur, Henry W. *President Lincoln's Attitude Toward Slavery and Emancipation.* Philadelphia, PA: W.H. Jenkins, 1914.

Williams, T. Harry. *Lincoln and His Generals.* New York, NY: McGraw-Hill Co., 1989.

Williams, T. Harry. *Lincoln and the Radicals.* Madison, WI: University of Wisconsin Press, 1960.

Wills, Garry. *Lincoln at Gettysburg: The Words that Remade America.* New York, NY: Simon & Schuster, 1993.

Zilversmit, Arthur, Editor. *Lincoln on Black and White: A Documentary History.* Belmont, CA: Wadsworth Publishing Co., 1971.

YOUNG ADULT BIBLIOGRAPHY

D'Aulaire, Ingri. *Abraham Lincoln.* New York, NY: Doubleday, 1957.

Elliot, I., Editor. *Abraham Lincoln, 1809-1865: Chronology, Documents, Bibliographical Aids.* Dobbs Ferry, NY: Oceana, 1969.

Judson, Clara. *Abraham Lincoln, Friend of the People.* Chicago, IL: Wilcox & Follett Co., 1950.

Kigel, Richard. *The Frontier Years of Abe Lincoln: In the Words of His Friends and Family.* New York, NY: Walker, 1986.

Lee, Andrew. *Lincoln.* North Pomfret, VT: Trafalgar Square, 1989.

McNeer, May. *America's Abraham Lincoln.* Boston, MA: Houghton-Mifflin, 1957.

Melzer, Milton, Editor. *Lincoln, In His Own Words.* New York, NY: Harcourt, Brace, 1993.

Morgan, Lee and Pietro Cattaneo. *Abraham Lincoln.* Morristown, NJ: Silver Burdett Press, 1990.

North, Sterling. *Abe Lincoln: Log Cabin to White House.* New York, NY: Random Books, 1987.

O'Neal, Michael. *The Assassination of Abraham Lincoln: Opposing Viewpoints.* San Diego, CA: Greenhaven, 1991.

Sandburg, Carl. *Abraham Lincoln Grows Up.* New York, NY: Harcourt, Brace, 1928.

Shorto, Russell. *Abraham Lincoln: To Preserve the Union.* Morristown, NJ: Silver Burdett Press, 1991.

Williams, T. Harry. *Lincoln and His Generals.* New York, NY: McGraw-Hill Co., 1989.

INDEX

ALSO AVAILABLE FROM EXCELLENT BOOKS

LANDMARK DECISIONS OF THE UNITED STATES SUPREME COURT
Maureen Harrison & Steve Gilbert, Editors

The actual text of 44 Landmark Decisions of the United States Supreme Court, carefully edited into non-legalese for the general reader, in four volumes.

"Remarkable." - Booklist
"Especially recommended." - Midwest Book Review

ABORTION DECISIONS OF THE UNITED STATES SUPREME COURT
Maureen Harrison & Steve Gilbert, Editors

The text of 20 major Abortion Decisions of the United States Supreme Court, published on the anniversary of *Roe v. Wade*, edited for the general reader, in three volumes.

"Wherever hands-on interest in abortion law runs high, these three unpretentious paperbacks are a good investment."
- Booklist

CIVIL RIGHTS DECISIONS OF THE UNITED STATES SUPREME COURT
Maureen Harrison & Steve Gilbert, Editors

The text of 26 major Civil Rights Decisions of the United States Supreme Court, published on the fortieth anniversary of *Brown v. Board of Education*, edited for the general reader, in two volumes.

ALSO AVAILABLE FROM
EXCELLENT BOOKS

John F. Kennedy:
Word For Word

A representative selection of thirty speeches by President John F. Kennedy, looking back on his life and times, not in the words of others, but in his own.

Includes his acceptance speech, his inaugural address, speeches on the Berlin Wall and the Cuban Missile Crisis, and the ungiven speech scheduled for Dallas on November 22, 1963.

"A fine collection; useful for scholars." - Bookwatch

Thomas Jefferson:
Word For Word

A selection of the lifetime writings of Thomas Jefferson, looking back on his times in his own words.

Includes his draft of the Declaration of Independence, his Presidential Papers, his autobiography, and the complete Jefferson Bible, the Gospels according to Jefferson.

"Strong coverage of an historic collection." - Bookwatch

EXCELLENT BOOKS ORDER FORM

(Please xerox this form so it will be available to other readers.)

Please send

Copy(ies)

_____ of ABRAHAM LINCOLN: WORD FOR WORD @ $19.95 each
_____ of THOMAS JEFFERSON: WORD FOR WORD @ $19.95 each
_____ of JOHN F. KENNEDY: WORD FOR WORD @ $19.95 each
_____ of CIVIL RIGHTS DECISIONS: 19th CENTURY @ $16.95 ea.
_____ of CIVIL RIGHTS DECISIONS: 20th CENTURY @ $16.95 ea.
_____ of LANDMARK DECISIONS @ $14.95 each
_____ of LANDMARK DECISIONS II @ $15.95 each
_____ of LANDMARK DECISIONS III @ $15.95 each
_____ of LANDMARK DECISIONS IV @ $15.95 each
_____ of THE ADA HANDBOOK @ $15.95 each
_____ of ABORTION DECISIONS: THE 1970's @ $15.95 each
_____ of ABORTION DECISIONS: THE 1980's @ $15.95 each
_____ of ABORTION DECISIONS: THE 1990's @ $15.95 each

Name: _____

Address: _____

City: _____ State: _____ Zip: _____

Add $1 per book for shipping and handling
California residents add sales tax

OUR GUARANTEE: Any Excellent Book may be returned at
any time for any reason and a full refund will be made.

Mail your check or money order to: Excellent Books,
Post Office Box 927105, San Diego, California 92192-7105
or call (619) 457-4895